THE ARMY IN TRANSFORMATION, 1790–1860

Recent Titles in

The Greenwood Press "Daily Life Through History" Series

Nature and the Environment in Nineteenth-Century American Life
Brian Black

Native Americans in the Twentieth Century
Donald Fixico

Native Americans from Post-Columbian through Nineteenth-Century America
Alice Nash and Christoph Strobel

Cooking Europe, 1250–1650
Ken Albala

The Black Death
Joseph P. Byrne

Cooking in America, 1590–1840
Trudy Eden

Cooking in America, 1840–1945
Alice L. McLean

Cooking in Ancient Civilizations
Cathy K. Kaufman

Nature and the Environment in Pre-Columbian American Life
Stacy Kowtko

Science and Technology in Medieval European Life
Jeffrey R. Wigelsworth

Civilians in Wartime Africa: From Slavery Days to the Diamond Wars
John Laband, editor

Christians in Ancient Rome
James W. Ermatinger

THE ARMY IN TRANSFORMATION, 1790–1860

James M. McCaffrey

The Greenwood Press "Daily Life Through History" Series

American Soldiers' Lives
David S. Heidler and Jeanne T. Heidler, Series Editors

GREENWOOD PRESS
Westport, Connecticut • London

Library of Congress Cataloging-in-Publication Data

McCaffrey, James M., 1946–
The Army in transformation, 1790–1860/James M. McCaffrey.
p.cm.—(The Greenwood Press "Daily life through history" series, ISSN 1080-4749)
Includes bibliographical references and index.
ISBN 0-313-33172-3 (alk. paper)
1. United States. Army—History—18th century. 2. United States. Army—History—19th century. 3. United States. Army—Military life—History—18th century.
4. United States. Army—Military life—History—19th century. I. Title. II. Series.
UA25. M395 2006
355.00973′09034—dc22 2006015365

British Library Cataloguing in Publication Data is available.

Library of Congress Catalog Card Number: 2006015365
ISBN: 0-313-33172-3
ISSN: 1080-4749

First published in 2006

Greenwood Press, 88 Post Road West, Westport, CT 06881
An imprint of Greenwood Publishing Group, Inc.
www.greenwood.com

Printed in the United States of America

The paper used in this book complies with the Permanent Paper Standard issued by the National Information Standards Organization (Z39.48-1984).

10 9 8 7 6 5 4 3 2 1

CONTENTS

SERIES FOREWORD

More than once during the military campaigns undertaken by American armies, leaders in both civilian and martial roles have been prompted to ask in admiration, "Where do such people come from?" The question, of course, was both rhetorical and in earnest: the one because they knew that such people hailed from the coasts and the heartland, from small hamlets and sprawling cities, from expansive prairies and breezy lakeshores. They were as varied as the land they represented, as complex as the diversity of their faiths and ethnic identities, all nonetheless defined by the overarching identity of "American," made more emphatic by their transformation into "American soldiers."

They knew and we know where they came from. On the other hand, the question for anyone who knows the tedium, indignity, discomfort, and peril of military service in wartime is more aptly framed, "Why did they come at all?"

In the volumes of this series, accomplished scholars of the American military answer that question, and more. By depicting the daily routines of soldiers at war, they reveal the gritty heroism of those who conquered the drudgery of routine and courageously faced the terrors of combat. With impeccable research and a deep understanding of the people who move through these grandly conceived stories—for war, as Tolstoy has shown us, is the most grandly conceived and complex story of all—these books take us to the heart of great armies engaged in enormous undertakings. Bad food, disease, haphazardly treated wounds, and chronic longing for loved ones form part of these stories, for those are the universal afflictions of soldiers. Punctuating long stretches of loneliness and monotony were interludes of horrific violence that scarred every soldier, even those who escaped physical injury. And insidious wounds could fester because of ugly customs and ingrained prejudices: for too long a span, soldiers who happened to be minorities suffered galling injustices at the hands of those they served, often giving for cause and comrades what Lincoln called "the last full measure of devotion," despite unfair indignities and undeserved ignominy. And sadly, it is true that protracted or unpopular wars could send veterans returning to a country indifferent about their sacrifices, sometimes hostile to the cause for which they fought, and begrudging even marginal compensation to their spouses and orphans. But quiet courage, wry humor, tangible camaraderie, and implacable pride are parts of these stories as well, ably conveyed by these gifted writers who have managed to turn the pages that follow into vivid snapshots of accomplishment, sacrifice, and triumph.

Until recently the American soldier has usually been a citizen called to duty in times of extraordinary crisis. The volunteer army of this latest generation, though, has created a remarkable hybrid in the current American soldier, a professional who nevertheless upholds the traditions of American citizens who happen to be in uniform to do a tough job. It is a noble tradition that ennobles all who have honored it. And more often than not, they who have served have managed small miracles of fortitude and resolve.

Walter Lord's *Incredible Victory* recounts the story of Mike Brazier, the rear-seat man on a torpedo plane from the carrier *Yorktown* in the Battle of Midway. He and pilot Wilhelm Esders were among that stoic cadre of fliers who attacked Japanese carriers, knowing that their fuel was insufficient for the distance to and from their targets. Having made their run under heavy enemy fire, Esders finally had to ditch the spent and damaged plane miles short of the *Yorktown* in the rolling Pacific. He then discovered that Brazier had been shot to pieces. Despite his grave wounds, Brazier had managed to change the coils in the radio to help guide the plane back toward the *Yorktown.* In the life raft as he died, Mike Brazier never complained. He talked of his family and how hard it had been to leave them, but he did not complain. Instead he apologized that he could not be of more help.

In the great, roiling cauldron of the Second World War, here was the archetype of the American soldier: uncomplaining while dying far from home in the middle of nowhere, worried at the last that he had not done his part.

Where do such people come from?

We invite you to read on, and find out.

David S. Heidler and Jeanne T. Heidler
Series Editors

PREFACE

Bell Wiley's seminal works, *The Life of Johnny Reb* and *The Life of Billy Yank*, laid the groundwork for those interested in the study of the everyday life of soldiers, and were the books that sparked such an interest in me.[1] This social history of soldiers is something that one comes to after having read and digested the books on warfare that deal with strategy and tactics and the "big picture." Understanding what motivated soldiers to do the things they did—whether it was enlisting in the first place, or getting drunk, or deserting from the army, or any number of other activities—helps to complete the study of how the army was able to succeed as it did and, perhaps, why it failed to accomplish even more.

Throughout the present work, *The Army in Transformation, 1790–1860*, volume one of *American Soldiers' Lives*, I have attempted to let the long-dead soldiers of the antebellum (pre–Civil War) era speak for themselves, through their letters, diaries, and journals. Admittedly, this only allows us to "know" those men who were literate and whose written records are available for research, but the number of such sources is not small.

The first chapter is an overview of the antebellum army in the United States. Here I have introduced the difficulties threatening the young country's security, both internally and externally, and outlined the progression of the conflicts that resulted.

The second chapter discusses the experiences of a man from the time he decided to enlist until he became a soldier. Just who were these men? where did they come from? What prompted them to enlist? This chapter also covers the newly enlisted soldier's training. This training varied somewhat depending upon whether the recruit was assigned to the infantry, the artillery, or the mounted service, but included everything from how to march to how to make use of the weapons upon which his life might come to depend.

Chapter 3 outlines the typical day-to-day routine of most soldiers. Many soldiers spent their entire enlistments without ever having fired their weapons in anger, but they generally stayed busy in other endeavors. These activities ran the gamut from chopping and hauling firewood to planting and harvesting crops. And afer those none-too-frequent visits from the paymaster, the soldiers often spent all their money within a few days-gambling, drinking, or pursuing some other dissipations.

The fourth chapter continues the thread of everyday life, discussing the food, medicine, and clothing made available to American soldiers. The Army diet was not very imaginative, and soldiers found many ways, both legal and otherwise, to supplement their rations. Army medical officers were surprisingly well-trained and provided care that was certainly comparable to what most American civilians enjoyed.

It was not always easy for young men in the army to amuse themselves in their off-duty hours without running the risk of falling afoul of regulations. Chapter 5 examines the system of military justice. Many of the transgressions were the result of drinking to excess, but there were other causes as well. And although the Articles of War, the basis for the military justice system, allowed courts-martial to impose death sentences for a wide variety of offenses, the percentage of such sentences actually handed down was rather small. There were many other ways to command the obedience of troops.

The next chapter, Chapter 6, addresses the activities of soldiers on campaign. These campaigns could be something as simple as merely relocating from one frontier fort to another, or they could embrace actual warfare. This chapter explores not only how the American soldiers fought their enemies, but also how they interacted with them in non-combat situations.

The final chapter draws the curtain on the antebellum army. With the onset of the Civil War, many American soldiers found themselves facing their former comrades across a battlefield. Many others, too old to fight with muskets, had to fight with pen and paper to get pensions from a sometimes penurious government.

This book also includes a timeline of the important events that fall within the chronological scope of this volume, 1790–1860. This feature provides readers with a convenient way to scan the most important historical and military incidents discussed.

Finally, an extensive, topically arranged bibliography provides more than 500 sources for the interested reader to investigate for more information and research. These materials range from historical surveys and illustrated histories to articles, diaries, and primary documents from the U.S. government and other sources.

NOTE

1. Bell I. Wiley, *The Life of Johnny Reb*, New York: Bobbs-Merrill, 1943; Bell I. Wiley, *The Life of Billy Yank*, New York: Bobbs-Merrill, 1951.

ACKNOWLEDGMENTS

I wish to thank Ms. Anita Garza and Ms. Alice Lewis, both of the interlibrary loan department at the University of Houston-Downtown. Without their cheerful help, this book would have taken much longer to complete.

TIMELINE

April 1790	Congress passes legislation that establishes a three-year army
October 1790	Brigadier General Josiah Harmar's army defeated by Indians in the Ohio Territory
November 4, 1791	Major General Arthur St. Clair's army defeated by Indians in the Ohio Territory
March 1792	Congress authorizes the Legion of the United States
August 20, 1794	Major General Anthony Wayne leads the Legion to victory over the Indians at the Battle of Fallen Timbers in the Ohio Territory
1802	United States Military Academy founded
1804–1806	Army expedition under Captain Meriwether Lewis and Lieutenant William Clark explores the American northwest
1806–1807	Army expedition under Captain Zebulon Pike explores the west
November 1811	Governor William H. Harrison leads troops to victory over the Shawnee at the Battle of Tippecanoe
June 18, 1812	Congress declares war on England
December 24, 1814	Diplomats meeting in Belgium sign the Treaty of Ghent, bringing the War of 1812 to a close
January 8, 1815	Major General Andrew Jackson's troops defeat a British force near New Orleans
1817–1818	First Seminole War
1835–1836	Texas Revolution

March 6, 1836	General Antonio López de Santa Anna's Mexican troops defeat Americans at the Battle of the Alamo
April 21, 1836	General Sam Houston's troops defeat Santa Anna at the Battle of San Jacinto
1835–1842	Second Seminole War
1846–1848	Mexican War
1857–1858	Mormon War
1861–1865	Civil War

1 INTRODUCTION

THE ARMY AFTER THE WAR OF INDEPENDENCE

The ink was scarcely dry on the treaty that brought an end to America's hard-fought War for Independence when the army that had fought it was reduced to a mere corporal's guard. And most Americans wanted it that way. The national government was almost bankrupt by the end of hostilities and did not have money enough to pay soldiers their wages. In fact, General George Washington had faced a near mutiny in 1783 over the issue of insufficient, or nonexistent, pay. The cost of maintaining an army, now that independence had been achieved, seemed unjustifiable. Perhaps more important was the idea that, as elucidated by one of the signers of the Declaration of Independence, "standing armies in time of peace, are inconsistent with the principles of Republican governments, dangerous to the liberties of a free people, and generally converted into destructive engines for establishing despotism."[1]

THE BEGINNINGS OF A NATIONAL ARMY

Many Americans seemed content to rely on the various state militias to serve the nation's defense needs. They perhaps had an inflated opinion of the citizen-soldiers' role in the recent war and were content to have them continue to ensure national security. General Washington, who was able to gauge the militia's effectiveness more accurately than most, declared that "to place any dependence upon [the] militia is assuredly resting upon a broken staff." He shared the commonly held opposition to a *large* standing army when there was no war for it to fight, but he believed that the young nation needed enough of a force "to awe the Indians, protect our Trade, prevent the encroachment of our Neighbors of Canada and the Floridas, and guard us at least from surprises." The militia could then be used to back up the regular army, but it had to be a well-trained, well-led, and well-supplied militia for it to be effective.[2]

The members of Congress seemed not to pay much heed to Washington's well-reasoned approach to national defense. It is likely that a sense of euphoria still attended the "victory" over the British, but it is more likely that they just did not want to spend any more of their extremely limited funds on national defense at a time when there was no immediate threat. The Congress, after all, had almost no power to generate revenue and had to depend on the good will of individual states to provide money for an army or for any other purpose. By the summer of 1784, therefore, the regular army of the United States consisted of just eighty enlisted men and a handful of officers, none of whom ranked higher than a captain!

That same year, a growing Indian menace along the western frontier prompted Congress to pass a law calling for the enlistment of 700 volunteers for one year, but because Congress had no power to compel enlistments, this force never reached its authorized strength. In spite of the poor turnout, Congress soon decided to extend the life of this force for three more years, and Brigadier General Josiah Harmar, a veteran of the war against England, manfully led this force into the trans-Appalachian west. By late 1786, the army's short statutory life had almost expired, but the influx of settlers into the area meant that conflict with Indians was becoming more and more common.

Meanwhile, in the more settled areas of the country along the eastern seaboard, Americans were beginning to get used to the idea of political independence from Great Britain. Avowed nationalists had taken it upon themselves to revamp the system of government that had emerged during the Revolutionary War, and they had written a brand new constitution that saw former General George Washington elevated to the position of President. The newly reorganized Congress also had the power now to levy taxes and raise an army without having to depend upon the individual states to provide funds or manpower voluntarily. At the end of April 1790, Congress passed legislation calling for an army that would be maintained for three years. The 1,273 officers and men authorized were to make up a three-battalion regiment of infantry and one battalion of artillery. President Washington received authorization to call for militia on an ad hoc basis. One outspoken critic assured Secretary of War Henry Knox "that the people of this Country will not inlist [*sic*] upon the terms proposed" and that the troops thus raised would "consist of a set of Vagabonds ... and the very *dregs* of other *nations*."[3]

A month later, Indians attacked an army supply convoy, and war seemed inescapable. General Harmar received instructions to punish the Indians responsible and restore peace to the frontier, but to say that success was elusive would be to vastly understate the case. His mixed force of regulars and volunteers finally set out in October of that year. The volunteers, who made up the majority of his force, were untrained and undisciplined. When Harmar's force finally met the Indians, it was soundly thrashed and sent scurrying back to the relative safety of Fort Washington, near Cincinnati.

A year later, another amalgamated force, this time under the command of Major General Arthur St. Clair, also met an overwhelming defeat. His losses numbered over 900, with 657 fatalities. In addition to the military casualties, thirty of the women accompanying the army were killed, many of whom, according to one observer, "were inhumanely butchered, with every indecent and aggravated circumstance of cruelty that can be imagined."[4]

Once again, the reliance on untrained militia proved to have been misplaced. One government official suggested that the low pay offered to soldiers only attracted men who could not earn a living doing anything else. "Too great a proportion of the privates," he believed, "appeared to be totally debilitated and rendered incapable of service, either from their youth (mere boys) or by their excessive intemperance and abandoned habits. These men who are to be purchased from the prisons ... and brothels of the nation at two dollars per month, will never answer our purpose of fighting Indians." A regular officer was equally uncomplimentary when he wrote in his diary:

> Picked up and recruited from the offscourings of large towns and cities; enervated by idleness, debaucheries and every species of vice, it was impossible they could have been made competent to the arduous duties of Indian warfare. An extraordinary aversion to service was also conspicuous amongst them and demonstrated by the most repeated desertions, in many instances to the very foe we were to combat. The late period at which they had been brought into the field left no leisure or opportunity to attempt to discipline them. They were, moreover, badly clothed, badly paid and badly fed.[5]

Congress reacted in March 1792 to this latest military disaster, once again enlarging the size of the army. This legislation provided that the existing artillery battalion and both infantry battalions of the regular army were to be recruited up to their fully authorized strength. The act also added four companies of mounted troops and three more infantry regiments to the national force—but only on a temporary basis. The firmly entrenched fear of standing armies meant that the new units would only exist for three years, and less than that if the problems with the Indians were settled sooner. This new force brought the total authorized strength of the army to 5,000 officers and men. It was organized along the lines of the old Roman legions; in fact, the army now became the Legion of the United States, and it was broken up into four sublegions. Each sublegion was authorized eight infantry companies, four rifle companies, one light dragoon company, and one artillery company. Thus each sublegion was relatively self-contained and could, theoretically, campaign effectively against any kind of enemy.

Then in May, Congress sought to further strengthen the military by passing the "Act for making further and more effectual Provision for the Protection of the Frontiers of the United States." Known more familiarly as the Militia Act of 1792, this legislation laid the groundwork for universal military training by requiring every healthy, white, male citizen between the ages of eighteen and forty-five to enroll in his state's militia. He was, furthermore, to furnish himself with a suitable firearm, ammunition, and other martial impedimenta. Until superseded by the Dick Act of 1903, this law, even though extremely unevenly enforced, was the cornerstone of the American militia tradition.

Major General Anthony Wayne came out of retirement to command the Legion and soon subjected its members to a vigorous training regimen. The Indians in the Ohio country, meanwhile, emboldened by the decisive victories over Harmar and St. Clair, demanded total white withdrawal from all lands north of the Ohio River. Negotiations failed to move them, so on August 20, 1794, Wayne's legion attacked a combined force of Indians and Canadians that had found refuge amid trees that had toppled in a severe storm some years earlier. Within forty-five minutes, this battle, dubbed the Battle of Fallen Timbers, was over and the Indians were on the run. The Indian threat in the Ohio country was soon at an end.

In 1797, relations between the United States and its recent ally France began to sour. Officers of the French court had insulted American diplomats in Paris and demanded large bribes of them. President John Adams asked Congress for a larger army and navy and permission to use them against France to defend American rights. Congress responded by giving him the authority to raise a 10,000-man-army for up to three years' service. George Washington agreed to come out of retirement with the rank of lieutenant general and lead this Provisional Army if necessary. Although the United States and France waged an undeclared naval war for almost two years, the Provisional Army was never called up, and Washington was allowed to remain the gentleman farmer he had become.

Major General Anthony Wayne. (*Courtesy of the Library of Congress*)

UNITED STATES MILITARY FORCES FROM THE EARLY 1800s TO 1860

Thomas Jefferson became President in 1801—after the threat of war with France had subsided, and with it the need for a large military force—and immediately took steps to cut back the size of the army. Within three years, he reduced army manpower from 4,410 to 2,579 and cut the military budget by two-thirds. It was under Jefferson, however, that the United States Military Academy at West Point, New York, came into being. There had been an earlier attempt, in 1794, to set up a training facility at West Point, but the prospective cadets rebelled and burned down the classroom building. In October 1802, however, twelve cadets reported for training, and this time there were no arsonists in their midst. Their daily routine consisted of four hours of classroom work in the morning (in which ***every*** student recited lessons ***every*** day) and field sports in the afternoon. The length of the curriculum varied at first, taking anywhere from nine months to six years, and the first two graduates finished up a year after they had started. Eventually, ten of the first twelve cadets graduated, and one was still on active duty as an artillery colonel over sixty years later during the Civil War.

Jefferson also presided over the acquisition of the huge Louisiana Territory from France, and he was quick to send army explorers into it. Captain Meriwether Lewis, the president's personal assistant in the White House, led the most ambitious of these efforts. Lewis was ably assisted by fellow officer William Clark and accompanied by a Corps of Discovery made up, for the most part, of enlisted soldiers. The journey began in May 1804 when the expedition left St. Louis for the upper reaches of the Missouri River. Twenty-eight months later Lewis and Clark returned. They had trekked by water, by horseback, and by foot all the way to the Pacific coast and brought back much valuable information on the land, the flora, the fauna, and the people they met along the way.

While Lewis and Clark struggled up the Missouri and then overland to the Pacific, another army officer led an exploration searching for the source of the Mississippi River. Captain Zebulon Pike's expedition was about half the size of the Corps of Discovery and not nearly as successful. Pike reached the site of present-day Minneapolis before returning to St. Louis, but failed to find the source of the great river. After only two-and-a-half months of rest, Pike was on the move again. This time, General James Wilkinson sent him into the southern reaches of the vast Louisiana Territory ostensibly to map the rivers he encountered but more likely to spy on the Spanish in neighboring Mexico. The results of this expedition were mixed. Poorly prepared for winter weather, Pike and his men nearly perished in the winter of 1806–1807 and were captured by Spanish troops. The main value of the mission was the military information Pike was able to glean from his captors before they escorted him back to the United States in July 1807. Over the next several decades, other army officers, such as Stephen Long in 1820 and John Frémont in the 1830s and 1840s, also penetrated into the West for the purpose of gathering data on the plants, animals, people, weather, and geography of the area.

Open warfare between England and France broke out anew in 1803, and that meant big profits for American merchants who traded with both countries. Both belligerents took steps to stop this trade. Britain seized American ships bound for France and confiscated their cargoes unless they stopped in England first and paid customs duties. Napoleon responded with the Milan Decree, whereby French ships seized any vessel that sailed to a British port, paid British duties, or allowed itself to be searched by British ships. This effectively made any trade with either warring nation almost impossible. The British also began impressing, or kidnapping, American sailors into the Royal Navy. They claimed they were only taking back British sailors who had deserted the Royal Navy. (By 1811, they had taken some 10,000 men.)

Events pushed toward war in 1807. On June 22, the American naval ship *Chesapeake* left Norfolk, Virginia, en route to the Mediterranean with a crew of 375 men. Among them were four alleged deserters from the Royal Navy. The *Chesapeake*'s captain, Commodore James Barron, had been in a hurry to leave and had temporarily cluttered his gun decks with various supplies that his men would stow properly while they were under way. About ten miles out, the British frigate *Leopard* signaled the *Chesapeake* and asked to deliver a despatch. When the ships pulled alongside to allow the British officer to come on board the *Chesapeake* with his message, the American gun crews were not ready for action—as they should have been, whenever they were that close to another country's warship.

The British officer's message was in the form of a demand that Commodore Barron allow him to search among the *Chesapeake*'s crew and retrieve the errant British seamen. Barron refused, of course, and the visiting officer returned to the *Leopard.* The British warship then fired three broadsides at point-blank range into the *Chesapeake,* killing three and wounding eighteen. The *Chesapeake* managed only a single shot in its own defense before hauling down the flag in abject surrender. British sailors then came aboard and removed the four "deserters," three of whom were native-born Americans. War seemed imminent, but Jefferson, as well as his successor President James Madison, used diplomatic measures to avert immediate bloodshed.

Even as trouble with England loomed, settlers continued to flood into the trans-Appalachian West. And as they moved into the Indiana Territory, there was renewed conflict with the Indians there. Successive treaties reserved more and more Indian land for the encroaching whites until an armed confrontation was almost inevitable, and the secretary of war ordered the Fourth Infantry Regiment from Pittsburgh to the territorial capital at Vincennes in July 1811. Governor William Henry Harrison met on several occasions with the Shawnee leader Tecumseh and his equally charismatic brother Tenskwatawa, or the Prophet, hoping to find some way to resolve their differences without bloodshed.

Early in August, negotiations having failed to achieve results, Tecumseh left Vincennes and journeyed south of the Ohio River to forge alliances with some of the southern tribes. While he was gone, Governor Harrison led a combined force of regulars and militia volunteers north from Vincennes to build a fort along the Wabash River, near present-day Terre Haute. Then in early November, the soldiers moved farther north toward the Shawnee village of Prophetstown, near the juncture of the Wabash and Tippecanoe Rivers.

By the afternoon of November 6, Harrison's command had reached a point within sight of Prophetstown, and Shawnee emissaries came out to parley with Harrison briefly. The soldiers went into camp within 150 yards of the town, though they were well aware of the potential danger in the situation. Not wanting to experience what had befallen St. Clair's careless troops twenty years earlier, they slept fully clothed and in combat formations with loaded muskets at their sides.

The Indians attacked the next morning about 4:30, hoping to catch the soldiers off guard, but the men were already up and were soon returning fire. The attack was not well coordinated. Some Indians swept forward yelling and shooting. Others crept through the grass and trees looking for every bit of concealment they could find on this cold, rainy morning. The soldiers' well-trained defensive fire soon took the fight out of the attackers, and by the time it was full light the Indians had withdrawn in defeat.

The Battle of Tippecanoe cost the soldiers some sixty or so killed and double that number wounded. Indian losses are unknown, but might have been less. The Shawnees and their Kickapoo and Winnebago allies scattered, but Indian troubles were not at an end.

THE WAR OF 1812

On June 1, 1812, President Madison, listing several specific complaints, finally asked Congress for a declaration of war. The British were still kidnapping sailors from American ships. The Royal Navy had set up a virtual naval blockade of the U.S. coastline in order to intercept American merchantmen bound for France. Americans suspected that British forces in Canada were inciting the Indians to attack American settlements, though the suspicion was unfounded. The Indians did not need encouragement to mount these attacks, and the British were in fact worried that such violence would provoke a larger problem with Americans. The Anglo-Indian alliance was a self-fulfilled prophecy for the Americans, because after Tippecanoe, the Indians were driven into the arms of the British. Congress responded on June 18 with a declaration of war. Ironically, Britain had conceded almost all points of contention and hoped to avert war. In fact, just two days before Congress's declaration of war, Britain agreed to reopen the seas to American ships.

The United States was woefully unprepared to fight one of the strongest nations in the world. The navy only had twenty ships, none of which could match the big 74-gun ships of the line of the British navy. Three of the American ships were 44-gun frigates left over from the Quasi War with France (the undeclared war that lasted from 1798 to 1800) and had done duty in the Mediterranean Ocean and against the Barbary Pirates. Three others were smaller 36-gun vessels and the remainder consisted of small sloops, brigs, and schooners.

Luckily for the Americans, British forces were tied up with Napoleon in Europe and did not devote much in the way of resources and men to fight the Americans. There were 7,000 British and Canadian regulars in Canada, plus 10,000 Canadian militiamen, and 3,500 Indians. By September 1812, the Royal Navy had eleven ships of the line, thirty-four frigates, and thirty-four smaller craft ready to do battle in the western Atlantic.

War began with a divided populace in America and no clear strategy as to how to conduct the war. As there was no way to match enemy sea power, a land invasion of Canada seemed to have been decided upon by default. There was an unrealistic belief that American militiamen could conquer Canada without breaking a sweat. Another big problem was that militiamen could legally refuse to participate in an invasion of Canada or any other country. By law they were to be used only in defense, and only within the borders of the United States.

The first two years of the war saw repeated attempts by the American army to invade British Canada repulsed. During the summer of 1814, after the collapse of French resistance on the Continent, Britain began to shuttle battle-hardened troops from Europe—where they had been battling Napoleon—to the United States. Going on the offensive, the British decided to attack out of Canada and to operate along the Atlantic coastline. Sir George Prevost, Governor-General of Canada, led 11,000 troops across the border on September 1, 1814 and headed for the American camp at Plattsburgh, New York. Brigadier General Alexander Macomb faced him with a mixed force of 4,500 regulars, volunteers, and militia. Prevost hesitated, waiting for a British fleet to support further movement against Plattsburgh. Meanwhile, a small American flotilla under Commodore Thomas Macdonough blasted the British squadron into submission before it could support Prevost. With this unlikely turn of events, Prevost, perhaps remembering that General John Burgoyne had been forced to surrender his entire army in this same area back in 1777, pulled up stakes and returned to Canada without offering battle.

Along the Atlantic seaboard, however, the British had more success. Naval superiority allowed them to raid coastal areas with impunity. In August 1814, they captured Washington, DC and burned the White House, the Capitol, and several other government buildings. They were unsuccessful, however, in their attempt on Baltimore. It was here that Francis Scott Key commemorated American defense of that city with his "Star-Spangled Banner."

The British next shifted their emphasis from the Atlantic to the Gulf coast and aimed at the important port of New Orleans. Veterans of the Napoleonic campaigns landed near New Orleans late in December 1814. Two weeks later, Major General Sir Edward Pakenham launched them in a direct frontal assault on the American position, commanded by Major General Andrew Jackson and composed of a mixed lot of regulars, militia, volunteers, and some of Jean Lafitte's pirates. American artillery, firing from across the Mississippi, shredded the tightly packed enemy formations with grapeshot and canister. American infantry, protected behind stout earthworks and cotton-bale barricades, added to the carnage. General Pakenham died on the field, one of more than 2,000 British casualties; American losses were fifteen.

The War of 1812 is barely a footnote to the Napoleonic Wars in British textbooks, but offered valuable lessons to the young United States. With proper training and leadership, both regulars and militia volunteers performed well in battle. The regulars pointed with pride to their efforts at places like Chippewa and Lundy's Lane, and were appalled when large numbers of militiamen refused to invade Canada in 1812 and also the pitiable "defense" of Washington, DC in 1814. The militiamen, on the other hand, were proud of their defense of Baltimore and New Orleans, and were equally horrified at the regulars' refusal to support militia Major General Stephen van Rensselaer's attack into Canada in 1812 and the poor overall performance of Major General James Wilkinson. The output of the infant military academy at West Point—engineer officers—proved its value by way of the fortifications erected at places such as Fort Erie, Fort Meigs, and Plattsburgh. Neither regulars nor volunteers had a monopoly on able leadership, as proven by the emergence of men such as Jacob Brown, Winfield Scott, and Andrew Jackson. Some lessons were apparently not learned, however. The nation still faced the problem of how to raise an army, not how to improvise in the face of the enemy, as had been done in this war.

THE U.S. ARMY PURSUES AMERICAN INDIANS

The army, now reduced to a maximum of 10,000 officers and men, would not face another foreign foe for almost three decades. Those years would not be entirely without conflict, however, as elements of this small army would be fairly busy trying to control various Indian outbreaks. The next problem area for the army was to the south—Florida. This Spanish colony had long been a haven for runaway slaves and a place from which Indians and pirates frequently raided American settlements and ships.

In December 1817, President James Monroe sent Major General Andrew Jackson into Florida to punish some of the marauding Seminole Indians. Not only did he defeat the Seminoles, he overthrew the Spanish government there and executed two British citizens whom Jackson alleged had incited the Indians against the Americans. Public reaction was mixed. Spain wanted Jackson punished, obviously. Nor was Britain very happy. Secretary of State John Quincy Adams, however, saw Jackson's deeds as positive, not negative. He assured the Spanish government that Jackson had acted within his rights under a 1795 treaty in which Spain promised to keep the Indians in Florida under control. Spain, sensing an inevitable takeover, ceded Florida to the United States in 1819 under the terms of the Adams–Onís Treaty.

The seemingly insatiable land-lust of the Americans moving into Florida actually intensified conflict with Indians in that part of the country. More and more white settlers, many with their black slaves, moved into areas already occupied by Indians. President Monroe had already let it be known in his first annual message that armed conflict between whites and Indians would be considerably alleviated by the removal of the Indians from lands coveted by the growing number of white settlers. The government proposed to exchange the fertile Indian lands of the southeastern United States for the considerably less attractive lands in present-day Arkansas and Oklahoma. In "justification" of this policy, the president informed his listeners that "the earth was given to mankind to support the greatest number of which it is capable, and no tribe or people have a right to withhold from the wants of others more than is necessary for their own support and comfort." He also stated, rather disingenuously: "The hunter state can exist only in the vast uncultivated desert."[6]

In 1820, the House of Representatives was once again in the mood to reduce the size of the Army, and solicited suggestions from Secretary of War John C. Calhoun on how best to accomplish this. The lack of preparedness at the outbreak of war in 1812 was a lesson that had not been lost on the secretary, and his recommendation showed much thoughtfulness. First, he proposed that there be no reduction in the sizes of the staff bureaus during peacetime. That way, when the next war came the basic staff structures would already be in place, thus avoiding the loss of valuable time. Similarly, he advised against the disbanding of existing regiments. Instead, the manpower of each regiment's component companies would be reduced. Then, in the event of another war, the strengths of these units could more easily be augmented by new recruits who would be injected into existing companies of experienced soldiers. In other words, Calhoun wrote, "At the commencement of hostilities there should be nothing either to new model or to create." Unfortunately, Congress did not see the obvious benefit of such an expansible army for another thirty years.[7]

The same Andrew Jackson who had invaded Florida and brought about a short-lived war with its native inhabitants in 1818 became president in 1829 and resolved to remove the Indians altogether. "Such a policy," he said, "will separate the Indians from immediate contact with settlements of whites; ... enable them to pursue happiness in their own way and under their own rude institutions; ... and perhaps cause them, gradually, under the protection of the Government and through the influence of good counsels, to cast off their savage habits and become an interesting, civilized, and Christian community." To save the Indian from "perhaps utter annihilation," he went on, "the General Government kindly offers him a new home, and proposes to pay the whole expense of his removal and settlement." Congress soon validated this plan with the Indian Removal Act of 1830, by which it appropriated half a million dollars to relocate Indians to the western lands.[8]

Indians of the combined Sac and Fox tribes, who had been relocated westward into Iowa from Illinois, faced conflict with other tribes there and sought to return to their former homes east of the Mississippi. What followed was the short Black Hawk War, named for the aged Indian leader. One of the ironies of this conflict was the presence of two men who would later assume great national importance: Lieutenant Jefferson Davis was one of the young West Point–educated officers in the regular army and a young man named Abraham Lincoln was among the Illinois militia.

Partly as a result of chasing Indians across the Illinois prairies, the army saw the wisdom of employing mounted troops instead of just foot-slogging infantrymen. The first tentative step in this direction was the creation, in the summer of 1832, of a battalion of mounted rangers, who volunteered for one year. It was obvious that the government was not fully committed to the idea of a mounted force, as each volunteer had to provide his own horse, his own weapons, and his own clothing. The operational success of the Ranger Battalion was less than sterling, but its mere existence showed the usefulness of having a well-trained, well-disciplined cavalry. Consequently, Congress authorized a regular dragoon regiment to succeed the rangers in the summer of 1833.

Meanwhile, reactions among the Five Civilized Tribes—the Cherokee, Choctaw, Chickasaw, Creek, and Seminole—to the Indian Removal Act were varied. The Cherokee mounted a spirited, if ineffective, resistance in the courts. Most of the Cherokee, Choctaw, and Chickasaw appeared to bow to the inevitable and headed west, whereas many of the Seminoles and Creeks resisted.

In Florida, the Seminoles—an offshoot of the Creeks—were the most recalcitrant. Indian leaders had signed the Treaty of Fort Moultrie in 1823 that guaranteed their continued unhampered occupation of some five million acres. Nine years later, faced with a growing white presence, they reluctantly signed the Treaty of Payne's Landing, which, in effect, nullified the earlier agreement. Under the new terms, a half dozen Seminole leaders traveled to the West to inspect the lands now set aside for them. Finding the region at least marginally acceptable, they signed yet another treaty at Fort Gibson that bound the rest of their tribe to emigrate. A large number of Seminoles remained obstinate, claiming that these chiefs had no right to sign treaties on their behalf. They repudiated this latest treaty and fell back on the terms of the agreement at Fort Moultrie, allowing them to stay in Florida for at least another twenty years.[9]

Troops were dispatched to Florida to begin the process of escorting "willing" Seminoles to their new homes across the Mississippi and to urge those reluctant to comply. There were scattered instances of violence by the Indians , but the most violent was the massacre of an army patrol on December 28, 1835. On that day, Major Francis Dade was leading a 100-man column of troops from Fort Brooke to Fort King (from present-day Tampa to Ocala). The weather was cold, and the men had donned their heavy greatcoats. Unfortunately, and certainly not anticipating any dangers other than the weather, they had not taken the time to unsling their cartridge boxes, but had merely thrown their coats on over them. Thus, when the Indians struck, the soldiers had a difficult time getting to their cartridges and were unable to resist effectively. The annihilation was almost complete. By the end of the fighting, Dade and all but three of his men lay dead on the field.

For the next several years, soldiers and marines tramped around in the forests and swamps of Florida trying to bring to bay the elusive Seminoles. Successes were small. Gradually, Indians in ones and twos surrendered or were captured and sent west. By 1842, the government decided that to continue this war was no longer valuable. The few remaining Seminoles were allowed to continue living in Florida.

This war had been costly. The government had spent millions of dollars and the lives of 1,500 soldiers had been lost. One young West Point–trained officer lamented the high cost incurred. He was sure "that it cost more than $100,000 to capture or kill one Indian. I believe it would have been much cheaper," he continued, "to let the matter out by contract." In other words, offer each Indian such a huge amount of money to move that there would have been no need for military coercion. "How could a soldier," he continued, "loaded down with his musket and cartridge box, his canteen and haversack succeed in catching wholly unencumbered Indians who knew every path and stream and culvert and who were not encumbered with any commissariat?"[10]

The Creeks, whose lands were in present-day Georgia and Alabama, signed a treaty in 1833 that allowed those who wanted to emigrate to do so while those who chose to remain received individual plots of land. These allotments—320 acres to most heads of families—were extremely generous by contemporary agricultural standards but did not leave the Indians much room to roam and hunt. By 1836, unscrupulous white speculators had swindled many of the Indians out of their lands. Many unhappy and dispossessed Creeks soon resorted to violence out of a sense of frustration and betrayal. Soldiers, both regulars and militiamen, soon put an end to the brief war that followed.

WAR IN TEXAS

Even while the U.S. Army was fighting Indians in Florida and Alabama, other American men were at war in Mexican Texas. Americans had begun emigrating to Texas under very favorable terms in the 1820s. But by the early 1830s, concerned by the extremely high percentage of Americans there, Mexican officials passed laws halting further immigration and putting strict controls on the activities of those already there. The Americans, meanwhile, unsuccessfully sought to have Texas recognized as a Mexican state—separate from its co-province of Coahuila. Finally, in the fall of 1835, hostilities began between the Americans living in Texas—the Texians—and the government of Mexican strongman Antonio López de Santa Anna.

After an initial skirmish near the village of Gonzalez, Texians swelled their ranks with a large influx of Americans from the United States eager for a fight. A ragtag army of these men forced the capitulation of a small Mexican garrison at San Antonio on December 9, but the war had just begun. Santa Anna led a hastily recruited army northward to avenge the insult to Mexico and to himself, for the defeated commandant at San Antonio was his brother-in-law.

By mid-February 1836, most of the Texians had left San Antonio. But about 150 men stayed behind and began fortifying the ruins of an old mission known as the Alamo. Santa Anna arrived on February 24 and immediately laid siege to the fort. For the next thirteen days, his soldiers pushed closer and closer to their objective while, inside the fort, Colonel William Travis, the commander, sent riders out with pleas for reinforcements. Finally, in the pre-dawn hours of March 6, a massive Mexican assault breached the walls of the old mission and the defenders were slaughtered.

Another Mexican army, under General José de Urrea headed up the coast toward the village of Goliad where a force of some 400 Americans, under the command of Colonel James Fannin, waited apprehensively in the old Spanish *presidio*. Fannin finally heeded the instructions of General Sam Houston to abandon Goliad and retreat northward toward the rest of the Texas army on March 19. After only a few miles' march, however, Mexican cavalry overtook the slow-moving troops and attacked. Fighting through the afternoon, Fannin realized that further resistance would only result in more casualties. He therefore surrendered his force the next morning; the Mexicans escorted the Americans back to Goliad and imprisoned them within the walls of the fort that they had only just abandoned.

A week later, Mexican soldiers organized those captives who were able to walk into three marching columns and headed them out of the fort in three different directions. The wounded remained behind. The Americans were told that they were marching to the coast where a ship would pick them up and return them to New Orleans. Instead, however, as each column reached a point about a mile or so away from the fort, the guards halted for a rest. As the men stood or sat in the grass, the *soldados* remained standing, formed a firing rank, and opened up on the terrified prisoners. There were not many survivors. Back at the fort, the wounded, including Colonel Fannin, were brought into the parade ground and shot.

Texas statesmen, meanwhile, passed a resolution of independence from Mexico, and more and more volunteers poured in from the United States to join General Houston's growing "army." These men were impatient to avenge the defeat at the Alamo and the slaughter at Goliad. General Houston, however, steadily led his army back, away from the advancing forces of Santa Anna. Finally, he stopped, along the banks of the San Jacinto River near the present-day city that bears his name. There, on the afternoon of April 21, 1836, his men attacked the Mexican camp. Screaming "Remember the Alamo!" and "Remember Goliad!" Houston's men showed little mercy. In a matter of minutes the Mexican army was shattered and Santa Anna was fleeing for his life.

The next day, a couple of mounted scouts captured the Mexican leader wearing the simple uniform of a Mexican private. His identity was soon revealed, and many of the Texians wanted the supreme revenge of killing him on the spot. Sam Houston, however, wounded in the ankle during the battle, recognized that Santa Anna was more valuable alive than dead and intervened. The Mexican leader was instead forced to sign the Treaty of Velasco recognizing the independence of Texas from Mexico. All Mexican troops north of the Rio Grande were ordered to retrace their steps across the river.

Following the Battle of San Jacinto and the Treaty of Velasco, Texas existed as an independent republic for the next nine years. Americans in Texas, however, wanted to join their newly won territory to the United States immediately. The United States finally annexed Texas by a joint resolution of Congress in 1845. The Mexican government, having understandably repudiated the Treaty of Velasco, looked upon annexation as nothing more than the theft of Mexican territory and, therefore, an act of war, and the Mexican diplomatic minister asked for the return of his passport and traveled back to Mexico. To make matters worse, Texas claimed a southern boundary of the Rio Grande River when the historic boundary for the Mexican province of Texas had been the Nueces River—some 125 miles farther north (when measured near the coast). So even if Mexico were to recognize the loss of Texas, the Rio Grande claim meant that the United States was trying to take part of Tamaulipas State along with Texas.

Brigadier General Zachary Taylor took about half of the small U.S. Army to the north bank of the Nueces, near present-day Corpus Christi, in the summer of 1845 as an Army of Observation. It was on ground that was indisputably part of Texas, and it was there to make sure that Mexico did not try to invade and take Texas back before the formal annexation proceedings could be completed.

In the fall of 1845, President James K. Polk learned that Mexico was willing to negotiate on some unpaid claims against it by American citizens due to losses incurred during various revolutions in Mexico. An international tribunal in 1842 had mediated

Not known for his sartorial splendor, Major General Zachary Taylor's nickname was "Old Rough and Ready." (*Courtesy of the Library of Congress*)

and set up a payment schedule, but Mexico had reneged a year later. So Polk sent John Slidell to negotiate. Slidell had instructions to try to offer to forgive this debt in return for recognition of the Rio Grande as the border of Texas. He was also to negotiate for the purchase of California and New Mexico Territory. Mexican officials were outraged! They would certainly not sell off half their country and in fact refused to talk to Slidell at all when they found out his entire mission.

WAR AGAINST MEXICO

By early 1846, the annexation of Texas was complete, and General Taylor moved his army down the coast to the Rio Grande—just opposite the Mexican town of Matamoros. His force was now known as the Army of Occupation. Mexican General Pedro Ampudia notified Taylor in April 1846 that he must immediately evacuate back to the Nueces because he was on Mexican soil. Taylor, of course, refused and began building an earthen fort on the north side of the river—Fort Texas. On April 25, a large force of Mexican dragoons crossed over and defeated an American mounted patrol. Taylor reported to Washington that war had begun.

President Polk, in fact, had already decided on war, and on May 11, after receiving Taylor's message, he told Congress: "Mexico has passed the boundary of the United States, has invaded our territory and shed American blood on the American soil. She has proclaimed that hostilities have commenced, and that the two nations are now at war." Congress responded two days later with a declaration of war and a call for 50,000 volunteers to help the army.[11]

Back in Texas, Taylor took most of his troops to Point Isabel for supplies on May 1, leaving some 500 men in Fort Texas. Major General Mariano Arista—having replaced Ampudia—took a large force over the river to confront the divided American force. He used some of his troops to bombard Fort Texas and took the bulk looking for Taylor. On May 7, Taylor's men, along with 200 supply wagons, started back from Point Isabel. The next day, Taylor found the Mexican army blocking the road and prepared for battle at a place called Palo Alto. The American army held firm in the face of repeated Mexican attacks. By the end of the day, Taylor's command had suffered fifty casualties: five killed, forty-three wounded, and two missing out of a force of 2,200 men. Arista's losses were much higher: 102 killed, 129 wounded, and 26 missing out of a force of 3,700 men. The next day, as Taylor prepared for the resumption of battle, his scouts discovered that the enemy had departed.

Arista had not gone far. He positioned his army in an old dry riverbed called Resaca de la Palma and waited for Taylor to attack. The Americans were again victorious, and the defeated Mexicans swarmed back to Matamoros. Many of them drowned in their haste to cross the Rio Grande.

By May 17, 1846, Taylor occupied Matamoros, and Whig politicians started talking about him as presidential material. The Mexican Army, meanwhile, fell back to Monterrey, and Taylor spent the next few months waiting for volunteers to arrive from the United States before engaging in any more active campaigning.

By September, Taylor was ready to move against the Mexican Army again. He reached Monterrey by September 19 and began a three-day battle on the 21st. Fighting was difficult in the city. Urban architecture promoted good defense. Parapeted buildings offered protection to soldiers on the roofs, and Mexican artillery took up positions at street intersections where they could sweep attackers from several directions. The Americans used the same tactic that had been used in San Antonio in 1835—they broke into the end building of a block and then went through the walls until they reached the other end of the block. They could then attack enemy gun crews close up and avoid dangerous crossfire.

By September 23, Americans had penetrated into the heart of the city, but both sides were exhausted. Taylor saw nothing to be gained by further battle and appointed a three-man commission to parley with the enemy. Negotiations resulted in a truce whereby Mexican troops evacuated the city with their small arms and some of their cannons. They were to withdraw several miles into the interior. American troops would not pursue. The truce was to last for eight weeks to give diplomats time to iron out a way to end the war.

But President Polk repudiated the armistice; the war did not end. Instead, General Santa Anna led a ragtag force northward toward General Taylor's position near a ranch called Buena Vista. The Mexican force attacked the outnumbered Americans on February 22 but was unable to defeat them in a two-day battle.

In the meantime, a second armed thrust had headed for Mexican California. Colonel Stephen Watts Kearny led a mixed force of regulars and volunteers—the Army of the West—from Fort Leavenworth toward Santa Fe. Kearny expected fierce resistance in a canyon near Santa Fe, but the Mexican troops decided not to challenge. The Army of the West took Santa Fe without firing a shot. Kearny subsequently kept part of his force on occupation duty in New Mexico while he led another part into southern California. Yet a third segment marched south into Mexico under the command of the renowned Missouri volunteer leader Alexander Doniphan.

With still no diplomatic resolution to the war, President Polk reluctantly ordered General Winfield Scott to lead an amphibious invasion of Mexico, with the ultimate aim of capturing the capital city. The resultant landing, south of the coastal town of Vera Cruz in March 1847, was America's first instance of a successful invasion of another country. The landing was unopposed; within a matter of a few weeks, the fortified city of Vera Cruz had capitulated and Scott led his troops inland and toward Mexico City. A string of victories followed, at places like Cerro Gordo, Padierna, Churubusco, Molino del Rey, and Chapultepec. Mexican leaders surrendered the capital on September 14; the war was soon over and the large army of American volunteers went home.

THE U.S. MILITARY AND THE CHURCH OF JESUS CHRIST OF LATTER-DAY SAINTS

Concurrent with the early stages of the war with Mexico, members of the Church of Jesus Christ of Latter-Day Saints—the Mormons—had begun an exodus from Illinois toward the West. These men and women, seen by many as somehow posing a threat to the more mainstream denominations, had decided to distance themselves from the animosity and prejudice that had been their lot throughout their church's short existence. Brigham Young, the church's leader after the murder of its founder Joseph Smith, sought to lead his flock completely out of the United States and into the northern vastness of the territory claimed by Mexico. With war and the subsequent movement of American forces in the same direction, some 500 Mormon men mustered into the army as a separate Mormon Battalion. The existence of this unit served a dual purpose for its members. It helped to show those who had persecuted them that they were just as loyal to the United States in its hour of need as anyone else was. And it was a way for these volunteer soldiers to have the federal government pay for their movement west.

By the time the war ended, the Mormons had begun to scrape an existence out of the harsh lands in the vicinity of the Great Salt Lake, in present-day Utah. Ironically, however, they had not actually escaped the reaches of the United States because Mexico had surrendered all of this land as a result of the Treaty of Guadalupe Hidalgo. The Mormons, nevertheless, were far removed from physical contact with most nonbelievers and worked hard over the next few years to make their desert oasis habitable.

As the population of Utah Territory grew, so too did friction between its inhabitants and those passing through on their way to California and Oregon. In late October 1853, Indians attacked a military surveying party in Utah, leaving eight fatalities. Almost immediately, rumors began to circulate that Brigham Young and the Mormon hierarchy had instigated the attack. Four years later Indians attacked a party of 137 emigrants from Arkansas on its way to California. During a lull in the fighting, a party of Mormon men approached the travelers under a flag of truce. The Mormons convinced them to lay down their arms and accept an escort to a safe place. Instead, however, the Mormons and Indians murdered all the unarmed settlers over the age of ten; a tragic event that became known as the Mountain Meadows massacre. By this time, President James Buchanan had already decided to send the army to Utah to maintain peace, to force Mormon leaders to respect federal law, and to replace Territorial Governor Brigham Young.

Brigadier General William S. Harney commanded the expedition originally, although without much enthusiasm, and Brigadier General Albert Sydney Johnston soon replaced him. A dragoon regiment, most of two infantry regiments, and two artillery batteries made up the force headed for Utah by mid-summer of 1857. As this force moved nearer its goal, irregular groups of Mormons successfully raided its supply trains, drove off its livestock, and hindered its progress. Winter snows soon made it impossible to traverse the passes through the mountains east of Great Salt Lake, forcing the troops to go into winter quarters where they suffered through bitter weather, short rations, and low morale.

In the spring of 1858, before active campaigning could begin anew, President Buchanan issued pardons to the Mormons, although many of them were still not sure what they had done wrong in the first place. The *New York Times* editorialized that "the whole story of the war is crowded by as much ignorance, stupidity and dishonesty, as any Government ever managed to get into the annals of a single year. An army was sent to chastise rebels before it was clearly ascertained whether or not there were any rebels to chastise. It was sent forward in the Fall, just when it ought to have reached its destination." An infantry captain listed the casualties of this "war" as: "Wounded, none; killed, none; fooled, everybody." In just a few years, however, this officer and every other soldier in the nation would have reason to reflect on this almost bloodless conflict with a degree of nostalgia.[12]

THE ARMY FACES ITS MOST DIFFICULT TEST

As the 1850s came to an end, the United States was about to face its most severe test—Civil War. As one state after another decided to leave the Union, it presented difficult choices for officers and men of the army. Each had taken an oath, upon enlistment or commissioning, to defend and protect the U.S. Constitution. And now some of them found their home states disregarding that document and attempting to sever all connections with the Union. Most Americans at that time—soldiers and civilians—still considered their first loyalty to be toward their states, and only secondarily to the nation. Soldiers from the southern states now had to choose from among three options: they could honor their oaths and remain in the U.S. Army; they could resign (or desert) and cast their lot with their home states; or they could leave the Army and hope to avoid service in either army in the approaching fratricidal strife.

NOTES

1. Francis Paul Prucha, *The Sword of the Republic: The United States Army on the Frontier, 1783–1846,* (Lincoln and London: University of Nebraska Press, 1969, 1986), 4–5.

2. James Kirby Martin and Mark Edward Lender, *A Respectable Army: The Military Origins of the Republic, 1763–1789,* (Wheeling, Illinois: Harlan Davidson, 1982), 45 (1st quotation); Dave Richard Palmer and James W. Stryker, *Early American Wars and Military Institutions,* The West Point Military History Series, Thomas E. Griess, Series Editor (Wayne, New Jersey: Avery Publishing Group, 1986), 41 (2d quotation).

3. Marvin A. Kriedberg and Merton G. Henry, *History of Military Mobilization in the United States Army 1775–1945* (Washington, D.C.: Department of the Army, 1955), 26; Colonel Henry Jackson to Henry Knox, May 16, 1790, in Ward, *Department of War,* 104 (quotation).

4. James T. Currie, "The First Congressional Investigation: St. Clair's Military Disaster of 1791," *Parameters: Journal of the U.S. Army War College* 20 (December 1990), 251; Sargent, "Diary," 269 (quotation).

5. Prucha, *Sword of the Republic,* 26–27 (1st quotation); Prucha, *The Sword of the Republic,* 28–29; Sargent, "Diary," 242. (2d quotation).

6. James Monroe, First Annual Message, cited in David Brion Davis, ed. *Antebellum American Culture: An Interpretive Anthology,* (Lexington, Massachusetts and Toronto: D. C. Heath, 1979), 240.

7. Frederic Louis Huidekoper, *The Military Unpreparedness of the United states: A History of American Land Forces from Colonial Times until June 1, 1915,* (New York: MacMillan, 1916), 72 (quotation); Huidekoper, *Military Unpreparedness,* 92.

8. Andrew Jackson's second annual message to Congress in Davis, *Antebellum American Culture,* 241–242.

9. Jacob Rhett Motte, *Journey Into Wilderness: An Army Surgeon's Account of Life in Camp and Field during the Creek and Seminole Wars, 1836–1838,* edited by James F. Sunderman, (Gainesville, Florida: University of Florida Press, 1953), 264n.

10. Abner Doubleday, *My Life in the Old Army: The Reminiscences of Abner Doubleday form the Collections of the New-York Historical Society,* edited by Joseph E. Chance (Fort Worth, Texas: Texas Christian University Press, 1998), 183–184.

11. James K. Polk to the Senate and House of Representatives, May 11,1846, in James D. Richardson,ed. *A compilation of the Message and Papers of the Presidents, 1789–1897* (Washington, D.C.: Goverment Printing office, 1897) Vol.4, 442.

12. *New York Times,* July 17, 1858, as cited in Norman F. Furniss, *The Mormon Conflict 1850–1859* (New Haven: Yale University Press, 1960), 204 (1st quotation); Furniss, *Mormon Conflict,* 227 (2d quotation).

2 MAKING SOLDIERS

During times of war, or other impending crises, there were usually—but not always enough young men willing to join the army to meet its manpower needs. Recruiting officers attempting to fill the ranks of General Anthony Wayne's legion made appeals to young men's patriotism, sense of adventure, anxiety to escape unpleasant domestic situations, and desire to participate in the opening of the West. One recruiter's notice in a New England newspaper urged "all those young gentlemen who are possessed of enterprise, and have a wish to render their country very important services, to repair without loss of time to his recruiting rendezvous … where they can be freed from the anxiety of providing a support by hard and constant labour [*sic*]." Another recruiter promised those who took the oath that their service would be "easy, pleasing and profitable," and offered to be the experienced guide to those who agreed to "take the road that leads to honor."[1]

REASONS FOR ENLISTING

Glory

In times such as these, many young men answered the call for soldiers so they would not miss what they assumed to be their generation's most important event—a war! They might have heard colorful stories of their fathers' military exploits in earlier crises and wanted chances to continue the families' fine traditions of military service to their country. As war with Mexico loomed, the Army's surgeon-general wrote to a fellow officer that "it is much to be feared that the Mexicans intend to content themselves with waging a war of threats and denunciations, and that, after all their blustering, they will not afford our gallant officers and men … sufficient pastime to keep their blood in circulation." During the early stages of the Mexican War, for example, an Indiana volunteer wrote that his comrades-in-arms were "impatient to have active service" so they could "exhibit more observable acts of patriotism." Another man expressed sincere regret at having missed a chance to earn martial glory. "Our position did not enable us," he wrote, "to participate in the glory of the fight at Monterrey [September 1846] but we are confident that we shall have a chance at Saltillo or Tampico to show what we are made of." In the fall of 1847, a disappointed volunteer lamented that there did not seem to be "the least chance for sport in the way of a fight." Three months later, still unblooded by combat and the war virtually over, he wistfully declared: "I wish to remain in this Country some two or three years longer and therefore would prefer to see hostilities keep up for that length of time."[2]

During times of peace, it was difficult for army officials to entice healthy, qualified men into the ranks. Some men saw army service as a way to keep body and soul together when no other source of employment offered itself. This was particularly true during national financial crises, such as those that shook the nation in 1819, 1837, and 1857. Some were simply honest men down on their luck while others were, through intemperance or laziness, unfit to do much of anything. One army doctor characterized a recently arrived group of such recruits in 1814 as "principally composed of the miserable refuse of society, who never had energy enough to demonstrate that they lived, and scarcely enough to prove that they existed." A prominent Virginian, writing in 1798, characterized soldiers as "loungers, who live upon the public, who consume the fruits of their honest industry, under the pretext of protecting them from a foreign yoke." An army officer expressed a widely held belief that "the material [recruits] offered in time of peace is not of the most desirable character, consisting principally of newly arrived immigrants or those broken down by bad habits and dissipation, the idle, and the improvident." The anonymous author of a letter to a Philadelphia newspaper from Fort Leavenworth in 1858 characterized the makeup of that force as "the lowest dregs of society." The letter writer, who was probably an officer, further expressed his belief that fully 99 percent of enlisted men were habitual drunkards. One might expect that enlisted men might have a different perception of their fellow soldiers. But since these men were usually not as well educated as their officers and often came from a lower socioeconomic standing, they did not leave as many first-hand accounts of life in the ranks. Surprisingly, however, there are at least some reports from men in the ranks that tend to bear out the negative impression of American soldiers of the time. One soldier, a European immigrant like so many of his comrades-in-arms, responded to a letter from his parents asking him to describe the men with whom he served. "The greater part of the army," he wrote in 1857, "consists of men who either do not care to work, or who, because of being addicted to drink, cannot find employment."[3]

This same soldier obtained his discharge a couple of years later and went to work as a common laborer in California. After a month at his new occupation, he wrote: "I have now survived the first and hardest month after my five years of idleness [in the army], and I am no longer afraid that work is too hard for me and that I should therefore have to enter the army again." A future lieutenant general in the Confederate army held a similar opinion as to the usefulness of his army experience. "I have no particular wish to stay in the army," wrote a youthful twenty-three-year-old Richard S. Ewell in 1840, "but a positive antipathy to starving or to doing anything for a living that requires any exertion."[4]

Recruiting enough soldiers to meet the needs of even the relatively small American peacetime army of the nineteenth century was a tedious task. The commanding officer of each regiment usually kept two or three officers and perhaps a handful of enlisted men on recruiting duty at all times. Occasionally, recruiting parties from more than one regiment found themselves competing for likely candidates from the same geographical area. In 1825, a General Recruiting Service came into existence to operate in the nation's larger cities and to supply recruits to those individual regiments that had trouble filling their quotas. It was not always enough just to discuss the benefits of army life to convince young men that the army was for them. Sometimes, lively demonstrations did the trick. In the summer of 1848, just after the end of the Mexican War, an army sergeant and two privates were manning a recruiting station in the Five Points area of New York city. Soon, some of the neighborhood bullies began roughing up the soldiers. Captain Phil Kearney, who had lost an arm in the recent conflict, next arrived on the scene, and, with only one arm, proceeded to give the most belligerent of the thugs a sound thrashing. Having thus administered "the stick," he now offered them "the carrot." "You're all supposed to be tough," he snarled. "Why don't you really prove it? The Army needs you! The Army needs men—even gutter rats like you! Come on, lads, chuck this life down here. Do your country and yourselves some good. Join up! That is," he continued, "if you're men enough!" The tough captain had his best day of recruiting that day.[5]

Escape

Sometimes, men enlisted to escape domestic situations that they found repressive. A Texas newspaper in 1847 carried an account of one such instance. According to the story, a veteran soldier was quizzing a new recruit about his reason for enlisting. "Why I volunteered," the proud young soldier replied, "because I have no wife, and go in for war." When the older man was questioned about his motive, he replied: "I have volunteered *because I have a wife, and go in for peace.*" At times, the army made a conscious effort to appeal to men such as this veteran. A recruiting notice, for example, appeared in a New Jersey newspaper in 1792 that promised that "all worthy fellows that are unfortunately connected with women who come under the denomination of termagants, now is their time to get clear of the greatest earthly curse possible" by enlisting. It is not known how many men answered the call to the military to wriggle out of such situations. One man who did so, however, left a wife and two children behind. This recruit's father and brother, reacting to the situation, used their influence with the Secretary of War, who agreed to release the man from service if the family hired a substitute to take his place, which they did. The recruit left the army, but he never returned home.[6]

WHO COULD BE SOLDIERS?

Since soldiering has always been a job for men in their physical prime, army regulations generally forbade the enlistment of men who were either too old—older than thirty-five years—or too young—under twenty-one years—from becoming soldiers. Older men who were already in the army were allowed to re-enlist, and younger men who obtained the permission of their parents or guardians were also allowed to join. Recruiting officers had no way to verify the ages of the men appearing before them, and many men entered service by falsifying their ages. One study, just before the Civil War, of sixty-six enlisted men, found that only thirteen of them had been truthful about their ages. Five men were over thirty-five and had to chop years off their actual ages to be accepted. (Some years earlier, a man enlisted who, later examination revealed, was probably twenty years past the maximum enlistment age and was, according to an army doctor, "so infirm that he cannot walk a mile.") Forty-eight others were under the minimum age, including one recruit who was only fifteen. The army did accept boys into the ranks as musicians, and these were often the sons of soldiers already serving. In what was perhaps the most extreme example of youngsters in the army were the two sons of a soldier serving in the Sixth Infantry Regiment in 1838. Their ages were eleven and six![7]

Foreign-Born Soldiers

The men who made up the army in the first half of the nineteenth century came from a wide variety of occupational, educational, and economic backgrounds, as one might expect, and a significant number were foreigners. There were various regulatory attempts to restrict enlistment to native-born American citizens, but they were often ignored in the face of manpower needs that could not otherwise be met. Finally, in 1828, the rules were relaxed to allow the enlistment of able-bodied citizens of the United States without regard to their nation of birth. One man who enlisted in 1849 left a vivid description of the polyglot of recruits he encountered. "The room contained from 60 to 70 persons from all quarters of the globe," he remembered.

> First was heard a Dutch song by a group of German representatives. In another place is heard "Sacre, Mon Dieu!" which emanates from a dark, curly headed Frenchman. We next hear a witty story, from a son of Erin's Isle, interrupted of course by long whiffs of smoke from his stump of a pipe. In another portion of the room is seen in earnest converse a party of Poles and Hungarians, perhaps sympathizing with each other upon their countries' recent annexation by Austria. We also see an Englishman complaining of the bill of fare while at one corner of the fireplace sitting "solitary and alone" whittling and whistling is a Yankee right out of Vermont.

In fact, during the early 1820s approximately 25 percent of the men in the American army were immigrants. By the mid-1830s that percentage had risen to about 40 percent, and in the early 1850s it was not unusual to encounter a unit that was made up of 70 percent foreign recruits.[8]

Many of these foreign-born soldiers, like their native-born counterparts, became disillusioned with army life after a while. And although desertion was certainly a common avenue of escape, some sought their releases from military service through other means. Near the end of the War of 1812, a native of England serving in the American army thought that he should be discharged because he was not just an alien, but an *enemy* alien—one who owed national allegiance to a country with which the United States was then at war. A U.S. federal court ruled against him, saying that he had voluntarily enlisted, that the recruiters had accepted him as a soldier, and that he could not now use his place of birth as an excuse to avoid his duty. Word of this decision spread throughout the army and no other alien soldiers used such an argument again for more than a quarter century. Then, in 1841, a Virginia court ruled in favor of another Englishman seeking his release, and in 1842 there was a similar ruling in New York. These rulings also made themselves known throughout the army and soon some 400 alien soldiers gained their release on similar grounds.[9]

A German soldier serving in the U.S. Army in the 1850s went to considerable lengths to legally gain his discharge as an alien. This man, Private Christian Bartholomus, began by placing anonymous notices in several German newspapers announcing the death of one of his near relatives. Since, according to the announcements, Bartholomus was an heir of the deceased, he was thus notified to appear in person to claim his inheritance. Next, the wily soldier had a friend of his in Germany clip the notices from the newspapers and mail them to him at Fort Union, New Mexico. He then wrote a plaintive letter to a German consular official in St. Louis woefully describing how, because of his being unable to speak or understand English, he had been tricked into enlisting. He included the newspaper clippings and asked the official to intercede on his behalf with Army officials in Washington so he could return to Germany and claim his estate. Before the soldier's chicanery was discovered, a sympathetic secretary of war, when presented with his sad story, ordered him discharged. Several other foreign-born soldiers used variations of this scheme to obtain their freedom as well.[10]

Of greater importance than place of birth to the smooth functioning of an army was the ability of all soldiers to understand commands. Although many of the immigrant soldiers in the ranks came from Ireland and England and would have no trouble understanding their officers, many others came from Germany and other countries where English was not the dominant language. In the 1830s, a captain complained that fully half of the men in his company did not understand the English language well enough to be able to comply with simple orders. These men, he complained, "never could comprehend the difference between the command to charge [load] their muskets, charge the enemy, and charge the United States for services rendered." Sometimes the existence of this language barrier resulted in some rather comical consequences. At about the same time that the company commander was bemoaning the inability of most of his men to understand his commands, Colonel Zachary Taylor experienced a similar situation within the ranks of his First Infantry Regiment in Michigan Territory. While reviewing his troops, Taylor noticed that one man was obviously not obeying some command—perhaps he was slouching when he should have been standing erect at attention. Taylor assumed that this soldier was purposely defying his orders and approached him to administer one of his favorite methods of getting a soldier's attention. He grabbed the miscreant by both of his ears and shook him violently. As it happened, this soldier, an immigrant from one of the German principalities and almost totally ignorant of the English language, had not understood the drill command that Taylor suspected him of ignoring. He was even less understanding of his commanding officer abusing him in front of the entire command, and when Taylor let go of his ears, the soldier knocked the colonel off his feet in retaliation. The colonel quickly realized the truth of the matter and ordered that the soldier not be punished. In fact, the man's boldness probably marked him as having the makings of a good soldier.[11]

African American Soldiers

Army regulations regarding who was allowed to enlist were usually fairly explicit, even if these rules were not always enforced. Not only were various efforts made to restrict foreigners from entering the army, but the ranks were likewise closed to nonwhite men and all women. Even though black Americans had performed creditably in the army during the emergencies of the Revolutionary War and the War of 1812, regulations throughout most of the antebellum period expressly forbade their enlistment. It was a simple matter in most cases for the recruiting officer and the accompanying physician to bar enlistment because of race, but it became more difficult in the case of young men of mixed racial heritage. An 1840 instruction manual titled *Hints on the Medical Examination of Recruits for the Army* alerted army physicians to other methods to determine if a young man presenting himself for enlistment might have African blood in his veins. When there was any doubt and where the prospective recruit's skin color was light, the examiners were to look for other clues in the shape of his head or the texture of his hair. There were undoubtedly at least a few soldiers whose physical characteristics did not cause the recruiters to question their ethnicity. During the excitement surrounding the opening days of the Mexican War in 1846, a potential enlistee showed up at a recruiting station in Virginia. Something about his physical appearance caused the examining physician to question his background. He consulted with another officer and both ultimately agreed that the man before them was white, and they proceeded to enlist him into the army. A few weeks later, and before this man's unit had left for the seat of war, a middle-aged white man came to claim him as one of his slaves. When officers expressed doubt to the man that the young recruit was of African ancestry, he explained to them that not only was the young man his slave but also his biological son![12]

Women Soldiers

The enlistment of women was another area of concern. Scholars now know that possibly as many as several hundred women passed themselves off as men and fought in the Civil War—on both sides—but as yet there is very little reliable information about women soldiers in earlier American wars. One woman, a Miss Eliza Allen, claimed in a book written after the War with Mexico that she had taken an active part in that conflict disguised as a man. She claimed that she was even able to keep her secret after having been wounded at the Battle of Cerro Gordo in 1847.[13]

Women enlisted, or tried to enlist, for a variety of reasons. In 1792, Peter Davis and his friend Jack Tarbox appeared before a recruiting officer ready to join the army. Davis was the taller of the two, at 5′4″, but both men were rather frail-looking. After accepting Davis, the recruiting officer rejected his friend. He just did not look as if he could hold up to the rigors of active campaigning. Both men were disconsolate at this rejection. Davis begged the recruiter to also accept Tarbox who, according to Davis, "was dam'd hardy, and could bear a devilish deal of fatigue." The officer could not be swayed, but when he saw how close the two young men were he cancelled Davis's enlistment and sent the two men on their way. Later the truth came out. Davis and Tarbox were, in reality, two young girls from a neighboring village who had tried to pass themselves off as young men on a dare.[14]

During the War of 1812, a Kentucky woman took part in the Battle of Chippewa to avenge the deaths of her father and one brother earlier in the war in an Indian massacre. This woman, reported a fellow soldier, was "remarkable for her height, muscular figure, for the loss of one eye, and for her volubility in oaths and queer modes of execration when jeered at or incensed." Although she wore masculine clothing, she made no effort to disguise the fact that she was a woman and performed as valuable service nursing wounded soldiers in the hospital as she did on the battlefield. In a somewhat similar vein, a young woman from Indiana sought to join one of that state's volunteer regiments during the early stages of the Mexican War. Her purpose was not one of vengeance, but rather an effort to be near her father, who was in the army and already in Mexico.[15]

Occasionally, a woman "of questionable virtue" tried to smuggle herself into an army uniform from whence she could ply her trade among a vast population of potential customers. Such was the case with a lieutenant in a Missouri volunteer unit preparing to march to Santa Fe, New Mexico, in 1846. He arranged to have a woman mustered in to his company as a soldier and, for quite some time, she was able to carry off the deception. She performed routine soldier tasks during the day and was the officer's paramour by night. She was successful in her deception until she discovered that she was carrying the officer's child. The lieutenant arranged for her to "desert" and to accompany a supply train that was headed back toward Missouri. That was when the deception fell apart. A court-martial declared that by "tenting, sleeping and co-habiting with the said female" the officer had deprived the United States "of the service of a good and competent soldier," and ordered him dismissed from the service.[16]

MEDICAL EXAMINATIONS OF RECRUITS

After the recruiting party successfully weeded out those who were legally barred from service, the rest of the men had to pass physical exams. "Surgeons shall be particularly attentive to the examination of recruits," read one early nineteenth century regulation,

> and will suffer no man to pass, who has not, at his examination, been stripped of all his clothes, in order to ascertain, as far as possible, that he has the perfect use of all his limbs; that he has no tumours [*sic*], ulcerated legs, rupture, nor chronic cutaneous affection, nor other infirmity which may render him unfit for the active duties of the field; and it shall be their duty to ascertain, as far as practicable, whether he is an habitual drunkard, or subject to convulsions of any kind.

In addition, a man with a missing or deformed arm or leg was obviously not a fit candidate for induction. And not only did he have to have all of his major limbs, but he had to demonstrate full flexibility of his joints. Abnormal curvature of the spine or flat feet also disqualified men. Likewise, a man who was missing one or both of his two front teeth would not be able to tear open paper cartridges for his musket, and was therefore rejected. Some physicians checked eyesight by standing on one side of a room and holding up a dime. The recruit, standing against the far wall of the same room, then had to tell whether it was heads or tails. A mid-nineteenth century manual for military physicians also carried this warning: "Some recruits are so offensive in their breath…as to be intolerable to their comrades; and, for these causes…ought, unquestionably, to be rejected from any army."

The recruits were supposed to disrobe entirely for these examinations but, in the haste of raising troops, this provision was not always observed. In one extreme case, doctors hurriedly "examined" almost a thousand men in one regiment bound for action in Mexico without having the men remove their clothing. Only forty men failed to pass this cursory examination, and the rest departed for the seat of war. Soon, however, many of these men were applying for and receiving medical discharges because they were unable to perform the duties of soldiers. Occasionally, there were complaints from the field about the physical quality of newly arriving recruits. "Recruits for this country should be of the first quality," grumbled an officer in Florida in 1820. "Of those that have arrived several were old men from 40 to 50, two or three idiots, and generally intemperate. Such men cannot last long in this climate."[18]

Prior to 1833, there was some monetary incentive for recruiting officers to overlook certain shortcomings because they received two dollars for every recruit they passed. However officers, whether line officers or medical officers, who failed to be scrupulous when passing judgment on the fitness of volunteers, could be expelled from the service. Sometimes, the recruiting officers and inspecting physicians were held liable for the expense of clothing and equipping enlistees who were later discovered to be unfit for service. At one recruiting station, in 1841, three men enlisted into the army with the approval of both the officer in charge and the inspecting physician. Subsequently, these three men sought their release from the army—after having pocketed the enlistment bonus—on the grounds that they should never have been allowed to enlist in the first place because of physical disabilities. An investigation bore out their claims of incapacity that were found to be due to pre-existing conditions, which should have barred their original enlistments. The enlisting officer and the original physician were then fined a total of $52.22 to cover expenses incurred for these three men. The medical doctor protested, claiming that the three men were no better than shirkers and had found a way to fake their disabilities. His argument lost a little strength, however, when it was shown that the legs of one of the men were of demonstrably different lengths, and he meekly paid his fine.[19]

By the late 1830s, there were apparently so many cases of recruits having second thoughts after having been sworn in that recruiting officers received additional instructions to allow the prospective enlistee time to reconsider: this might be as much as two days after his initial appearance at the recruiting office. One young man, presenting himself to an army recruiter in Boston in 1849, must not have made much of a positive impression on that officer because he tried to discourage him from enlisting. "Mark me, young man," he warned, "if you take this step you will regret it only once, and that will be from the time you become acquainted with your position until you get out of it; and another thing," he continued, "a large percentage of men never return to their friends [from the army]. If you have no friends you ought to have, and if for any reason you want to hide yourself from the world, try something from which you can free yourself if you so desire." He then instructed the young man to go home and think about what he had said. If he came back the next day still determined to sign up, the officer would enroll him. This young man would not be swayed.

> I was a persistent reader of voyages, travels, campaigns, explorations and history, and novels ... and the spirit of adventure was so strong that I determined to enlist in the mounted service [the dragoons], which was sure to place me on the great plains of the West, among Indians, buffaloes, and other big game, and the mountaineers and trappers of whom I had read so much.... It seemed to me that five years [the period of enlistment] in this kind of field would round out my education.

He returned to the recruiter the next day and soon took the oath of enlistment.[20]

OUTFITTING THE NEW SOLDIERS

The first order of business after swearing in the recruit was to get him at least looking like a soldier. This might begin with a good head-to-toe scrubbing and a haircut. The new soldier then received his first uniform, while he sent home or otherwise disposed of all his civilian clothing. The Army did this for a couple of good reasons. Allowing the soldier to pack along his civilian clothing to the training depot or, ultimately, his regiment unnecessarily increased the burden that he or a pack animal would have to transport. It had learned, through sad experience, that some men would enlist and collect any cash enlistment bonus that might be offered, sell their newly acquired uniform clothing to raise even more money, and depart for places unknown. Desertion still occurred at this early stage, but at least if a man's only clothing was what was on his back he could not sell it. Also, a deserter in uniform was much easier to spot than a man in civilian clothes.

Some men took great pride in their new military appearance. Others, depending upon the mood of the populace at the time, would rather not have been so conspicuous. In 1843, Ulysses S. Grant had just graduated from the Military Academy at West Point and was proudly wearing his uniform while on leave back home in Ohio. Seeing the uniform, a barefoot boy began making fun of Grant, saying that he must have entered the army because he was too lazy to work at an honest job. A few years later, another new graduate had a similar experience. He, too, had returned home on leave following graduation, and when a circus visited the town he and some of his friends decided to go. He proudly put on his uniform for the occasion, but was mortified when a citizen, apparently mistaking him for one of the circus clowns, asked him what time the next show began. "I returned to the hotel," he wrote almost forty years later, "where I cast off the uniform and clothed myself in citizen dress. From that day to this I do not remember to have ever worn uniform when it was not absolutely necessary."[21]

TRAINING

American soldiers during the last decade of the eighteenth century and most of the first half of the nineteenth century did not generally undergo military training of the kind experienced by soldiers in the twentieth and twenty-first centuries. Before centralized recruiting was introduced, about 1825, the individual regiments competed with one another for manpower. A recruit, for example, who had enlisted in one of the eastern cities, might report to an established military post nearby where he would receive introductory military training for some unspecified period of time before being sent with others to join his regiment. If, instead, he joined the army somewhat closer to the frontier, he would go directly to whatever post his assigned unit occupied at that time. There, he would be expected to learn soldiering "on the job."

Infantry Training

The first training manual for American soldiers was prepared for General George Washington's Continental Army by Friedrich Wilhelm Ludolf Gerhard Augustin, Baron von Steuben, late of the Prussian Army, in 1778. Based upon the *1764 Regulations* of the British Army, it remained in use until the conclusion of the War of 1812. By that time, in spite of the ultimate defeat of Napoleon's armies, American military thinkers became infatuated with French training manuals, and volumes based upon French army regulations of 1791 began appearing. Congress, therefore, authorized a board of Army officers in 1814 to provide a new, updated system of tactics and instruction. The result, published in early 1815, was essentially nothing more than a translation of the French volume by which Napoleon had trained his legions. Ten years later, an Army board published a revision that included, for the first time, a system of drill that was applicable to light infantry and to rifle units. In 1835, the Army adopted Brigadier General Winfield Scott's translation of the 1831 French regulations. For the next twenty years, Scott's *Infantry Tactics* remained the cornerstone of military training in the United States. In 1854, Major William J. Hardee, who, like Scott before him, had traveled extensively observing European armies, chaired an Army committee that reviewed yet another French system of drill and tactics, this one from 1845. It was ultimately translated and adopted the following year.[22]

These instructional texts shared a basic format. They began with such simple things as telling the recruit how to stand at attention, how to follow simple commands, and how to perform the manual of arms. Scott and Hardee labeled this section the "School of the Soldier," and it was used to instruct individuals and small squads. When the men had mastered this introductory phase of the transition from civilian to soldier, it was time for them to learn to act as parts of larger groups. The next step, then, was the "School of the Company," followed by the "School of the Battalion."

Learning to March

The first lesson that the new soldier learned was usually how to turn left, turn right, and turn to face the rear. The procedures were simple. If the drillmaster wanted the recruit to turn to the right, he ordered: "To the Right—Face!" When the trainee heard the words "To the Right," he mentally prepared himself to move but remained still until he heard the word "Face." At this point, he lifted the toes of his feet slightly and turned ninety degrees to the right on his heels. Upon completing the turn, his right foot was slightly in front of his left; so he immediately brought his right foot back into alignment with his left. He followed the same steps to the left when he received the command: "To the Left—Face!" When an officer wanted his men to turn toward the rear, it was important that they all turned in the same direction to avoid bumping into each other. Therefore, the command was, "To the Right about—Face!" At the command "To the Right about," the soldier moved his right foot so that its arch was directly behind and about two inches away from his left heel. Then, at "Face," he pivoted all the way around and brought his right foot back into line with his left. By about 1830, the words of command had been shortened to simply "Right—face!," "Left—face!," and "About—face!"[23]

Something seemingly as simple as marching could sometimes be the source of confusion among raw recruits, or even among inexperienced officers. Drill manuals specified that upon hearing the command to march, the soldier stepped out upon his left foot. Throughout the first half of the nineteenth century, however, many army recruits were illiterate or, at best, semi-literate, and had a difficult time discerning left from right. Most of them, however, could readily tell the difference between hay and straw, so enterprising drill instructors would sometimes fasten a small thatch of hay to one shoe and straw to the other. Then, when counting the marching cadence, they would call out "Hay foot! Straw foot!" instead of "Left! Right!" A dragoon recruit has left a colorful description of his first day's drill and the difficulty some of his fellow soldiers had in leading off on the proper foot. At the first attempt, he wrote, "some put forward the right foot, others the left, … and before we had got six paces ahead, there were no two marching together." Another attempt followed. "This time," the soldier recalled, "all except three put forward the left foot, and we managed to keep together for some fifteen or twenty paces; when, by that time our front becoming somewhat semi-circular, we again received the order to 'halt!' " One man in the company, even after repeated attempts, never was able to get it right. He deserted the following week, an event that, according to his fellow soldier, benefited both himself and the service.[24]

Contemporary manuals also specified different rates of march. Baron von Steuben defined "common time," for example, as consisting of seventy-five paces per minute, each pace to be of twenty-four inches. Scott's manual lengthened the pace to twenty-eight inches and the rate to ninety steps per minute. "Quick time" raised the speed, depending upon the manual in use, to anywhere from 90 to 110 steps per minute. Some manuals even had a "double quick time" that had the soldiers moving forward at a trot. In the mid 1840s, a captain of engineers became very frustrated when drilling his recruits. All he expected of them was to be able to march at common time—ninety steps per minute—but they just seemed incapable of exceeding eight-five steps per minute. After an exhausting and unsatisfactory day of drill, the captain's two lieutenants figured out the problem. Instead of counting every step, the captain only counted as each man's left foot came down, thereby only counting half of the steps. Instead of dawdling along at eighty-five steps per minute, the men were moving at 170 steps per minute, which, at four-and-a-half miles per hour, was even faster than double quick time. Thankfully, the mistake was discovered before the captain tried to push the men to march at his concept of double quick.[25]

Weapons Familiarization: Muskets

Weapons familiarization was understandably of immense importance. Loading and firing a .69 caliber infantry musket of the day was not particularly difficult, but soldiers spent hours and hours on the drill field learning to accomplish these tasks "by the numbers." After a considerable amount of practice, a soldier might reasonably expect to be able to achieve a rate of fire of three to four shots per minute. Contemporary drill manuals listed as many as fifteen separate steps that the soldier had to go through in order to load and fire his musket once, so constant practice was essential. The instructions from an 1836 manual will serve to illustrate.

"Load in twelve times—Load." At this command, the soldier, who had been standing at attention with his musket on his left shoulder with the cocking piece at the half-cock position, turned slightly to his right and placed his right foot immediately behind and at right angles to his left. At the same time, he brought his musket down from his shoulder until it was at waist level and the barrel was pointing up at about a forty-five-degree angle.

"Open pan." The soldier pushed the hardened steel frizzen forward with his right thumb, thus opening the weapon's priming pan. He then immediately reached his right hand around to his leather cartridge box, which he wore slung from his left shoulder and resting against his right hip, and pulled open its flap. His cartridges were made of paper and contained a measured amount of powder and the solid lead ball or other projectiles.

"Handle cartridge." The soldier withdrew one of his paper cartridges and placed the end of it between his teeth.

"Tear cartridge." The soldier tore open the end of the cartridge and placed it next to his musket's priming pan.

"Prime." The soldier poured enough of his cartridge powder into the pan to ensure ignition when he fired. He then pinched the cartridge closed so as not to inadvertently spill the remainder of its powder.

"Shut pan." The soldier now closed the frizzen over the priming pan.

"Cast about." The soldier, maintaining a secure grasp of his cartridge, now turned back toward the front while bringing the musket around in front of him, butt resting on the ground near his left foot, barrel angled slightly toward the right so as to bring the muzzle even with the center of his body. He then brought his cartridge up to the muzzle of the gun.

"Charge cartridge." The soldier now poured the rest of his cartridge powder down the barrel, making sure he shook it all out of the paper, and placed the lead ball into the end of the barrel.

"Draw rammer." The soldier pulled the ramrod from the channel beneath his musket's barrel, reversed it, and forced the head of it a few inches down the barrel.

"Ram cartridge." The soldier pushed the ball all the way down the barrel until it was seated against the previously introduced cartridge powder.

"Return rammer." The soldier removed the ramrod from the barrel and returned it to its place underneath the barrel.

"Shoulder arms." The soldier raised the loaded musket to the position at which he had started, with the musket resting vertically against the front of his left shoulder.

"Ready." The soldier now again moved his feet as if he were getting ready to load his musket. Instead of lowering his weapon, however, he held it vertically in front of him while he placed his right thumb on the top of the cocking piece and his right index finger just under and touching the trigger guard.

"Aim." The soldier cocked the musket, brought it down to a horizontal position, put his right index finger on the trigger, and sighted along the top of the barrel for a likely target. Men in the rear ranks took a small step forward and to their right at this point and aimed their weapons between the two men immediately in front of them.

"Fire." The soldier pulled the trigger, causing the sharpened flint to strike the hardened steel of the frizzen. The frizzen flew forward exposing the priming powder and sending a shower of sparks into it. In an instant, the priming powder exploded and part of the resultant flame passed through a vent hole and directly into the rear of the barrel where the main cartridge charge was seated. This charge exploded and sent the ball toward the target. After firing, the soldier remained in the position taken for the command "Fire" until he heard the next command. If it was "Load," he started the entire process over again. If it was "Shoulder—arms," he resumed that position.[26]

Under battle conditions the soldiers sometimes found ways to shorten this rather lengthy procedure. During the Battle of Chippewa, in 1814, a sergeant was able to increase his rate of fire somewhat by not returning his ramrod to its normal place after he loaded his musket. Instead, he stationed a young drummer boy at his side and, every time, after loading his weapon, handed the ramrod to the young musician, who then had it ready to hand back as soon as the soldier fired. Soldiers firing from behind trees also found that they could lean the rammer up against the trunk between shots.[27]

Weapons Familiarization: Accuracy

According to a contemporary drill manual, "The fire of the musket is inaccurate, but in a general action, where accuracy of fire is not attainable, it may be made effective up to 300 yards [by mass volley firing]; beyond 400 yards it is useless." The War Department conducted accuracy tests of these muskets at various distances and with various ammunition loads. Ten soldiers each fired fifteen shots with the standard round ball load at a square target a hundred yards away that was ten feet on a side. Even with such a huge target, 32 of the 150 shots missed it altogether, and only 15 shots landed within a foot of the aiming point at the center of the target. At longer distances, of course, the number of hits fell off dramatically. Only 23 of 150 shots hit the target when the men fired from 300 yards away. Using buck-and-ball cartridges—one ball and three buckshot—the accuracy was even worse. At 100 yards, almost a third, or 48, of the musket balls and almost half, or 205, of the buckshot missed the target. At 200 yards, 60 percent of the balls missed and 84 percent of the buckshot went astray. Accuracy such as this prompted Ulysses S. Grant to remark in his memoirs that "at the distance of a few hundred yards a man might fire at you all day without your finding it out."[28]

Battlefield tactics of the late eighteenth century and the first half of the nineteenth century took the inherent inaccuracy of these muskets into account. Soldiers stood shoulder-to-shoulder with their comrades and blazed away at a similarly arranged enemy formation perhaps only fifty to eighty yards away. There was no need for laser-like accuracy and, in fact, there was not much emphasis on aiming at specific targets. Such aiming would probably have only frustrated the shooters because the muskets were not equipped with rear sights. A soldier simply pointed his weapon in the general direction of the enemy and fired. If his musket ball did not hit the man at whom he was "aiming," it probably would hit some other enemy soldier. The individual soldier's goal, therefore, was not accuracy but volume. The faster he could load and fire, the greater the likelihood that his bullets would find targets. Even with this, some authorities have claimed that only three bullets hit enemy soldiers for every thousand fired! Nevertheless, the American infantryman's basic weapon remained unchanged from the Revolutionary War through the War of 1812, the Seminole (and other Indian) Wars, and the Mexican War.[29]

American soldiers of the early nineteenth century did not spend much time at target practice. Indeed, no official drill regulation for target practice was published until 1858. The intrinsic lack of accuracy of their weapons meant that most "target practice" was engaged in more to familiarize the soldiers with their muskets than out of any hope of developing superb marksmen. There were, of course, exceptions to this rule. In 1819, the men of the Rifle Regiment spent more than two weeks at a rifle range. Their target was a three-inch circle, placed at a distance of fifty yards. Each man fired six times, and any of them who hit the target at least three times repeated the process at one hundred yards. Those who hit this more distant mark at least three out of six shots were considered to be first class riflemen. A contemporary observer remarked: "There are but few who are not in the first class." In the mid-1840s, cadets at West Point practiced firing at a flour barrel a hundred yards away. One man later reminisced that "we managed sometimes, and only sometimes, to hit" it. A more normal performance was probably that turned in by some dragoon sentries at a western post in 1853. Over a four-month period, each of a dozen of them unloaded his weapon when he came off guard duty by firing at a target three-and-a-half inches in diameter set off at some unspecified distance. During this entire time, only four bullets hit the mark and only eight of the more than 1,400 rounds hit inside a seventeen-inch circle around the center of the target.[30]

Improving Weapon Design

Muskets: From Flintlock to Percussion

The first major change in the design of muskets in perhaps a hundred years was the manner in which the weapons actually fired. The flint-and-steel method of ignition was not very effective in rainy weather when the soldier found it almost impossible to keep the priming powder dry. And when the flint became too dull to generate sparks when it hit the frizzen, the soldier was left with a ten-pound club instead of a firearm. By the early 1820s, however, a new percussion ignition system was beginning to prove its worth on sporting arms. Instead of the shooter fumbling with the frizzen and trying to prime the pan, he now merely had to reach into another small leather box on his waist belt, pull out a copper or brass percussion cap, and affix it to the cone, or nipple, adjacent to his musket's lock. These caps resembled tiny top hats. In the top of each was an explosive mixture—fulminate of mercury for example. The cocking piece—now referred to as the hammer—fell onto the cap when the soldier pulled the trigger and exploded the small charge therein. The resultant flame traveled through the nipple directly into the barrel and the main powder charge. This system was much more reliable, particularly in damp weather. The leather cap box protected the caps until the soldier needed them, making it less likely that the muskets would misfire.

British army gunsmiths converted 200 flintlock muskets to the percussion system for trials in 1831. The tests yielded such positive results that by 1836 percussion weapons were being issued to the elite guards battalions and, three years later, army technicians were busy altering all of the flintlock muskets then in government arsenals to percussion. Across the English Channel, the French authorities arrived at a similar conclusion at about the same time, but the changeover in the United States was slower. Officials were concerned about what would happen when a soldier had used up or lost all of his caps. He would then be unable to fire his weapon. On the other hand, the soldier armed with a flintlock who discovered that his flint had gotten too dull to function, or whose flint had somehow come out of the cocking piece and gotten lost, could sometimes make do

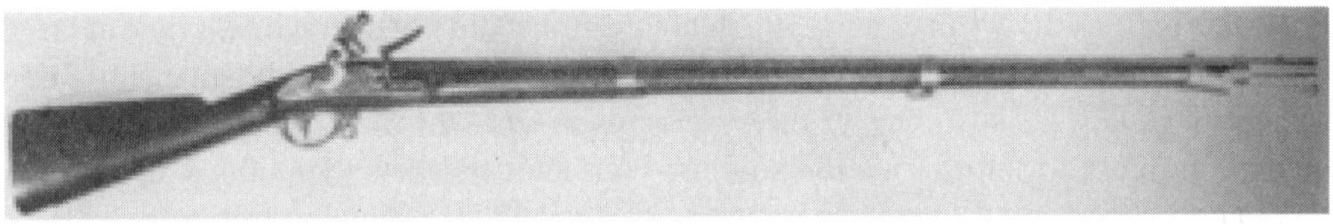

Typical .69 caliber flintlock musket as used throughout the first half of the nineteenth century. (*Courtesy of the Smithsonian*)

with small pieces of flint lying upon the ground. When the inevitable changeover to this system began in the mid-1840s, the government still had thousands of flintlock muskets in sound condition. Some, in fact, were still in the arsenals in brand new, unfired condition, and government armorers converted most of them to percussion.

The next significant advance in small arms came about with regard to their accuracy. Muskets were inherently inaccurate, especially when compared to rifles. The inside of a rifle's barrel had spiral grooves cut into it. These grooves acted upon the projectile as it was fired, giving it a spin, and imparting long range, stable flight. The disadvantage of rifles was that they were very slow to load. The rifle ball had to be a tight fit in the barrel if it was going to receive the benefit of the rifling. One way to achieve this was for the rifleman to carry soft lead balls that were barely larger than their barrel's inside diameter. He then forced the ball down the barrel with the ramrod so that it fit snugly all the way down. The more common method was to use an undersized ball, but to wrap a cloth or leather patch around it that would engage the rifling and give the ball the necessary twist as it exited the muzzle. This took more time than loading a musket, whose ball was somewhat undersized, and, after a few shots, the powder-fouling inside the barrel made it almost impossible to reload a rifle unless the soldier took a few minutes to clean it out. Rifles could be lethal at several hundred yards, but their rate of fire was much less than that of muskets. For most military uses, therefore, rate of fire was more important than pinpoint accuracy.

Mìníe's Improvement

By the 1830s, however, this began to change, as various tinkerers in Europe started to experiment with expansible ammunition. Near the end of the 1840s, Captain Claude-Etienne Mìníe of the French army perfected a rifle projectile that allowed the soldier to load and shoot as fast as a man armed with a musket. This new bullet had a pointed tip and a hollow base, and it was slightly smaller in diameter than the rifle barrel for which it was intended. Rifle accuracy was achieved when, upon firing, the explosion in the base of the bullet forced its sides out and into the rifling grooves.

A man firing these Mìníe or "minnie," balls had the rate of fire of a musket and the accuracy of a rifle. Using the Army's newest rifles, a ten-man team firing a total of 150 rounds at the 100-yard target hit it 148 times! And fifty of them fell within about a foot of the center! Even at 500 yards—a distance well beyond what any musket shooter would have attempted—more than a third of the rifle bullets hit the target.[31]

The U.S. Army was quick to take advantage of this improvement. By the mid-1850s, it had phased out the manufacture of smooth-bored muskets and had converted entirely to the production of rifled firearms. In fact, many muskets already in the hands of the troops or in government arsenals were updated by rifling their barrels and re-issuing them to the soldiers.

Not all infantry troops received these weapons. Volunteer soldiers, up until the Mexican War, usually reported for duty with whatever weapons they happened to have at home. This meant that not everyone in a particular unit carried the same kind of firearm. In fact, they might not even fire the same caliber of bullet. An Ohio volunteer during the War of 1812 described how the men in his company were "armed with their own rifles, and each had a tomahawk and large knife attached to their belts."[32]

On-Field Modifications

There were also field modifications occasionally. In 1792, General Anthony Wayne, for example, sought some way to increase the rate of fire produced by the muskets of his men, and he looked to the mechanics of the weapon rather than the method by which it was employed. He suggested that the touchhole linking the priming pan with the main powder charge be redesigned. He theorized that if it was bored slightly larger and at an angle toward the muzzle of the barrel, loading would be greatly facilitated. With a musket thus modified, and with the use of a much finer-grained powder in the cartridges, a soldier could eliminate several steps in the loading sequence. He would not have to carefully pour a small amount of precious cartridge powder into the priming pan, close the frizzen, and then load the rest of the powder, along with the bullet, into the barrel. Instead, some of the cartridge powder would automatically fall into the inclined touchhole from inside the barrel and dribble out into the priming pan, and the musket was then ready for firing. Wayne estimated that such a modification would increase the rate of fire by 50 percent. He was unable to convince President George Washington of the efficacy of this plan. The president thought that the chances of the enlarged touchhole becoming fouled offset any possible advantage. He saw no disadvantage in the present rate of fire because "every shot ought to be well and deliberately aimed" anyway. Still, some of Wayne's muskets were eventually modified according to this plan.[33]

Breech Loaders

By the 1850s, the impact of the industrial revolution began extending to the military, as many inventors produced firearms that loaded, more conveniently, from the breech. In anything but a small skirmish, musketry just was not enough to defeat an enemy force, and the army then turned to its big guns—the artillery.

ARTILLERY TRAINING

During the U.S. Army's infancy, its artillery was a conglomeration of French guns, captured British guns, and guns cast in the young nation itself. Over a dozen different calibers were represented, making ammunition supply a very difficult proposition. American artillerists continued to use these guns for some years after the end of the Revolutionary War, and when a system of domestic manufacture was established, it embraced the British calibers. These were measured differently than were the calibers of small arms. Whereas rifle and musket calibers were measured by the diameter of the bore, expressed in decimals of an inch, there were two systems for measuring the size of cannons. The first method did not depend directly upon the diameter of the bore but rather on the weight of cast-iron spherical projectile that the piece fired. The bore size of a 12-pounder gun, for example, was such that a cast-iron ball weighing 12 pounds would just fit. This translated to a bore diameter of about 4.62 inches. Common gun sizes during the antebellum period were 6-, 12-, 18-, 24-, 32-, and 42-pounders. A 42-pounder had a bore size of about 7 inches. Larger pieces went back to direct bore measurements, such as eight-inch and ten-inch.[34]

Gun Types

Artillery in the U.S. Army did not change appreciably from the Revolutionary War until after the Civil War. It consisted of heavy iron or bronze cannons that were loaded from the front, much like the personal weapons of the time. Throughout the early nineteenth century, artillerists had several types of weapons at their disposal, each with a specific use or application. Artillerists classified their weapons as guns, howitzers, or mortars. Guns were for battering down targets with solid shots at long range and on relatively direct lines of fire. Howitzers fired explosive shells on moderately curving trajectories to hit less distant targets. The squat, short-barreled mortars fired their projectiles at a high angle and were most effective against fortified positions. Whereas the flatter-firing guns and howitzers would have to batter down the walls of a fort, for example, the mortar could throw its shells high into the air so they would fall down within the confines of the enemy fortifications before bursting. They were also effective in seacoast forts where, in some instances, their shells could plunge through the decks of enemy ships and explode below the waterline.

The lightest were the field pieces. Although relatively heavy, they were of sizes such that teams of horses could move them into and out of position in fairly short order as the tide of battle shifted. Field artillerists generally marched as infantry or rode on the caissons but, in 1808, the army provided horses for the men to ride so that they could put their guns into action more quickly. Although this horse, or "flying," artillery held great promise, a parsimonious Congress decided the very next year that the cost of upkeep for the additional animals was unjustified. When horse artillery was reintroduced, some three decades later, it proved very effective. The heavier guns, those that could do the most damage, were situated in the permanent forts along the Atlantic coast. In addition to heavy mortars, these were the weapons whose projectiles could reach out to sink attacking ships.

Field Artillery

The field artillery most often used 12-pounder guns or smaller, although larger pieces were not unheard of in the field. The barrels of the 12-pounders ranged from just over 5 feet long to the Model 1839, which sported a tube that was more than 8.5 feet long. Barrel lengths had an obvious impact on the weight and, therefore, on the maneuverability of the guns. These field guns usually weighed anywhere from 2,500 pounds to perhaps as much as 5,000 pounds. The weight of larger caliber pieces went up significantly. The barrels of most contemporary 24-pounders weighed more than the heaviest complete 12-pounder gun, and the tubes of 42-pounders, often exceeded 4 tons. Likewise, the weight of most mortars was such as to relegate them to use in permanent forts where they would not have to be transported over great distances.[35]

Most field guns of the antebellum army had sufficient range to hit targets over a half mile away. The range of a 6- or 12-pounder with a 5-degree elevation was almost a mile. The range of howitzers, because of their greater trajectories, was less, but still upwards of a thousand yards. The heavier guns placed in permanent forts could, of course, reach targets at much greater distances. A 10-inch gun, for example, firing at an elevation of almost 40 degrees and with a powder charge of 20 pounds, could put a 127-pound shell more than 3 miles downrange. Of course, actually hitting targets at the extreme ranges, whether from a field gun or a garrison piece, had as much to do with the skill and luck of the gunners as with the gun's capabilities.[36]

Artillerymen had to be proficient in both infantry drill and artillery drill because many of them served the majority of their enlistments without ever firing one of the big pieces. Instead, they served as infantry. So only after mastering the School of the Soldier, as it was applied to the infantry, did they advance in their training to more specific artillery training.

Contemporary drill manuals describe the duties of a gun detachment as follows: The man in charge of the gun, usually a sergeant or a corporal, was known as chief of the piece, or the gunner. All the other members of the detachment were simply known by numbers. In battle, it was the gunner who estimated the range to the target and decided whether to use solid shot, shell, or something else. He passed this information along to Number 6, stationed at the ammunition chest well behind the gun, who withdrew the proper projectile and prepared the fuse for the estimated range. Number 6 or Number 7, who was also at the ammunition chest, handed the projectile along with a flannel bag holding a powder charge to Number 5, who put them into a leather pouch slung over his shoulder. Number 5 then moved forward on the left of the gun to Number 2, stationed near the muzzle. Number 2 removed the powder charge and pushed it into the muzzle of the gun. He then placed the projectile just at the muzzle. At this point, Number 1, stationed on the opposite side of the gun, employed his ramrod to push powder charge and projectile all the way to the base of the breech end of the barrel. Number 3, standing on the right of the gun near the breech, now jabbed his sharpened priming wire into the vent of the gun in order to punch a hole in the flannel of the cartridge. This allowed the flame from the primer to reach the main powder charge and fire the piece.

The gunner, having already estimated the distance to the target and computed the necessary angle of elevation, then used a detachable sighting mechanism and the threaded elevation screw under the rear of the barrel to achieve it. He sighted down the barrel to obtain the necessary lateral position. When the point of aim was too far to the left, he tapped that side of the carriage with his left hand. This was a signal to Number 4 to roll the left wheel slightly forward to move the point of aim to the right. Similarly, if the gun was pointing too far to the right, Number 1 heeded the gunner's signal and made the requisite adjustment.

With the piece now aimed accurately, Number 4, standing to the left of the gun, stepped forward to prime it. This task changed somewhat over the course of the first half of the nineteenth century. Some guns, at the beginning of this period, were equipped with flintlocks. These made use of the same principles as those found on shoulder-fired weapons but were, of course, much larger. The simplest manner of priming, however, saw Number 4 sprinkle some very finely ground gunpowder from his powder horn directly into the vent. Artillerists soon improved on this method by having special, self-contained priming tubes made. Sometimes constructed from carefully rolled tin and at other times from goose quills, these tubes contained a compound of fast-burning powder. By mid-century, some manufacturers were equipping their cannons with percussion locks, following the trend of infantry weapons. A lower cost option, also gaining popularity by the late 1850s, was the use of friction primers. These mechanical devices fit into the cannon's vent, much like the earlier priming tubes.

The gun was then ready to fire. The gunner checked to make sure that no one was standing directly behind the wheels of the cannon before he gave the command to fire. At this signal, Number 3 applied his slow match: a chemically treated length of rope wrapped around a wooden staff that, when lit, burned at a slow rate, to the vent of the piece if it used loose powder or priming tubes. Guns fitted with either flintlocks or percussion locks were fired by a lanyard that actuated them. Likewise, lanyards attached to friction primers were yanked briskly to ignite the powder charge.

Upon firing, the gun rolled back several feet under the force of its recoil. If it was to continue firing, the men had to manhandle it forward again and re-aim it. Then they began the loading cycle all over again, but this time there were some extra duties for Number 1 and Number 3. Number 1's ramrod had a large sponge on one end and, as soon as the gun fired, he would dip this into a bucket of water and begin swabbing out the barrel. This was to extinguish any lingering sparks before the next powder charge went down the barrel. While Number1 sponged out the barrel, Number 3 held his thumb over the vent to prevent air from entering and fanning any embers to life. He wore a heavy leather thumbstall to avoid burning his thumb on the hot barrel of the gun, and he kept the vent closed until Number 2 had inserted the powder bag for the next shot. Keeping the vent closed was of vital importance to the gun crew and to the gun itself. If embers existed in the barrel when another powder charge was pushed home, they might well cause it to explode as Number 1 was pushing the projectile into place. If the cannon fired prematurely, at the very least, this would probably cost Number 1 his arms, if not his life. In some instances, an early detonation could blow up the gun itself and subject everyone nearby to flying pieces of iron.[37]

In actual battle, of course, one could expect casualties within the gun detachment, so every man had to train in every position. Each man had to be able to carry out the duties of every other man on the crew. During heavy fighting, each man might find himself liable for the duties of two or three of the original detachment.

Sometimes, too, during the heat of battle, members of the gun detachment took dangerous shortcuts to increase their gun's rate of fire. In one instance, Number 1 decided that swabbing out the hot barrel after every shot was taking too much precious time, so he only applied his sponge after every fifth shot or so. Not only did this increase the chances of a premature detonation, but it also meant that the gun barrel became so hot that it was almost impossible for Number 3 to keep the vent covered during loading. Number 3's leather thumbstall was soon burned completely through, and the skin on his thumb was blistered. He begged Number 1 to start swabbing the bore more often, but that grizzled cannoneer simply told him that when he had burned all the flesh completely off his thumb that he should then "thumb it with the bone." Luckily for Number 3, the action soon subsided, and he quizzed Number 1. "Suppose I had let go of that hot vent when you wouldn't sponge," he queried, "and there had been a premature discharge in consequence?" "Well," the other man replied, "I had thought of that, and had made up my mind to brain you at once with the rammer-head if that occurred!" The irony, of course, is that in case of a premature discharge there would have been very little left of Number 1.[38]

Heavy Artillery

The larger pieces of artillery, those positioned in permanent forts along the east coast, did not require men or horses to move them from place to place. These guns were usually of much heavier caliber than those employed in active campaigning—up to ten-inch—so their rate of fire was slower. It might take two men, for example, to load a projectile, which often weighed more than a hundred pounds, into one of these pieces. Similarly, it took brute human strength to muscle one of these guns back into battery after it had fired. The heaviest of these cannon could easily weigh in excess of eight tons! It might take even a well-drilled crew over a minute to load and fire one shot, and a rate of twelve aimed shots per hour was considered adequate.[39]

During the Mexican War, General Winfield Scott's field army did use heavy siege guns to force the surrender of Vera Cruz in 1847, even borrowing some heavy naval guns to do so. Scott also employed seven ten-inch mortars to fire over the city's walls. An American volunteer observed the fire from a safe vantage point and was certain that every one of the mortar rounds exploded with great effect inside the walls of the enemy city. Another soldier described what it was like to be on the receiving end of such a fire when the Mexican artillery responded. "Perhaps Milton's description of the harsh, thunder-grating of the hinges of the infernal gates approaches to a faint realization of the indescribable sound."[40]

Projectiles

Cannons fired an array of projectiles. The easiest to manufacture, of course, was solid shot, which were simply cast-iron balls. They could be very effective against the massed formations popular among European and North American armies throughout the first half of the nineteenth century. Artillerists were occasionally able to multiply their deadly effect on rocky terrain by purposely aiming low and skipping the ball across the ground into the attacking force. The ball thus sometimes created secondary projectiles, as it struck and shattered rocks in its path before plowing into the ranks.

Shells were hollow balls filled with gunpowder. When the powder detonated, it shattered the iron shell and strewed deadly pieces of jagged iron in all directions. Different types of fuses regulated when the shells exploded. Some were impact-fused and exploded when the shells struck solid objects, such as trees, the walls of a fort, or even the ground itself. Others were time-fused, allowing the gunners to estimate the distance to the enemy force and the time it would take for the shell to travel that far. They would then set the fuses to explode the shells at the precise moment when they had arrived directly over the enemy.

For close work, as when an infantry force of some strength attacked a gun position, there were two extremely effective antipersonnel rounds available. The simplest of these was simply called canister. A canister round consisted of an open-ended cylinder of sheet metal filled with iron balls or, in some cases, lead musket balls. It had a thin top crimped over the open end. When fired, the blast blew the cover away almost immediately and sprayed the balls in a deadly cone of destruction. It turned the cannon into a huge shotgun. In extremely desperate circumstances, two—or sometimes even three—canister rounds would be loaded over the powder charge, multiplying the lethality of the shot. One such instance occurred during the Battle of Buena Vista in 1847. Major General Zachary Taylor came upon Captain Braxton Bragg's artillery battery as it furiously fired at attacking Mexican infantrymen. The general asked Bragg if he was using single or double canister. When the reply was "single," Taylor is reported to have yelled, "Well, double-shot your guns and give 'em hell, Bragg."[41]

Grapeshot was another effective round, and its larger components made it particularly devastating against attacking cavalry. The sub-diameter shot were tied up in a bag and lashed to a central wooden—and later iron—spindle. When fired, the bag disintegrated and the heavy shot splayed outward. A variation had nine balls arrayed in three tiers with iron plates on top and bottom and iron rings holding the balls together at the sides, all held in place by a bolt passing through both plates. Upon firing such a round, the concussion sheared the bolt, and the contents—this time including the two iron plates and the two rings—dispersed into the enemy ranks.[42]

For extreme conditions, artillerists might load grape *and* canister at the same time. During the Niagara campaign of 1814, the gunners of one American battery sewed the canvas scraps from an old tent into bags, which they then filled with musket balls. One of the men later wrote that his cannon was "filled with round shot, grape, canister, and bags of musket-balls, at discretion, till I could touch the last wad, with my hand, in the muzzle of the piece." Such a practice would likely have had one of two results. A gun fired with so much iron and lead in front of the powder ran the risk of exploding from the build up of pressure in the barrel. Or, an immense amount of death and destruction would result among any troops unlucky enough to be in the path of all these projectiles. Since this soldier is silent on which of the two took place, and since he survived this battle, one must assume that the latter case prevailed.[43]

The other common type of projectile for use in the field was called spherical case shot and had been developed by a British artillery officer named Henry Shrapnel. Lieutenant Shrapnel was looking for some way to combine the best effects of shells and canister. Shells were able to reach fairly significant distances before shattering, but the resultant shards of iron were relatively few. Canister, on the other hand, was extremely effective out to about 500 yards, at which point the individual balls had lost most of their energy and had dispersed so widely as to be no longer effective. To solve this, Shrapnel devised a shell with a thinner wall than the standard one. Then, instead of

This faithfully recreated shell shows how metal strapping was used to secure the shell to its wooden sabot. The sabot was necessary to ensure that the fuse remained oriented toward the muzzle while loading. (*Courtesy of the author*)

filling the shell with powder, he specified a charge of powder just sufficient to break up the shell. He had this smaller bursting charge surrounded by as many musket balls as could fit in the remaining space. He now had a projectile that could carry well beyond the range of canister and grapeshot before it exploded. And then, when it did, it rained down a much larger number of potentially lethal musket balls. An artillery battery provided with spherical case shot and experienced gunners could now break up a massed attack of enemy infantry before it even had a chance to leave its marshalling area.[44]

Another variation in the use of solid shot was known as "hot shot." This consisted of a cannon ball that had been heated to an extremely high temperature before firing. It was intended to hit an enemy building or ship and set it ablaze. The use of hot shot in the field required the digging of a pit, perhaps six feet across and three or four feet deep, in which the soldiers built a very hot fire. Solid shots were then placed in the coals until they glowed. It was shot prepared by French artillerists in such a manner as this that burned the 44-gun British frigate *Charon* to the waterline during the siege of Yorktown in 1781. Similarly, during the War of 1812, American gunners used hot shot to burn four block houses inside the walls of British Fort George and three storehouses outside the walls.[45]

Upon the recommendation of one of Napoleon's former generals, American forts built along the Atlantic and Gulf coasts after about 1817 all included permanent brick furnaces for heating shot. These furnaces varied in size depending upon the number of guns in a fort that might be used to fire hot shot. Indeed, some of the larger forts had more than one such furnace. The firebox was at one end of the furnace and the balls were loaded onto inclined metal racks at the other end. Thus, when a ball directly over the fire had reached cherry red or white color it was removed, allowing the ball directly behind it on the rack to roll into position for maximum heating. It took slightly more than an hour from the time that a fire was started until the first shot was ready for firing: after the fire was hot enough to heat the first cannon ball, each ball thereafter required about twenty-five to thirty minutes of heat.

When a ball reached the desired heat, one of the men opened the door and removed it with a long iron fork while another man used a rasp to quickly knock off the scale that had formed as an inevitable byproduct of the heating. Then one of them carried the ball in a specially designed apparatus to a gun for immediate use. (If the ball was larger than a 24-pounder, 2 men delivered it to the gun.) In the meantime, the men of the gun detachment had loaded a relatively light powder charge into the gun and then followed it with a thick piece of sod or wet hay—or maybe even a tightly fitted wooden plug. After all, the last thing the cannoneers wanted was to load a red-hot ball down onto a powder bag that was not carefully insulated against premature detonation. The light charge was desirable so as to keep the shot from penetrating completely through a ship or other target without setting it ablaze. Tests showed that if a hot shot penetrated more than a foot or so into a wooden structure, it would not have sufficient oxygen to encourage flames.[46]

Steam often issued from the cannon's vent when a red-hot ball came in contact with a wet hay wad, but accidents were relatively infrequent. Contemporary drill manuals urged the gunners to fire their pieces as soon as the loading process had been completed so as not to allow enough time for the heat from the ball to burn through the wad and ignite the main charge. During the War of 1812, however, there was a tragic accident involving hot shot, but it was not due to insufficient wadding. A hot ball, having expanded from the heat of the furnace, was not seated all the way down on the wad when the gunners loaded their 12-pounder. Instead it stuck fast some two feet away from the wad. Then, when the gun fired, the cannon ball served as a very effective barrel plug. Instead of the ball leaving the muzzle, the cannon barrel exploded and sent hot

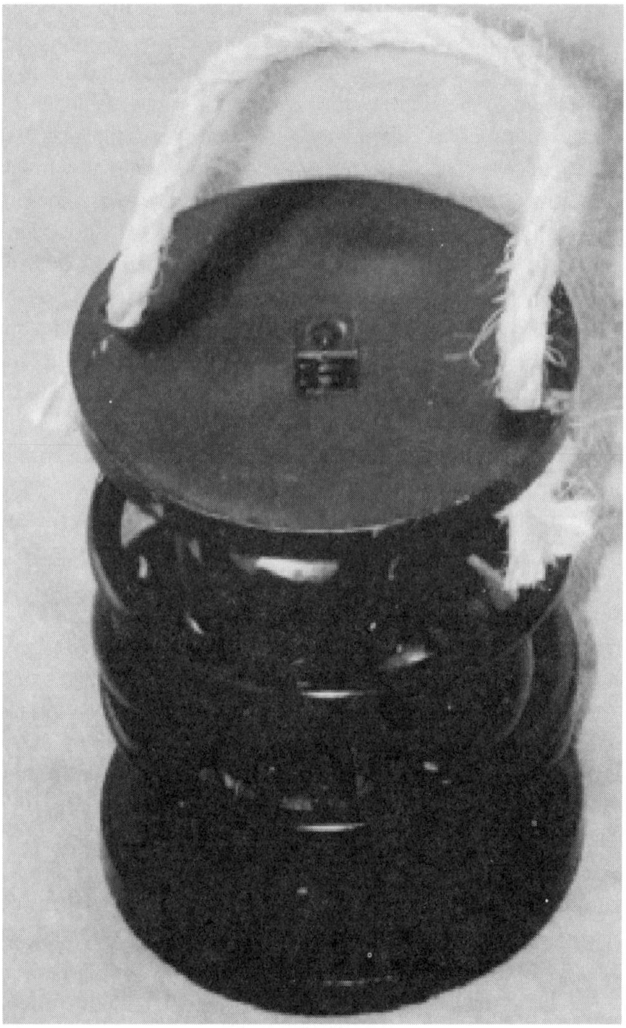

This recreated stand of grapeshot for a 12-pounder gun shows the nine individual grapes, each just over two inches in diameter. The rope on the top plate aids the artillerist in handling this round. (*Courtesy of the author*)

shards of steel in several directions, killing one man and wounding four others.[47]

Another weapon that was sometimes used was the rocket. The British inventor, Sir William Congreve, had begun working on rocket design in about 1804, and his government quickly adopted it as part of its arsenal of weapons. Perhaps the most common size of rocket was four inches in diameter and forty-two inches long and filled with black powder. It could deliver warheads of various sizes, but the most common was probably the 32-pounder. The British navy used rockets aboard some of its ships during the Napoleonic Wars, and with great effect against land targets. Francis Scott Key saw Congreve rockets being fired from a British ship at Fort McHenry, and they helped inspire him to write the poem that eventually became the national anthem of the United States. Not all who saw their use were as impressed by them, however. A Pennsylvania volunteer officer commented upon their use at LaColle Mill in March 1814: "In this affair I saw the Congreve rocket used for the first time. The enemy threw a number which passed over and burst in the air harmless. They might answer a good purpose for burning a town or for frightening raw troops, but in the field they are a poor contrivance for killing men, when compared to the rifle and musket." Another American, perhaps witnessing the same battle, thought that rockets "served only to frighten a few horses and set fire to a tent or two, although our enemy seemed to set a high value upon its destructive powers." A British officer, who witnessed a rocket attack on American troops several months later, held a much different opinion of its effectiveness. "Never," he observed, "did men with arms in their hands make better use of their legs."[48]

In 1847, the U.S. government adopted a rocketry system developed by an American named William Hale. Hale's rockets were smaller than Congreve's, the largest being only three inches in diameter and about fifteen inches long. Although American artillerists fired rockets into the Mexican city of Vera Cruz and used them again a few weeks later at Cerro Gordo, most contemporary accounts suggest that rockets in the American service were more useful as signaling devices or to awe the Indians than as actual weapons. Rockets remained in the nation's weapons inventory for some time—and saw occasional use by both sides during the Civil War—but the advent of accurate, long-range field artillery soon made rockets superfluous.[49]

Mounted Troop Training

The training specified for a mounted soldier was, of course, markedly different from that for an infantryman. Whether destined for a dragoon, cavalry, or mounted rifle regiment, the recruit had first to learn how to ride a horse. It seems rather unlikely that men without prior riding experience would have offered themselves up for one of these regiments but, as with any such organization, the amount of skill exhibited by the incoming soldiers varied considerably, and familiarization with horseflesh was of primary importance to men in these branches of service. The recruit soon learned that the welfare of his horse had to take precedence over his own. He had to ensure that his horse was fed and watered before he fed himself. He had to learn the proper way to saddle his mount so as to avoid causing the horse discomfort. He had to learn to recognize symptoms of potential ill health in his horse and tend to them before the animal became unable to perform the necessary functions of a cavalry mount. A cavalryman who did not take care of his horse soon became a soldier on foot. Not only was this personally embarrassing to the soldier but, if a large number of men showed such callous disregard for their mounts, they could jeopardize an entire military mission. A cavalry recruit, therefore, who had the luxury of extensive formal training, spent a major part of his first week learning to take good care of his horse.[50]

Human and Horse

During this first week, the novice soldier learned the proper way of mounting his horse from either side—so as not to startle the animal—and the importance of properly saddling and bridling his horse. He was to lay the saddle upon the animal's bare back to make sure that it conformed to the shape of his particular horse. Next, he removed the saddle and placed his saddle blanket, "folded into 12 or 16 thicknesses," on the horse's back, being careful to smooth the animal's hair down in the process. He adjusted the stirrups so that later, when he was mounted, there would be a six-inch space between him and the saddle when he stood up in the stirrups. After fastening the girth and the breast strap, the soldier then proceeded to load the various other articles necessary to the life of a mounted trooper. This might include his pistol and holster, a hatchet, a saber, a watering bridle, extra clothing, and a carbine, all of which had to be placed on the horse in such a way as to distribute the weight symmetrically.[51]

After a week's familiarization training, the soldier began several weeks of dismounted drill. Dismounted drill was important because cavalrymen and dragoons would often find it necessary to dismount and fight on foot—as infantry. Twice a day, for an hour and a half each time, the recruit learned the rudiments of military life. It began with such basic information as how to correctly perform the various infantry facing movements—left face, right face, and others. Over the course of time, his lessons became more and more advanced until, usually by the end of the sixth week, he was capable of mounting guard.

Here he began to learn the many bugle calls by which cavalry officers transmitted orders, sometimes on noisy battlefields. In addition to a dozen such signals, there were two dozen more that regulated camp life. There were bugle calls that instructed the troops when to wake up, when to go to each meal, when to report for drill, when to water the horses, when to go to sleep, and many other routine duties.

Next, he received a gentle horse, one that was already trained as a cavalry mount, upon which to continue his own training. For the next six months, he learned the School of the Trooper, the object of which, according to a contemporary drill manual, was "to make troopers skilful in the management of their horses and arms, in all directions, and at all gaits." This segment of cavalry training taught such basic lessons as how to sit on a horse with the least amount of discomfort for both man and animal. The recruit learned how, while mounted, to change direction and speed by the application of pressure on the reins, pressure from his knees on the flanks of the horse, and, occasionally, by the judicious use of spurs. He learned the different speeds that his horse might be required to maintain: the walk, at three-and-a-half to four miles per hour; the trot, at eight-and-a-half miles per hour; and the gallop, at eleven miles per hour.[52]

Occasionally, one of these training horses was not so docile, and recruits dreaded the day that found them assigned to such a mount. One former cavalryman described such a horse as having "his own views regarding the proper duration of riding exercises, and when that time had expired he could not be persuaded to remain any longer on the field but would break for the stables like a 'quarter horse' generally leaving his rider on the ground more or less demoralized." After one such episode, the platoon commander badgered the would-be horseman sitting in the dust. When asked why he had insisted on using his spurs on the animal after the officer had expressly told him not to, the hapless recruit said that it was only the spurs sticking into the animal's sides that had allowed him to stay on as long as he had! The lieutenant was not amused. He set out to demonstrate to his pupils how to control even as fractious a horse as this one. Everything proceeded smoothly as this more experienced horseman bent the animal to his will—or so it seemed. All of a sudden, the horse bolted for the stables, and managed to unseat his unwelcome rider along the way. Some horses, it seemed, were just not meant to be ridden.[53]

A similar incident occurred in the mid-1830s but, in this instance, it was a seasoned dragoon noncommissioned officer rather than a recruit who drew upon himself his commander's ire. "You bestride your horse," bristled the captain, "as if she was a beer barrel; dismount sir, and let me show you how to manage her." The captain climbed into the saddle and put his spurs to use. "The next moment," reported a witness, "the Captain was seen describing a parabolic curve similar to the trajectory of a ten inch shell; his neck and head resembling the fuse, and alighting on his seat of honour [*sic*] at the feet of the unskillful Sergeant." Embarrassed, but still able to see the humor at his own expense, the captain ordered the sergeant to dismiss the company. "And," he continued, "the next time I attempt to break a jade of a young filley [*sic*], may I never be promoted."[54]

In spite of the occasional ill-tempered horse, most of the trainees learned to ride with a minimum of major mishaps. Then it was on to the next stage of training, where the horse soldier learned to load and fire both his pistol and his rifle or carbine. An added element of difficulty in this segment of his training, which the infantryman did not encounter, was having to do these things from the back of a horse. Quite often, as in the heat of battle, this animal would be prancing, squirming, or just stomping his feet out of nervousness or fear. All of these movements made aiming a firearm rather difficult, and loading it even more so.

From here the cavalry recruit entered the School of the Troop (or Company) where he became a part of a bigger organization. By this time, he had become a confident horseman, and it only remained to coordinate his movements with those of dozens of other men. Exercises that were relatively simple to accomplish for individual troopers on horses that were walking took on a considerable amount of difficulty when fifty or a hundred men had to synchronize their movements with one another, with their animals trotting or galloping. It was at this stage of his training that the soldier learned how a marching column of horsemen deployed into a line of battle, for instance. Here, too, was where the fine points of the cavalry charge were practiced. The men learned to charge in a long line parallel to the enemy position. They learned how to maintain proper intervals between platoons and to charge in narrow columns. And they learned to charge as foragers, or skirmishers, where there was no need to observe the niceties of formations, and the troopers had a tremendous freedom of movement as they attacked.[55]

Finally, the cavalrymen and dragoons graduated to the School of the Squadron and, sometimes, to the Evolutions of the Regiment. Two cavalry troops, or companies, made up a squadron, and four to five squadrons comprised a regiment. For the most part, the training at these levels was an expansion in scale of what had composed the School of the Troop. Except in times of war, it was unusual for an entire cavalry or dragoon regiment to be stationed at one place, and the largest unit most men saw was a squadron.

The effectiveness of mounted combat probably depended as much on the amount of drill that the horses had undergone as it did on the drill of the men. The men had to train their mounts, for example, to stand under fire. If a man's horse bolted at the first loud noise it heard in battle his value to his unit would be almost zero.

During the 1790s, General James Wilkinson decided to test the training that a company of dragoons under his command had received. After putting them through their paces on the parade ground, he managed to align them so that they faced his quarters, specifically the stone wall surrounding his vegetable garden. He gave the command to charge, and then waited to see how close to the wall the men would ride before halting. To his dismay and shock, the captain commanding the company leapt his horse over the wall and into the garden beyond—followed by every man in the company. The horses' hooves quickly churned his plants into the soil as the general looked on in amazement. Recovering his composure, Wilkinson decided to give them another test, or perhaps he was trying to find a way to punish them for having followed his orders. This time, the troopers came to a halt facing a river. Again came the order to charge, and again the soldiers responded as ordered. At least one man was swept from his mount and nearly died in the crossing, but soon all of the dragoons scrambled up the opposite bank. The general realized that these troops were indeed trained to follow orders, no matter how foolhardy they appeared to be.[56]

Weapons

Carbines

Weapons training differed for the horse soldiers as well. An infantry musket, with a forty-two-inch barrel, was almost impossible to wield on horseback, and there was little chance that a man could reload his piece after he had fired its one shot. Cavalrymen, therefore, often carried shorter rifles, or carbines, that were at least a little easier to load. Some, specially designed for use atop a horse, had the ramrods permanently attached to swivels under the barrel, so a horseman would not accidentally drop his ramrod and lose the use of his weapon in the heat of battle. At different times during the antebellum period, the Army experimented with different weapons that loaded from the breech, or rear. A soldier equipped with such a breechloader could dispense with the cumbersome ramrod, giving him one less thing to deal with at such a critical time.

The earliest attempt to arm these men with breechloaders was a result of a patent issued to John Hall and William Thornton in 1811. It was several years before the weapons covered by this patent went into production, and then it was only the longer, rifled, infantry model. By 1837, there were two dragoon regiments in existence, and the government arsenal at Harper's Ferry, Virginia, began producing Hall flintlock carbines. These were smooth-bored and fired a .64 caliber ball. The barrel was barely more than two-feet long, and the entire weapon was about the length of the standard infantry musket's barrel. Slightly more than 3,000 pieces were manufactured over the next 6 years. They met with mixed reactions. While it was certainly true that they were easier to load than muzzleloaders, they had a tendency to leak hot ignition gasses where the breech and barrel came together. It could be rather disconcerting when a trooper fired and had burnt powder flare up in front of his face. Another problem with the early breechloaders arose due to the effect of gravity. The horseman carried his carbine in a nearly vertical position with the muzzle downward. During the course of a long day's jostling ride, the powder charge often compacted itself near the forward end of the chamber. Then, if the trooper had to make quick use of his weapon, he might find that there was no powder adjacent to the flash hole from the priming pan or the percussion nipple, and the weapon would fail to fire. An army officer, inspecting dragoons at a frontier post in 1836, wrote: "The chief complaint [with regard to this carbine] is the uncertainty of its fire, which on an average does not take place oftener than eight out of twelve trials." He revised his opinion downward slightly when he estimated the carbine's reliability at no more than sixty percent a few years later.[57]

Born the very year that Hall and Thornton obtained their patent, Christian Sharps had learned much of the gunmaker's art working for Hall at the Harper's Ferry Arsenal, beginning around 1830. In 1848, he obtained a patent for a breechloader that proved to be much more reliable than the older Hall model. A board of ordnance officers tested the weapon in late 1850 and remarked favorably upon its power, accuracy, and speed. "This arm was fired ten times per minute," the committee's report crowed, "and when discharged over water, a second charge was fired before the ricochet of the first had ceased." The U.S. government placed an order for 200 Sharps carbines in the summer of 1854 and issued them to various units of mounted troops on the frontier. Even though these early models were prone to a certain amount of gas leakage around the breech, it was not as serious as that in the Hall models, and most of the reports from the field were highly complimentary. Minor improvements continued to be made, and the government bought almost 90,000 .52 caliber Sharps rifles and carbines during the Civil War.[58]

Pistols

Mounted troopers also often carried pistols in lieu of, or perhaps in addition to, their shoulder arms. For most of the antebellum period, these were single-shot muzzle-loading pistols that operated in the same way as the muskets of the period. They employed flintlock ignition up until the mid-1840s, by which time the government began producing new percussion-fired pistols and converting the flintlocks to the more modern system.

Arms manufacturers and inventors had sought for years to design and build a reliable repeating firearm. As early as 1819, Elisha Collier, in England, was producing guns capable of firing seven times without reloading. Each of these weapons made use of a metal cylinder that revolved around a rod that was coaxial with the barrel. There were seven parallel cylindrical holes bored into the cylinder to serve as ammunition chambers. The shooter loaded gunpowder and a ball into each chamber, and when the cylinder was rotated it brought each of these chambers successively into line with the barrel and ready for firing. The firing mechanisms of Collier's weapons were flintlocks, however, and that meant that the priming pan had to be refilled after every shot. It would not be until the advent of reliable percussion gunlocks that multishot guns would become reliable and, therefore, economically feasible.

In the United States, it was Samuel Colt, of Connecticut, whose persistence finally drew the Army's attention to his repeating pistols and carbines. Colt had formed a friendship with Colonel William S. Harney, and it was this relationship, along with the superiority of Colt's product, that led to Harney procuring fifty repeating rifles for his dragoon regiment in Florida in 1838. The following year, the Navy of the young Republic of Texas bought 180 carbines and an equal number of 5-shot pistols. These weapons soon proved their value in the hands of the Lone Star sailors and, later, the Texas Rangers, and by the late 1840s, selected units of U.S. mounted troops received Colt revolvers as their sec-

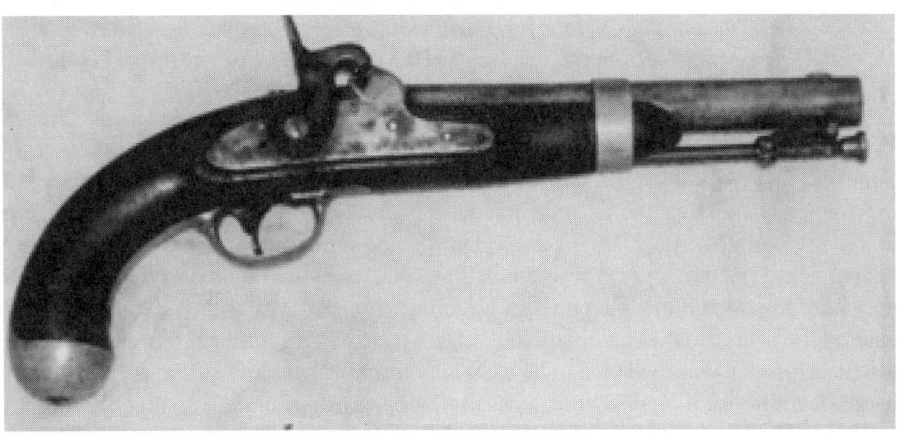

This handsome brass-mounted Model 1842 pistol fired a round .54 caliber bullet. The ramrod was secured to the underside of the barrel by a swivel to prevent its loss. (*Courtesy of the author*)

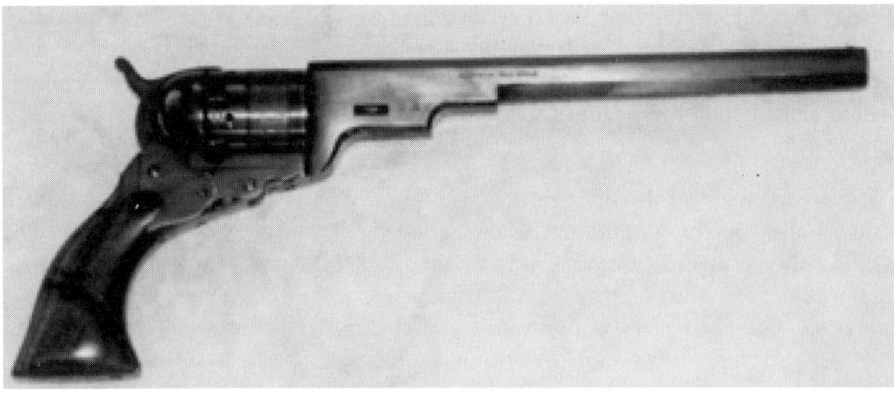

One of Samuel Colt's earliest successful revolver designs, the Patterson Colt, resulted in this five-shot, .36 caliber model manufactured in Paterson, New Jersey. These were made without trigger guards. Instead, the hidden trigger drops into position when the hammer is cocked. This replica features a seven-inch barrel. (*Courtesy of the author*)

ondary firearms.[59]

Although Colonel Harney was among the first military men to express confidence in Colt's products, this same level of trust did not necessarily extend to the ability of his soldiers to care for them. Some years after Harney had first obtained repeating carbines for his men, he received a shipment of new Colt's pistols for field trials. When distributing the new arms among his troops, Harney's well-known penchant for colorful language came to the fore. (A contemporary wrote that Harney "had the reputation of having at his command an original and exhaustless vocabulary of cumulative and energizing profanity.") The colonel calmly and carefully explained to the men that each pistol came with an extra cylinder, and that they should always have the spare cylinder loaded and ready to use when the need arose. Then, warming to his topic, Harney let loose. "No man," he charged,

> can be such a blankety blank fool as not to see the importance of not losing this extra cylinder, for if lost you will have only six shots and when they are gone you will be at the mercy of your enemy and if you have lost it I hope to God that he'll kill you, and if he don't by the blankety blank blank I will, but I expect to hear that they are all lost before you ever get a chance to use them and if I do, the very first one that is lost the blankety blank idiot that lost it will wish that all the blankety blank Indians in Florida had him instead of me, blank blank him. Now go and lose them, blankety blank.[60]

Sabers

Weapons training at this time included instruction in the one weapon that was unique to mounted troops—the saber. This was the weapon that, more than any other, distinguished the cavalryman from his fellow soldiers in the infantry and artillery. And no matter how much prior experience a recruit may have had with firearms before he entered the army, this was a completely new weapon for him. It was a weapon, unlike his firearms, that was designed to be used *only* from the back of his horse. He therefore had to learn to use it against enemy cavalry and against infantry. Although the slightly curved, three-foot long blade of this cut-and-thrust weapon made it appear quite formidable, it was usually only employed when the trooper's firearms were empty or broken. The neophyte horse soldier learned how to thrust his sword at a mounted enemy on either side of him and to front and rear. He employed the same technique against infantrymen. He likewise learned to employ a sweeping cutting motion and to use his weapon to parry the cuts and thrusts of enemy soldiers.

No matter how rigorously officers drilled their troops the true test of their training only came when they faced armed enemies in combat. But combat only filled a small percentage of the soldiers' time in the service. They also faced day-to-day routines that were often long on hard, physical labor and tedium and short on strictly military activities.

NOTES

1. Alan D. Gaff, *Bayonets in the Wilderness: Anthony Wayne's Legion in the Old Northwest* (Norman, Oklahoma: University of Oklahoma Press, 2004), 39.

2. Thomas Lawson to William Worth, October 13, 1845, as cited in Mary C. Gillett, *The Army Medical Department, 1818–1865* (Washington, D.C.: Center of Military History, United States Army, 1987), 96 (1st quotation); J. S. Arthur to David W. Dailey, December 1, 1846, David W. Dailey Collection, Indiana Historical Society, Indianapolis, Indiana (2d quotation); Henry Smith Lane to Samuel Stone, November 5, 1846, Henry Smith Lane Papers, Filson Club, Louisville, Kentucky (3d quotation); George M. Burton to James Burton, October 8, 1846, George M. Burton Letters, Illinois State Historical Library, Springfield, Illinois (4th quotation); George M. Burton to Alex Montgomery, January 16, 1848, George M. Burton Letters, Illinois State Historical Library, Springfield, Illinois (5th quotation).

3. W. E. Horner, "A Military Hospital at Buffalo, New York, in the year 1814," *The Medical Examiner and Record of Medical Science,* New Series, Number 97 (January 1853), 10 (1st quotation); Arthur A. Ekirch, Jr., *The Civilian and the Military* (New York: Oxford University Press, 1956), 43 (2d quotation); James O. Breeden, "Health of Early Texas: The Military Frontier," *Southwestern Historical Quarterly* 80, Number 4 (April 1977), 371–372 (3d quotation); *Philadelphia Daily Evening News,* May 28, 1858, cited in *To Utah With the Dragoons and Glimpses of Life in Arizona and California 1858–1859,* edited by Harold D. Langley (Salt Lake City: University of Utah Press, 1974), 22; Eugene Bandel, *Frontier Life in the Army 1854–1861,* translated by Olga Bandel and Richard Jente, edited by Ralph P. Bieber (Glendale, California: Arthur H. Clark, 1932), 114 (3d quotation).

4. Bandel, *Frontier Life in the Army,* 300 (1st quotation); R. S. Ewell, *The Making of a Soldier: Letters of General R. S. Ewell,* edited by Percy Gatlin Hamlin (Richmond, Virginia: Whittet and Shepperson, 1935), 34 (2d quotation).

5. Dale Richard Steinhauer, "Sogers": Enlisted Men in the U.S. Army, 1815–1860," Ph.D. diss. (University of North Carolina at Chapel Hill, 1992), 23.

6. *Northern Standard* (Clarksville, Texas), February 13, 1847 (quotation); Gaff, *Bayonets in the Wilderness,* 41, 138.

7. Steinhauer "Sogers," 46–48, 62 (quotation).

8. James A. Bennett, *Forts and Forays: A Dragoon in New Mexico, 1850–1856,* edited by Clinton E. Brooks and Frank D. Reeve, (Albuquerque: University of New Mexico Press, 1948), 4–5 (quotation); Francis Paul Prucha in George Croghan, *Army Life on the Western Frontier: Selections from the Official Reports Made Between 1826 and 1845 by Colonel George Croghan,* edited by Francis Paul Prucha (Norman, Oklahoma: University of Oklahoma Press, 1958), 42.

9. Stanley S. Graham, "Life of the Enlisted Soldier on the Western Frontier, 1815–1845," Ph.D. diss. (North Texas State University, 1972), 45–46.

10. Dale Frederick Giese. "Soldiers at Play: A History of Social Life at Fort Union, New Mexico, 1851–1891" (Ph.D. diss., University of New Mexico, 1969), 170–171.

11. Steinhauer, "Sogers," 99 (quotation); Graham, "Life of the Enlisted Soldier," 41–42.

12. Thomas Henderson, *Hints on the Medical Examination of Recruits for the Army and on the Discharge of Soldiers from the Service on Surgeon's Certificate* (1840, Rev. ed. by Richard H. Coolidge. Philadelphia: J. B. Lippincott, 1856), 32–33.

13. *The Female Volunteer; or The Life and Wonderful Adventures of Miss Eliza Allen, a Young Lady of Eastport, Maine,* cited by Robert W. Johannsen in *To the Halls of the Montezumas: The Mexican War in the American Imagination* (New York and Oxford: Oxford University Press, 1985), 137.

14. Gaff, *Bayonets in the Wilderness,* 51–52.

15. Horner, "A Military Hospital at Buffalo," 772 (quotation); Indiana *Democrat,* June 22, 1846.

16. Leo E. Oliva, "Missouri Volunteers on the Santa Fe Trail, 1847–1848," *Trail Guide* 15, Number 3 (September 1970), 4; Thomas L. Karnes, "Gilpin's Volunteers on the Santa Fe Trail," *Kansas Historical Quarterly* 30, Numberl (Spring 1964), 5–6.

17. *General Regulations for the Army; or, Military Institutes*—hereinafter *Army Regulations for 1821*—(Philadelphia: M. Carey and Sons, 1821), 288 (1st quotation); Henderson, *Hints on the Medical Examination of Recruits for the Army,* 87–90; John C. Tidball, "Getting Through West Point: The Cadet Memoirs of John C. Tidball, Class of 1848," edited by James L. Morrison, Jr. *Civil War History* 26, Number 4 (1980), 312; Henderson, *Hints on the Medical Examination of Recruits for the Army,* 87–90 (2d quotation).

18. Henderson, *Hints on the Medical Examination of Recruits for the Army,* 79–80; Charles W. Ayars, Some Notes on the Medical Service of the Army, 1812–1839," *The Military Surgeon: Journal of the Association of Military Surgeons of the United States* 50 (May 1922), 511 (quotation).

19. Ayars, "Some Notes on the Medical Service of the Army," 510; Graham, "Life of the Enlisted Soldier," 65; *Army Regulations for 1821,* 288, 312; Gillett, *The Army Medical Department, 1818–1865,* 76–77.

20. *General Regulations for the Army of the United States, 1841* (Washington, D.C.: 1841), 119; Percival G. Lowe, *Five Years a Dragoon ('49 to '54) And Other Adventures on the Great Plains* (Norman, Oklahoma: University of Oklahoma Press, 1965, 3–4 (quotation).

21. Marcus Cunliffe, *Soldiers and Civilians: The Martial Spirit in America, 1775–1865* (Boston and Toronto: Little, Brown and Company, 1968), 102; R. W. Johnson, *A Soldieris Reminiscences in Peace and War* (Philadelphia: J. B. Lippincott, 1886), 35–36 (quotation).

22. Donald E. Graves, " 'Dry Books of Tactics': U.S. Infantry Manuals of the War of 1812 and After, Part I," *Military Collector and Historian* 38, Number 2 (Summer 1986), 50–61; Donald E. Graves, " 'Dry Books of Tactics': U.S. Infantry Manuals of the War of 1812 and After, Part II," *Military Collector and Historian* 38, Number 4 (Winter 1986), 173–177.

23. Friedrich Wilhelm Ludolf Gerhard Augustin, Baron von Steuben, *Regulations for the Order and Discipline of the Troops of the United States* (Philadelphia: 1779; reprinted as *Baron Von Steuben and His Regulations,* edited by Joseph R. Riling, Philadelphia: Ray Riling Arms Books, 1966), 12; *Abstract of Infantry Tactics; including Exercises and Manoeuvres of Light Infantry and Riflemen; for the Use of the Militia of the United States* (Boston: Hilliard, Gray, Little, and Wilkins, 1830), 15.

24. [James Hildreth], *Dragoon Campaigns to the Rocky Mountains* (New York: Wiley and Long, 1836; reprint, New York: Arno, 1973), 41–42.

25. Steuben, *Regulations,* 13; *Abstract of Infantry Tactics,* 15; James M. McCaffrey, *Army of Manifest Destiny: The American Soldier in the Mexican War, 1846–1848* (New York: New York University Press, 1992), 43–44.

26. S. Cooper, *A Concise System of Instructions and Regulations for the Militia and Volunteers of the United States, Comprehending the Exercises and Movements of the Infantry, Light Infantry, and Riflemen; Cavalry and Artillery; Together with the manner of doing duty in Garrison and in Camp, and the forms of Parades, Reviews, and Inspections, As established by authority for the government of the Regular Army* (Philadelphia: Robert P. Desilver, 1836), 13–17,

27. Jarvis Frary Hanks, "A Drummer Boy in the War of 1812: The Memoir of Jarvis Frary Hanks," edited by Lester W. Smith, *Niagara Frontier,* 7 (1960), 56.

28. William Gilham, *Manual of Instruction for the Volunteers and Militia of the United States* (Philadelphia: Charles DeSilver, 1861), 59 (1st quotation); "Records of the firings and opinions of The Board assembled at Washington Arsenal for the Trial of Small Arms according to Special Orders Number23 War Department, February 1st 1860," in Claud E. Fuller, *The Rifled Musket* (New York: Bonanza Books, 1958), 73–78, 129–130, 132, 135; Ulysses S. Grant, *Personal Memoirs of U.S. Grant,* 2 vols. (New York: Charles L. Webster, 1885), I: 95 (2d quotation).

29. Paddy Griffith, *Forward Into Battle: Fighting Tactics from Waterloo to Vietnam* (Chicester, Sussex: Antony Bird Publications, 1981), 31.

30. John Gale, *The Missouri Expedition 1818-1820: The Journal of Surgeon John Gale with Related Documents,* edited by Roger L. Nichols (Norman, Oklahoma: University of Oklahoma Press, 1969), 57 (1st quotation); Tidball, "Getting Through West Point," 314 (2d quotation); Stanley S. Graham, "Routine at Western Cavalry Posts, 1833–1861," *Journal of the West* 15 (July 1976), 53.

31. "Records of the firings ... of Small Arms ... February 1st 1860," in Fuller, *The Rifled Musket,* 59–65.

32. John Jackson, "'We Lay There Doing Nothing": John Jackson's Recollection of the War of 1812," edited by Jeff L. Patrick *Indiana Magazine of History* 88 (June 1992), 116.

33. Gaff, *Bayonets in the Wilderness,* 60, 107.

34. Albert Manucy, *Artillery Through the Ages: A Short Illustrated History of Cannon, Emphasizing Types Used in America* (Washington, D. C.: United States Government Printing Office, 1949, reprint 1962), 10.

35. Warren Ripley, *Artillery and Ammunition of the Civil War* (New York: Promontory Press, 1970), 366–379.

36. Ripley, *Artillery and Ammunition of the Civil War,* 366–379.

37. Gilham, *Manual of Instruction,* 491–500; Cooper, *A Concise System of Instructions and Regulations,* 181–185.

38. Peterson, *Round Shot and Rammers,* 119.

39. Peterson, *Round Shot and Rammers,* 121; Ripley, *Artillery and Ammunition of the Civil War,* 228.

40. Clarence H. Frick to his brother Arthur W. Frick, March 28, 1847, Clarence Frick Collection, US Army Military History Institute, Carlisle, Pennsylvania; George Ballentine. *Autobiography of an English Soldier in the United States Army, Comprising Observations and Adventures in the States and Mexico* (New York, 1853), 155 (quotation).

41. McCaffrey, *Army of Manifest Destiny,* 145.

42. Grapeshot used by the Navy often contained anywhere from twelve to fifteen balls, but the Army's seemed always to have had only nine. Ripley, *Artillery and Ammunition of the Civil War,* 379.

43. David Bates Douglass, "An Original Narrative of the Niagara Campaign of 1814," edited by John T. Horton, *Niagara Frontier* 11 (Spring 1964), 26, 28 (quotation).

44. Harold L. Peterson, *Round Shot and Rammers: An Introduction to Muzzle-Loading Artillery in the United States* (New York: Bonanza Books, 1969), 80.

45. Peterson, *Round Shot and Rammers,* 64; Isaac Roach, "Journal of Major Isaac Roach, 1812–1824," *The Pennsylvania Magazine of History and Biography,* 17, Number 2 (1893), 145.

46. Much of the information on hot shot and its preparation and uses comes from: Herbert E. Kahler and F. Hilton Crowe, "Hot Shot Furnaces," *The Regional Review,* 2, Number 2 (February 1939) at http://www.cr.nps.gov/history/ online_books/regional/vol2-2d.htm, accessed on March 7, 2005 and Paul Branch, "Hot Shot Furnace to Become a Reality," *Ramparts,* Fall 1995 at http://www.clis.com/friends/HotShot.htm, accessed on March 8, 2005.

47. George McFeely, "Chronicle of Valor: The Journal of a Pennsylvania Officer in the War of 1812," edited by John C. Fredriksen, *The Western Pennsylvania Historical Magazine,* 67 (July 1984), 251.

48. McFeely, "Chronicle of Valor, 275 (1st quotation); Douglass, "An Original Narrative of the Niagara Campaign," 33 (2d quotation); A. D. McCaig, "The Soul of Artillery": Congreve's Rockets and Their Effectiveness in Warfare," *Journal of the Society for Army Historical Research* 78 (2000), 260 (3d quotation).

49. Journal entries for June 21, 1825 and July 5, 1825, Russell Reid and Clell G. Gannon, editors, "Journal of the Atkinson-O'Fallon Expedition," *North Dakota Historical Quarterly,* 4 (October 1929), 22; Journal entries for March 24, 1836 and March 30, 1836, A. B. Meek, "'The Journal of A. B. Meek and the Second Seminole War 1836," edited by John K. Mahon, *Florida Historical Quarterly* 38 (1960), 314–315.

50. "The Union Cavalryman in the Civil War," http://www.bufordsboys.com/UnionCavalrymanIII.htm, accessed December 13, 2004; *Cavalry Tactics,* 1841, http://www.9thVirginia.com/poinsett1.htm, accessed December 13, 2004.

51. *Cavalry Tactics;* Gilham, *Manual of Instruction,* 359.

52. Gilham, *Manual of Instruction,* 334 (quotation); Cooper, *A Concise System of Instructions and Regulations,* Part 2, 9.

53. William Woods Averell, *Ten Years in the Saddle: The Memoir of William Woods Averell,* edited by Edward K. Eckhardt and Nicholas J. Amato (San Rafael, California and London: Presidio Press, 1978), 60.

54. Jacob Rhett Motte, *Journey Into Wilderness: An Army Surgeon's Account of Life in Camp and Field during the Creek and Seminole Wars,* 1836–1838, edited by James F. Sunderman (Gainesville, Florida: University of Florida Press, 1953), 163–164.

55. Gilham, *Manual of Instruction,* 383, 390–392, 430.

56. Gaff, *Bayonets in the Wilderness,* 208–209.

57. Arcadi Gluckman, *Identifying Old U.S. Muskets, Rifles & Carbines* (New York: Bonanza Books, 1965), 173–177, 315–317; Croghan, *Army Life on the Western Frontier,* 97 (quotation); Croghan, *Army Life on the Western Frontier,* 99.

58. "Report of the Board of Ordnance Officers on Patent Small Arms Other Than Repeating Pistols," in Winston O. Smith, *The Sharps Rifle: Its History, Development and Operation* (New York: William Morrow, 1943), 9, 11, 19.

59. William B. Edwards, *The Story of Colt, Revolver: The Biography of Col. Samuel Colt* (New York: Castle Books, 1957), 68, 94–99.

60. Averell, *Ten Years in the Saddle,* 88–89.

3 DAY-TO-DAY LIFE IN THE ARMY

DAILY ROUTINE

A soldier's typical day—if indeed there ever was such thing as a "typical" day—began early when the company bugler or drummer sounded reveille, the wakeup call. This was usually at first light, which might be as early as 4:30 a.m. in the summer time. At this call, the men were to rise from their slumbers and begin preparing themselves for the day at hand. The first order of business was roll call—the first of several that would be held throughout the day. The troops then had a little time to get dressed and clean up the area around their quarters. Those in the mounted units—dragoons and cavalry—used this time to water their horses and move them to fresh grazing ground. Since a cavalryman without a strong, well-fed mount soon finds himself walking, he tended to his horse's nourishment before his own.[1]

Sick Call

"Surgeon's call" was usually the next signal the men heard. It was then that the first sergeants of each company escorted any man feeling too ill to perform his duties that day to the resident medical officer. Reporting sick led to one of several outcomes. The doctor might administer some medicine and send a man back to his quarters for a day or so of rest if his complaint did not seem too severe. A more seriously ill patient could be admitted to the hospital for continued treatment and monitoring of his symptoms. The quality of the hospital facilities often depended upon the size and permanency of the post. A well-established installation near a major city would likely have a solid wooden or masonry building with adequate ventilation in the summer months and sufficient heat in the winter. At a lonely, one-company camp on the frontier, the "hospital" might consist of nothing more than a leaky tent. From the hospital the man would recover, die, or be invalided out of the service and sent home.

Guard Mount

Guard duty was a constant necessity. In secure areas, its main value was as an aid to training. In areas where there was even the slightest threat of enemy attack, its value was obvious. Different guard posts were established around the perimeter of the camp, where perhaps as many as a dozen guards took up a twenty-four-hour residence. Dividing themselves into three or more relief shifts, the men then disbursed themselves to one- or two-man posts, where they were expected to be intensely alert for anything out of the ordinary for up to two hours. Then each, relieved by another soldier, returned to the guard post for rest. Sometimes, as in the dead of winter on the northern plains, two hours of walking a guard post posed a tangible threat of frostbite, so the time on duty was often reduced to one hour, or even less.[2]

An officer often visited the individual sentries to make sure they were staying alert and remembered the day's particular countersign. Sometimes, they quizzed the men with hypothetical situations to see how they reacted. One officer, apparently believing that too often the guards merely memorized instructions without actually thinking about them, asked one of his men what he would do if he saw a steamboat approaching the camp from over a nearby hill. The enlisted man promptly answered that he would of course alert the corporal of the guard, so that he, in turn, could notify the officer of the day for any special instructions.[3]

Sometimes, the combination of the need for camp security and the desire for personal comfort resulted in, if not always disaster, humor. In 1814, a sentry left his assigned post and ventured a short way into the woods to relieve himself. No sooner had he dropped his trousers and begun to heed the call of nature, than an inspecting officer approached his vacant post. Terrified that he might be court-martialed and executed for abandoning his post, the guard grabbed up his now soiled clothing with one hand and his musket with the other and scurried back to his station. "He only went to s—t," observed another of the sentries, "and he didn't know there was any harm in it. What was a man to do?" Luckily, the officer appreciated the situation for what it was and did not press charges.[4]

During the Mexican War, an officer of the guard overheard one of his sentries muttering loudly to himself as he approached his post. Unseen by the unhappy soldier, the officer stopped to listen. "Well this is the G—d damnedest shot of work I ever saw yet. I voted for old Polk G—d d—n him and here I am in the wind & rain & misery. I came out here to fight and instead of fighting I have to tread this [illegible] for four hours. What a d—d fool I was. I ought to be in Hell for a d—d fool." By this time the officer had decided to have a little fun with the man. As he approached, the guard dutifully challenged him by asking, "Who comes there?" Then, instead of responding with the proper countersign, the officer said, "James K. Polk." The sentry, not seeing any humor in the situation, raised his bayoneted musket and called out, "Stand, James K. Polk for I'll be d—d if I don't shoot you if you give me the least chance."[5]

Breakfast and Fatigue Duty

After guard mounting, there was another roll call before breakfast. Following the morning meal, the company officers assigned various fatigue tasks to their men. The nature of these tasks varied considerably. The Army used soldier labor to construct its frontier posts. This included erecting barracks, officers' quarters, headquarters buildings, post hospitals, and, in many cases, surrounding palisades. Even after construction was complete, some men at frontier forts would necessarily be required to bring in firewood, cut and store ice, and tend vegetable gardens. Troops at Fort Mackinac in the mid-1830s traveled across twelve miles of ice to another island to get the necessary 600 cords of firewood for the winter. The garrison of Fort Snelling in the mid-1820s, for example, needed 1,200 cords of firewood and 500 tons of hay every year, and acquiring them required a lot of man-hours that might otherwise have been devoted to perfecting the practice of the military duties of soldiers and officers. In fact, one officer had spent so much time tending to these nonmilitary tasks, that he estimated that it had been four or five years since he had last participated in a military drill.[6]

An inspection of a fort on the Northern Plains revealed that the absence of training time had led to a woeful inability to perform even necessary defensive functions in case of an attack. Officers had no idea what roles they were to play in such an event. The commanding officer required several hours in which to round up competent gun crews to man the fort's small cannons. The soldiers then had to locate proper ammunition for the cannons and bring it to the guns. The inspector's report on the defensive capabilities of Fort Howard, Wisconsin, in 1826 fairly drips with frustration:

> With a view to test the state of preparedness of the garrison for defence [*sic*], in whatever this particular arm is concerned, I directed a few shells to be fired. The officer of ordnance begged time to prepare some fuses, as they required paring down, being all too large for his shells. Some hours were occupied in this preparation; at length the fuses were driven and a trial made, sufficient to prove that but few present knew either how to prepare a shell, to load the piece, or to fire it when loaded, and that the fuses which cost such length of time to get ready were not equitable, nor to be made so by any means at hand to use. Out of perhaps a dozen shells fired, not more than two burst.[7]

LIVING QUARTERS

Eastern Forts

Living quarters were, like almost everything else in military life, of great variety, depending upon geographical location and other considerations. The young United States, although fairly well isolated from any potential European enemies, nevertheless had to protect its shoreline and its coastal cities from any seaborne threats. In the spring of 1794, therefore, Congress authorized a limited amount of funds to construct a series of fortifications to fill this need. The resulting installations generally consisted of earthen walls protecting cannons that were relatively unprotected from the elements or from enemy fire. These forts rapidly gave way to the ravages of the elements. With the threat of war with France in 1798, Congress earmarked more money to build forts, but their design was not much different than those already crumbling away. International relations remained relatively calm for the next few years, and it was not until war with England seemed possible in 1807 that Congress again loosened its purse strings. The designs now implemented began to include more and more masonry, both as reinforcement to the earthen walls and as the primary building materials. When war with England finally did come, in 1812, there was no extra money or manpower to devote to the construction of permanent forts but, as soon as the war ended, the government once again turned its attention in that direction. The forts that army engineers then designed were built of stone or brick, and sometimes a combination of both materials, and were impervious to all but the most sustained artillery bombardment that an enemy could bring to bear. Cannons were placed in vaulted masonry chambers called casemates with walls five feet thick or more. Some of these forts had two levels of casemates; with perhaps a third level of guns, with minimal protection, on the roof. There was no uniformity as to the size of these forts. Fort Massachusetts, on an island off the coast of Mississippi, was among the smallest, mounting thirty-seven cannons, while Fort Adams, in Rhode Island was over a mile in perimeter and was designed for 468 cannons.[8]

Frontier Forts

As settlements extended across the Allegheny Mountains and into Indian territory, the Army moved with it to offer protection. The forts that sprang up in the interior were vastly different than those along the Atlantic and Gulf coasts. The most important difference was due to the different enemy encountered in the woods and forests. Because the Indians did not possess artillery of even the smallest caliber, there was no need to build expensive masonry forts to protect against them. Fortifications of timber were stout enough, if properly designed and constructed, to stop the arrows and musket balls most likely to be encountered here. Most of the forts east of the Mississippi River were enclosed in stout log palisades, while those to the west were often simply a collection of houses, barracks, and storerooms, with no encircling protective works.

A fort built on the frontier in 1790 employed perhaps the simplest construction. It was a small, square work, barely a hundred feet on each side with bastions in each corner. Two hundred soldiers labored to erect the walls from logs laid horizontally, and then they built their barracks against the inside of these walls. A few years later, soldier-laborers built another one nearby, and they set the logs for the walls vertically this time. These thirteen-foot logs were hewn square on two sides, so they fit together without leaving gaps, and buried some two and a half feet deep in a trench dug for that purpose. Then, because a few gaps were inevitable, a second set of smaller logs was erected just inside of the main wall,

This painting shows Fort Snelling, a masonry fort near the headwaters of the Mississippi River. (*Courtesy of the Library of Congress*)

Solidly re-built blockhouse at Fort Massac on the Ohio River. (*Courtesy of the Fort Massac State Park/Illinois Department of Natural Resources*)

such as to close up these gaps and make it virtually impossible for an Indian arrow or musket ball to penetrate into the interior of the fort. The men cut loopholes into the walls to allow the defenders to fire on any attacking enemy without exposing themselves to return fire. These loopholes were cut some seven feet or so above ground level and a firing step, or banquette, provided for the riflemen to stand on. The height of the loopholes prevented an enemy from sneaking up to the walls of a fort, perhaps at night, and firing through the loopholes into the fort. At each corner of the fort stood a two-story, square blockhouse. The lower level of each provided living quarters for the soldiers, and the upper story of each contained a small cannon. Sometimes, a ditch some seven or eight feet deep encircled the entire fort to carry off excess rainwater and to serve as an additional deterrent to any attacker.[9]

Living quarters within forts ran the gamut from sturdy frame barrack buildings in some of the seacoast forts—where two soldiers shared a wooden bunk that might be stacked two or three high—to leaky tents in some of the frontier forts. A young lieutenant reporting at Fort Lauderdale for duty against the Seminoles described the fort as being nothing more than "a cluster of cane-built huts and a few Indian wigwams. I was shown my quarters, or a thatched hut of one room. The floor was of unplaned boards laid on the sand." To add to his discomfort, he was incessantly beset by cockroaches, mosquitoes, and an "army of fleas." Huts of similar construction were common throughout the Southwest as well, and they were only a little better protection against the elements than nothing. A junior officer at Fort Duncan, Texas, in 1854 noted that the predominant dwelling was built of vertical pickets set about eighteen inches into the ground for walls and a roof of thatch. The walls of these huts, or jacales, as the neighboring Mexicans called them, were finished off by compacting mud and small sticks in the spaces between the pickets. The young lieutenant's first experience in a Texas rainstorm in his leaky hut was not a pleasant one. Try as he might, he and his comrade were unable to find a dry enough space in which to sleep. A soldier at Fort Harker, Kansas, described a similar experience in such a dwelling:

Students visit the re-built officers' quarters at Fort Massac. (*Courtesy of the Fort Massac State Park /Illinois Department of Natural Resources*)

> The roof is a heterogeneous mass of mud, sticks, straw and boughs. The former, owing to its profound respect for the law of gravitation, would persist, at first, in falling in clods at all hours. It dropped upon our plates at dinner and into our mouths in dreams, till finally, a bright idea striking us, we stretched a piece of tent cloth above our bed and defied the mud. It snowed the night of our experiment, and a bushel or so of snow sifted into the tent cloth. Toward morning came a thaw. We were dreaming ourselves a victim of the Spanish Inquisition, and they were trying on us the torture of the shaven head and ice-cold drops of water. Just as we were about to renounce Protestantism in toto, we were awakened to a sense of the reality. The water was dripping from our cotton roof in quarts, and, as we wrung ourselves out, a few clods of mud fell with a loud thump, in the opposite corner, as if to remind us that in an uncivilized country man can never war successfully with the elements.[10]

Foul weather was not the only thing that intruded upon a soldier's comfort in his quarters. At various times, tiny winged pests—such as mosquitoes, fleas, gnats, and bedbugs—made it almost impossible for men to get a good night's sleep. It was not at all uncommon, at many posts, for the troops to not even bother trying to sleep in the barracks because of the bedbugs. Instead, weather permitting, they slept outside. Some dragoons on the Great Plains gave up the relative protection from the elements that their sod houses offered because of the fleas and mice and snakes with whom they shared quarters. "Compared to fleas," one discriminating trooper related, "bedbugs are pets. Spread out a soldier's blanket and see thousands of fleas hopping from an inch to a foot high, enjoying the warm rays of the sun and exercise, after a successful night with a soldier." A dragoon with a dry sense of humor described how numerous were the hungry mosquitoes during a march in Minnesota. He was convinced that there were enough of them to carry off some of the dragoon horses. "Poor hungry things," he commiserated. "How would they have been saved from starvation, but for this expedition of ours?" Nor were mosquito bars always an effective defense. An officer traveling aboard a steamboat on the Mississippi River found himself tormented by the tiny blood-suckers. "An old mosquito bar let in millions of mosquitoes that could not find their way out again," he grumbled. "After enduring tortures from them all night, I let them out this morning." A couple of engineering officers in Mexico seemed to have hit upon an effective, although somewhat repulsive, method of prophylaxis. They greased themselves from head to toe in salt pork and then climbed into canvas bags to sleep with only their heads exposed.[11]

OPINIONS OF OFFICERS

Whether ensconced in a permanent fort or cantonment or living under canvas while on campaign, soldiers had definite opinions about their officers. They liked and admired some, and they hated others. The written record probably shows a higher percentage of negative evaluations than is accurate because of the greater human tendency to condemn than to praise. A soldier's expressed impression of his officers was often influenced by some discrete incident that might have passed between them. A kind word, for example, could go a long way toward fostering a positive valuation. Likewise, a man disciplined for some breach of the rules by an officer might harbor an unjustifiably harsh opinion of him. Different soldiers, perhaps at different times, held diametrically opposed views of some of their superiors. General William H. Winder serves as a case in point. Whereas one soldier, writing in 1813, considered him "the best of the bunch" of the officers under whom he had served, another wrote that the general "before he was appointed knew no more of military matters than his horse, and I am satisfied he could not put a company in motion now after two year's experience." Upon the death in 1834 of Brigadier General Henry Leavenworth, a soldier memorialized him as "a man universally beloved by those under his command, as well for his unassuming manners, as for the natural mildness and clemency of his disposition." It is difficult to reconcile this glowing tribute with another account, written a few years earlier by an officer of the Sixth U.S. Infantry Regiment, whose acquaintance with proper grammar was somewhat lacking:

> we have a man to Comg [command] us that none of us Can Love or even Respect further than Duty Requires. Colonel Levingworth [Leavenworth] has applied for the Second Regt. of Artillery. I hope in God he may get it for then we Should be Clear of him which would be a jubilee to nearly all the Garrison. thare are Damned few that would Pick him up if his Leg was broke if Duty did not Compel them. To Sum up the [w]hole … I am not well and Damned Miserable under my Pres[en]t Com[mandin]g officer. if … Colo[nel] Levingworth will be Promoted to this Regt … we Shall be as Good as Gone for if he was Colo[nel] of the 6th Regt. I would as Soon be in Hell and have the Devil for my Com[mandin]g officer.[12]

Well-Liked Officers

Obviously not all officers enjoyed the unalloyed adulation of all enlisted men, nor were they universally reviled. Even though the human animal seems much more likely to complain about his superiors than to commend them, there is ample evidence of capable and well-liked officers. During the War of 1812, Brigadier General Scott seems to have been particularly well regarded by his troops. One man was sure that Scott was "the best officer in the whole army of any grade" and further characterized him as "the life and soul" of the army. Another noted that one of his officers commanded "immediate attention and respect, and while under him we consider ourselves as having a commander, a friend and instructor." Colonel Stephen W. Kearny was another man who drew praise. He displayed a rare ability to engender respect without pandering. Writing in the early 1840s, a dragoon described him as "the best exemplification of a … Soldier possible, rigorously strict almost to severity when on duty, but affable, just and kind when off duty." A few years later, another soldier, equally impressed with Kearny's ability to maintain proper military decorum without sacrificing his personality, said that he was "a universal favorite in the army, a rigid disciplinarian, and … respected and esteemed as a gentleman well qualified for anything in life."[13]

Scoundrels

Sometimes, the objects of the men's scorn were officers in general. An infantryman, writing in 1813, for example, characterized the bulk of the officer corps as "the most Ignorant and ugly parcel of rascals that I ever saw." Similarly, a soldier writing in 1836 dismissed the majority of his officers as "a trifling set of fellows." He then gave vent to his feelings about a particular, although unnamed, officer. "How mortifying," he wrote, " to be a soldier to be commanded by an old woman! Even a slave," he postulated, "feels proud of having a great man for his master." (There does not appear to be any documentary evidence to support this last statement, however.) A soldier, participating in the Utah campaign in 1858, loosed a tirade against the products of the United States Military Academy in a letter he wrote to a Philadelphia newspaper. "Fellows are let loose from West Point, full of the idea that they are born to rule, and soon they let out their dignity in everything that affects their subordinates. Men, in many cases better men than themselves, are treated as brutes by these new fledged cadets, and they lord it over the veterans of the service with rods of iron."[14]

Usually, the unhappy soldiers singled out specific officers for their comments. A Pennsylvania volunteer in the War of 1812 thought his colonel "entirely unfit to be a lieutenant, let alone a field officer." Another man, himself a junior officer and aiming farther up the chain of command, thought that the brigadier general commanding his brigade was merely "a man of very ordinary abilities and totally unfit for the command of an army." Yet another soldier discussed the growing unpopularity of his company commander and observed that some of the men under his command "would not lift their hand to save his life." A veteran of the Seminole fighting in Florida believed that Major William G. Belknap was "the most disagreeable man to serve with that one can find. I find him prudent to timidity and more cautious of his person than a miser of his money." "It was very evident," wrote another, "that the major thought no more of a private soldier than if he were a dog." A few years later, a young subaltern of dragoons described Major E. V. Sumner as "the greatest martinet in the service, who for our sins has got command of us." He told his brother he was "in perfect purgatory here, and Major Sumner would be the chief devil anywhere." He did find a silver lining of sorts. "Old Sumner has had one good effect on us," he admitted. "He has taught some of us to pray who never prayed before, for we all put up daily petitions to get rid of him." And, finally, an exasperated infantry officer on the Utah Expedition repeatedly referred to his commanding officer as an old woman. "But alas, the weakness of old women!" he complained, in a long-winded letter to his wife.

> It has been a severe trial for us all that we are humiliated into the position that we have an officer in the army, yes, at the head, by accident, of this gallant little army, and still more in personal point of view, a colonel of the 10th Inf. who is no more qualified for

> his position than a child ten years old, who changes his mind as often as the wind blows, who does not know what to do or how to do, whose intellect is blunted, who issues orders to do one thing and the next breath do the contrary, whose whole care is a grass plot for his tent and a feeding spot for his own animals, whose conduct is that of an insane man, who has marched up and down this valley to his eternal disgrace and injury to an immense amount of public property, such as loss of mules, wagons, cattle, etc., etc.[15]

Some officers were so unpopular that their men sought to assassinate them! During the War of 1812, troops under Colonel Alexander Smyth tried to burn down his tent and openly taunted him by snapping unloaded muskets in his direction. By the time he finally left the army, things had escalated to a point that Smyth felt safe only with a heavy guard around him while he slept, and he seldom slept in the same place for more than a few nights. Sometimes, unhappy soldiers did more than just snap empty muskets at unpopular officers. Among the slain at the Battle of Buena Vista, in 1847, was Colonel John J. Hardin, commander of the First Illinois Volunteer Infantry Regiment. Soon after the battle, rumors began to circulate that buckshot had been discovered in the colonel's body and that it had come from the buck-and-ball cartridges of his own men. "This was considered accidental," wrote one of his men, "but believed otherwise, as battles often decide private grievances, as well as those of nations." During that same conflict, Captain Braxton Bragg, a regular artillery officer, nearly became a victim of what became known in the late twentieth century as "fragging." A soldier with a grudge of some sort placed a very large artillery shell inside Bragg's tent and directly under his bed, or cot, and fashioned a powder train that passed under the tent wall to the outside. Then, after the unpopular officer had retired for the night, the soldier returned and applied a match to the powder train. Miraculously, Bragg survived the ensuing blast without so much as a scratch. Such manifestations of dislike for their officers were extremely rare. Most men vented their frustrations in conversations with one another or in letters to family and friends.[16]

GETTING ALONG WITH ONE ANOTHER

Whenever men are forced to live in relatively close quarters with one another, as soldiers are, they are likely, occasionally, to get on one another's nerves. Sometimes, this led to physical confrontations. The authors of the *Articles of War* could not possibly have foreseen every type of misbehavior that could occur within the military. The *Articles,* for example, do not specifically address fighting within the ranks between fellow soldiers. When instances of such conduct occurred, however, they tended to undermine good order and morale, so authorities had to find ways to deal with them. During the War of 1812, a Solomonic officer came upon two of his men fighting. After breaking them up, he decided to see just how badly they wanted to continue the fight. He gave each of them a stout stick and ordered them to resume their fight. And just in case a little of their original ardor had died, he gave sticks to two more men and told them that they were to use them on the combatants if they did not sufficiently whip one another. At Fort Fillmore, New Mexico, in 1851, another officer used a similar punishment against two quarreling soldiers. Instead of sticks, however, he supplied each man with a black snake whip—probably borrowed from the teamsters for the occasion—and ordered them to whip one another until they each had had enough.[17]

Altercations between officers also occasionally led to violence, but followed a more formal set of rules. Because promotion was glacially slow in the army, officers were very protective of their ranks. An officer was quick to take offense, therefore, at the slightest comment or action that he construed as somehow impugning his honor or reputation. He might then issue a formal challenge to the offender to meet him upon the "field of honor" and settle the dispute by a duel. The *Articles of War* expressly forbade dueling, and although it was slowly going out of fashion by the beginning of the nineteenth century, it definitely had not become extinct. Vice-President Aaron Burr, after all, killed former Secretary of the Treasury Alexander Hamilton in a duel in 1804, and Commodore James Barron (ill-starred commander of the *Chesapeake* in 1807) similarly dispatched Commodore Stephen Decatur in 1820. Nevertheless, army regulations were very explicit. "No officer or soldier shall send a challenge to another officer or soldier, to fight a duel, or accept a challenge if sent, upon pain, if a commissioned officer, of being cashiered; if a non-commissioned officer or soldier, of suffering corporeal punishment, at the discretion of a court-martial." As with everything else in the disciplinary code, however, not all infractions were treated with equal weight.

Dueling among officers in General Anthony Wayne's Legion became almost routine—averaging more than one per month in 1794. One of these petty quarrels resulted in the death of an officer under rather unusual rules. The two duelists stood about eight yards apart and facing away from one another. At a signal, they were both to turn and advance, firing whenever they felt ready. By the time they were slightly more than two yards apart one of the men fired—and missed! His opponent took one more step and, from a distance that must have been close enough for him to rest the muzzle of his pistol against his antagonist's chest, fired a fatal ball into him.[18]

Several junior officers at a frontier fort in 1844 decided to employ dueling to rid themselves of an unpopular fellow officer. They intended to issue formal challenges to him, one after another, forcing him either to accept them and fight duels with them, or to refuse to accept the challenges and appear to be unmanly. When the officer received the first challenge, he found himself in a bit of a quandary. He did not want to fight. Not because of cowardice, but because he knew that he was a deadly accurate pistol shot and did not unnecessarily want to kill a brother officer. He confided his concerns in the post sutler with whom he had become good friends, and the sutler apprised him of the officers' plan to oust him. After mulling over this bit of information, the officer said that he intended to fire over his challenger's head, but the sutler convinced him that he would never be able to find acceptance—or peace—at the post if he shirked his "duty" in this matter. "Well if you think it necessary," he told his friend, "I will fire at him and hit just exactly at the second button on his coat." When the time arrived for the duel, both men fired simultaneously, and the challenger went down with a bullet through his second button and into his chest. Turning to the spectators, the victorious officer said: "I have understood it was your intention to force me out of the regiment in this way. Will you, sir," he asked one of the assembled throng, "take a shot? Or you?" he asked another. "Or you?" All had apparently lost their zeal for dueling, and the unpopular officer eventually gained the acceptance of all those in the camp.[19]

PAYDAY

The arrival of the paymaster always created a lot of excitement. Soldiers' pay increased slowly through the first half of the nineteenth century. In 1790, a private soldier received $4 per month, and this increased to $11 per month by 1854. Higher ranks earned correspondingly higher pay. A sergeant's salary, for example, rose from $6[20] per month to $17 per month. As a soldier presented himself at the paymaster's table, a company officer checked his name against an official roster, and totaled up any debts the man might have accrued since the last payday. He might, for example, have had to be issued an item of clothing that was beyond his normal allotment. If so, the cost was deducted from his pay. Likewise, if he owed the company laundresses or the post sutler any money the officer deducted it from his earnings.[21]

Spending Money

On Gambling

Some men had very little money left after paying their bills, but they were anxious to spend whatever there was. This often meant gambling, whoring, or drinking, or all three. A soldier recorded in his diary in 1851:

> Paymaster arrived yesterday. Paid off the troops. Night came. The long rows of beds in our quarters were occupied. Benches were all full. All were interested in playing cards. Money exchanged hands as fast as possible. Up jumped one cursing himself, his parents, his God, his evil fortune. Another that fiendish smile exhibited because he had won his fellows' money. All much engaged. Morning found many still gambling. Lost their sleep and their money. This is a practice followed very much by soldiers.[22]

On Women

Soldiers with money in their pockets often looked for female companionship. The likelihood of finding a woman with whom to form a lasting relationship was exceedingly slim in and around army posts. The few women usually in residence were either the wives or daughters of officers, or they were the company laundresses. Officers' wives were obviously out of reach and so too, in most instances, were their daughters. It was highly doubtful that an officer would allow his daughter to establish a romantic relationship with a mere enlisted man. And of the four laundresses allotted to each company, some or all of them were usually already married to soldiers. Some men bucked the odds. In 1796, a junior officer at Fort Massac, right on the Ohio River, seduced the wife of an enlisted man serving at the post and openly kept her as his mistress. Several years later, a captain, living with his wife at the same post, tried to find someone to murder the husband of his mistress there! The record is mute with regard to the reactions of the cuckolds in these cases, but not in another. In 1841, a young second lieutenant of dragoons, only a couple of years removed from the Military Academy, became infatuated with the wife of a civilian living near Fort Gibson. The two lovers were in the woman's home when her husband returned unexpectedly and confronted them. After an angry exchange, the officer returned to the fort, and the betrayed husband beat his wife for her infidelity. The bruised and battered woman made her way to the fort and related the story of her mistreatment to the lieutenant. The next day, the angry soldier returned to the settler's home and fatally shot him in the back with a shotgun from a distance of only fifteen to twenty feet. After the officer's arrest, he was paroled on his honor to await trial. He must have realized that there was not much defense against a charge of shooting an unarmed man in the back, and he fled.[23]

The scarcity of women living in army posts left only the few women in nearby towns (except, of course, for prostitutes). With the odds thus stacked against them, the soldiers generally did not look for lifetime commitment, but they were more than willing to engage in business transactions with "women of negotiable virtue." And, apparently, there was no lack of such women in the vicinity of most military posts of any size. A soldier in Santa Fe, New Mexico, in 1847, was certain that "every House in Town is a Whore House or a Grog Shop" and another was only slightly less condemning when he wrote of the "various miniature hells which are found at every corner" in that city. Prostitution in this new American territory became such a problem that, only a few years later, the territorial legislature enacted harsh new laws with respect to how women found guilty of plying the world's oldest profession would be punished. They were to be given thirty lashes with a whip and then sentenced to three months' hard labor with their ankles chained together. It was not long before authorities arrested several prostitutes in the environs of Fort Union and applied a modified punishment. Instead of the thirty lashes, they received ten—lightly—and had their heads shorn before being banished from the area.[24]

When it came to procuring women for these short-term assignations, even highly placed government officials sometimes became involved. During the Utah expedition of 1857 and 1858, the Territorial Chief Justice apologized to an army officer for not having "yet procured you a bedfellow for the coming winter. I have spoken to one woman," he wrote, "and she says if her husband is agreed to it she would like to go but not until she is freed from her present *interesting* condition." The record is mute with regard to just what this condition might have been, but it is not unlikely that she was pregnant at the time, or, perhaps, was undergoing treatment for a venereal disease. At any rate, the woman let it be known that if she was unable to accept this new offer that she would let her sister know about it. The sister was also married.[25]

Many of the women with whom soldiers, and officers, had intimate relations were women of other cultures. They were Mexican, or Indian. It was easy in these situations for the men's feelings of racial superiority to justify using women to satisfy their base desires. It was not uncommon for soldiers on the frontier to follow the lead of civilian hunters and trappers who took Indian women for their wives or mistresses. Sometimes, too, soldiers stooped to behavior that would have scandalized them to have witnessed, let alone performed, in polite—American—society. During the Mexican War, for example, a couple of junior officers—one of whom later rose to the rank of major general—took mistresses from among the civilian population, including one who was reputed to be only fourteen years of age. Another officer was mortified by the public display these officers made when openly squiring their "ladies" around town in an open carriage. "They don't know what chastity is," wrote another, describing his encounter with the residents of Baja California. "I have seen mothers selling their daughters for two, three, four and six dollars." Evaluations by soldiers of Indian morality were often equally low.[26]

With so many soldiers looking for a connection and so few available women, even those women who might not have turned a man's head back east were able to find numerous suitors. One young officer, writing from Jefferson Barracks, near St. Louis, in 1844 wrote: "This is the best country for single ladies I ever saw in my life. They are hardly allowed to come of age before they are engaged to be married however ugly they may be." Beauty, however, as the saying goes, is in the eye of the beholder, and soldiers' ideas of what constituted feminine beauty varied with time and circumstances. This was particularly true when it came to evaluating Mexican or Indian women. Many men described the Mexican women they had seen as "handsome" or as "som of the hansomist girls that I Ever saw." One soldier described the beauty of Mexican women as "far surpassing any beauty I have ever seen," while another wrote that they possessed "more than their share of beauty." A similar percentage of observers had quite the opposite opinion. Many men discovered that the images of dark-eyed senoritas that they carried with them to Mexico did not bear up under the cold light of reality: "Well for my own part," wrote one such disillusioned soldier, "I have seen but few women that are worthy of the name[.] They are not good looking either in form or feature and the most of them are rather disgusting in their manners otherwise." "And as to the black-eyed señoras we all longed to see," wrote another, "we find nothing but old hags, worse looking than Indians." Other soldiers did not see any local women whom they would consider "more than third-rate beauties," or that were "half so beautiful" as American women. An Ohio volunteer wrote his wife that "not a female have I seen more winning and attentive in appearance than the majority of negro wenches about Cincinnati." Sometimes, opinions changed as the soldiers spent more and more time away from American women and among the native populace. "The first sight I got of the Mexican ladies," remembered one man, they "appeared exceedingly disgusting to me, but those feelings gradually wore off, until I began to think that some of them were pretty."[27]

Members of occupying armies seldom have much social interaction with the upper levels of the local society, and this was certainly the case for American soldiers in Mexico. American officers sometimes gained entrée into polite society, and there were even cases of intermarriage, but the enlisted men generally associated with members of the lower social classes. This, then, colored their perceptions of morality among the local women. Letters from soldiers are peppered with such comments as: "They [Mexican women] ... do not seem to know what virtue or modesty is and are very fond of the attentions of strangers," and "The women are bold and not overloaded with modesty." "They are not backward in letting a fellow put his hand in there [*sic*] bosom," wrote another. "Ah, Boy, theres [*sic*] great temptation set before men here."[28]

American soldiers found the Indian culture even more unfamiliar to them than that of the Mexicans, and the majority of those who commented upon the beauty of Indian women registered negative opinions. A member of the Mounted Rifles, writing from the Columbia River in 1849, said that he had seen no Indian women "who possessed the least beauty." One officer wrote, "Occasionally a good looking half breed may be seen, but generally they are [a] dirty set and all have a smoky odor about them which is particularly disagreeable to me at the distance of ten yards for I was never closer."[29]

Some observers also called into question the morality of Indian women. Indian "marriages," wrote one man, "are a mere formality which can be dissolved any minute on the part of the man." Because of this, he theorized, Indian "women are never particularly virtuous." This same soldier was certain that some of the Indians he met in Arizona supplemented their meager existence "by the profits of an infamous trafficking in their wives and daughters." He was perspicacious enough to realize that contact with whites had done much to undermine this tribe's sense of values. Another recognized the impact on Indian culture that "the vices and vicious habits introduced amongst them by the whites" was having. A veteran of the wars in Florida had stated earlier that "the presence of whites is a blight upon the Indian character, which, in its own native simplicity, is far less objectionable than is generally supposed."[30]

On Drink

Drinking was a fact of life. Benjamin Franklin is reputed to have said that it was obvious that God had never intended man to drink water, or he would not have blessed him with elbows capable of lifting wine glasses. Consumption of up to a quart per day was not unusual. When farmers gathered to help one another with the harvest, or to raise a new barn, or to clear more land for planting, they did so with plenty of whiskey available. City workers often had a couple of drinks during the workday, much as twenty-first-century workers have coffee breaks. Businessmen sealed deals with drinks. Drinks were served with meals. Militia muster days often dissolved into drunken parties. One newly elected militia colonel thanked those who voted for him by saying: "I can't make a speech, but what I lack in brains I will try and make up in rum." During the early stages of the War with Mexico, as Illinois volunteers were organizing themselves and electing company officers, the captaincy of one company went to the man who promised a hundred dollars worth of whiskey upon his election.[31]

In 1821, a prominent Bostonian predicted: "If the consumption of spirituous liquors should increase for thirty years to come at the rate it has for thirty years back we should be hardly better than a nation of sots." Estimates are that at that time Americans were drinking distilled liquor—rum, whiskey, gin, brandy—at a greater rate than ever in national history. The per capita consumption reached more than five gallons during the first three decades of the nineteenth century. This ranked Americans ahead of such stereotypically heavy drinking nations as Ireland and Prussia. Many Americans drank alcohol because of the unavailability of healthy alternatives. An early nineteenth-century medical journal noted that a "dread of water" was at epidemic proportions, and perhaps with good reason. River water was sometimes so loaded with silt as to be undrinkable, and well water might also have impurities. It was said that water from the shallow wells in New York City had the added effect of being a fairly efficient purgative. A visitor to that city inquired of a resident as to the quality of the drinking water, to which the local man replied: "Really, I cannot pretend to say, as I never tasted water there that was not mixed with some kind of liquor." Along the same lines, an army officer in Florida during the Seminole Wars also expressed an aversion to drinking water. "I don't see how we can possibly live here for a month," he wrote, "and drink such villainous water. Besides its warmth and discoloration by the infusion of noxious stuffs, it generates myriads of wiggle tails and pollywogs which are anything but palatable in a state of animation." But this captain also had a remedy: "A slight infusion of 'Old Rye' removes all deliteries [*sic*] and gurgleitis [*sic*] and cooks the animalculae to perfection and renders the mixture quite agreeable."[32]

Contemporary accounts seem to validate the stereotype of the hard-drinking soldier. An army doctor in the late 1850s was convinced, after having interviewed a number of soldiers, that the almost unbelievable quantity of "*three quarts* of whiskey was the customary daily allowance of quite a number of the men; one quart, as they expressed it, being required to 'set them up before breakfast.'" A young Ulysses S. Grant, himself no stranger to the bottle, remarked in 1846 that "soldiers are a class of people who will drink and gamble let them be where they may." An infantry lieutenant surveyed the thirty-five men in his company and declared that twenty-nine of them were drunkards, five drank every day, and one was sick. Likewise, of the 109 artillerymen stationed at Fort Moultrie, South Carolina, in 1852, only fifty were teetotalers, while thirty-five were characterized as drunks, thirteen as heavy drinkers, and eleven merely as "drinkers." An officer with first-hand knowledge of the various army posts on the western frontier commented that "the soldier who *will* have whiskey *can* procure it."[33]

And many were the ways in which drinking soldiers procured their liquor. Thirsty soldiers smuggled bottles into camp concealed in loaves of bread or in watermelons. Sometimes, they connived with laundresses, who would bring full canteens into camp under their petticoats. Some managed to sneak liquor into camp by using their musket barrels as canteens. The procedure was to whittle a small wooden plug to fit into the flash hole at the breech end of the barrel, and then pour whiskey down the muzzle and cap it all off with a cork. The standard forty-inch-long, .69-caliber musket barrel held about a cup of liquid when thus prepared. In one instance, the commander of a fort happened to look out of the second floor window of his quarters just as a soldier was about to enter the camp with two buckets of liquid. The officer could see that one of the pails clearly contained water, but the suspicious brownish color of the liquid in the other caused him to suspect that it was whiskey. As he continued to watch, he saw the soldier cover up both buckets and carefully hide one of them behind a bush in the post garden before going on his way. Unknown to the officer, the soldier had noticed him in the window, knew that he had been discovered, and altered his plans accordingly. Therefore, when the commander dispatched an orderly to retrieve the pail in the garden, he was dismayed to find that it contained nothing but water. One evening at Fort Crawford, Wisconsin, a couple of officers were out for an evening stroll and noticed what appeared to be a cat heading straight toward the walls of the fort. Something about the way it moved caused them to take special notice of it, thinking that perhaps it was sick. As they positioned themselves to intercept the animal, one of them noticed a string that appeared to line up directly with the cat. Stepping on the string brought a halt to the animal's movement, and a quick examination revealed that some ingenious soldiers had stuffed a cat's skin with a bladder full of whiskey and were now trying to sneak it into the fort. It was a little more difficult, but not impossible, to smuggle whiskey into a fort that was on an island. In the early 1850s, troops stationed at Governor's Island in New York harbor devised a method that worked fairly well. When men returned from legitimate passes to the mainland, they had to pass under the scrutiny of a noncommissioned officer once they stepped out of the boats. Therefore, any attempt to openly bring in liquor would quickly be discovered. So they filled small bladders with whiskey and tucked them into the tops of their boots. Then, when safely past the guard they would empty the whiskey into bottles, which they would then sell to other soldiers. On at least one occasion, one of these smugglers got safely into the barracks only to discover that the fragile bladders had somehow burst inside his boots. Undaunted, he carefully removed his boot and soaking wet sock and then wrung the whiskey out of the sock and into an acceptable container.[34]

Many soldiers believed in the therapeutic value of alcohol. In the summer, so the reasoning went, liquor was vital to maintaining healthy bowels, while during the rest of the year it helped prevent colds and chills. Even some doctors, according to a resident of Natchez, Mississippi, "believed in the hygienic virtues of alcoholic drinks, and taught that doctrine by precept and example." An army doctor in Mexico recommended that an Ohio volunteer officer drink a couple of glasses of beer every day as a guard against diarrhea. Other physicians, perhaps most others, made no such assertions regarding the medicinal values of alcohol. Instead, the general belief was that excessive intemperance lowered an individual's resistance to certain diseases like yellow fever and malaria. Among the soldiers who also believed this was a man who wrote home from Mexico to reassure his father that he was maintaining good health. "I have no fears of loosing [*sic*] my health here," he wrote, "as long as I refrain from the use of intoxicating liquors but the intemperate use of liquor in this country will kill any person in time I care not how vigorous a constitution they may possess."[35]

Soldiers campaigning in Mexico and, later, those who were on occupation duty in lands acquired from Mexico, encountered a very different culture. Not only were the language, the people, the dress, and the food alien to them, but so too was the liquor.

Mescal, pulque, and aguardiente were plentiful and inexpensive. A soldier who drank a glass of mescal that his friends had assured him was of high quality did not share that evaluation. "It appeared to draw my tongue half way down my throat," he remembered, "and took my breath away for an instant. It was the first and last glass of mescal I ever drank." A contemporary description of pulque is of equal interest:

> Here also I first tasted pulque; and on a first impression it appears to me, that as nectar was the drink in Olympus, we may fairly conjecture that Pluto cultivated the maguey [from which pulque is derived] in his dominions.... It is said, that when one gets over the first shock, it is very agreeable. The difficulty must consist in getting over it.

Another soldier compared aguardiente with smallpox:

> A little goes a long ways. I think that it is the meanest liquor in the world for a man to drink. As he gets ornery and mean. I have heard it said that when a man drinks a little of it he wants to steal something, and I have heard it said that when he can't find anything else to steal he will steal his own knife from one pocket and hide it in another, just so as to steal something.[36]

Alcohol abuse The abuse of alcohol among soldiers and officers led to a wide range of discipline problems within the antebellum army, and yet the army itself contributed to the problem for a number of years. Prior to 1830, each soldier was furnished one gill—about half a cup—per day of intoxicating liquor as a part of his daily ration. Army officials undoubtedly believed that not much harm could result from allowing soldiers this rather meager amount. Trouble arose, however, when the men saved up several days' worth of the liquor ration and then went on a spree. Soldiers performing hard physical labor while on detached duty qualified for additional amounts, and this sometimes led to abuse. A soldier at Fort Atkinson, Nebraska, for example, drew the additional whiskey ration for a six-man wood chopping detail, but neglected to share it with any of the other five men.[37]

When soldiers found that their legal allotments did not satisfy them, they frequently left post, sometimes against express orders, and visited the small shops—or "groceries"—nearby that sold liquor. Since camp commanders had no authority over civilian concerns that were located on private property, they were almost powerless to address the problem. General Anthony Wayne, however, was one who did not let legal niceties stand in the way of problem-solving when a liquor dealer set up shop within sight of Legionville in 1792. Wayne believed that the government-supplied whiskey ration was sufficient for his soldiers and resented the temptation that this shop provided to his men to give in to their base desires thereby also undermining military efficiency. He ordered one of his artillery crews to unlimber a cannon and place a ball in a tree that stood immediately adjacent to the offending vendor's place of business. It did not cause the man to close up shop, but he did, from then on, refuse to sell to the soldiers.[38]

Military authorities could, however, control whether or not sutlers sold whiskey to the soldiers. Some forbade the practice entirely, while others allowed it in certain circumstances. In early 1846, the sutler at Fort Gibson was allowed to sell liquor to the dragoons stationed there, but only as long as they remained sober. During the War of 1812, an officer sought to combat the growing problem of drunkenness within his command by restricting sutler sales of alcohol only to those who could produce written or oral authorization for the sale from a commissioned officer. Enterprising troops under his command were not long in figuring a way to get around this restraint. Several of them pooled their limited funds and bought a sword, the type a junior officer might wear. Then, one of them would take the sword and accompany others to the sutler's store with an empty canteen and an interest in seeing it filled with whiskey. The sutler asked for their written authorization, but, of course, they had none. Instead, they produced the spurious officer and quickly obtained his oral approval for the purchase.[39]

Some soldiers went to excessive lengths to satisfy their cravings. In 1795, a soldier in the Ohio country finally succumbed to a life of drunkenness, but before he died he confided in a surgeon's mate about his struggle with strong drink. He was, the mate later recorded,

> from his fortitude & perseverance in the wars of Bacchus, admitted as a member of the "Damnation Club;" where an essential requisite was to be ever ready to receive 100 lashes if it might be the means of procuring a pint of whiskey for the good of said society: He informed me that he had absolutely received seven hundred lashes in that *noble pursuit*.

Others soldiers also found it impossible to resist the lure of strong drink. While stationed at Fort Terrett, Texas, one such man deserted on December 23, 1852. He apparently did not make much effort to cover his tracks and was easily apprehended and returned to camp, still drunk, on Christmas day. In early January, after having been admitted to the post hospital, he determined to desert again, and after obligingly leaving a note on his bunk explaining that he had grown tired of the military life, he departed for a grog shop only a mile away. After three and a half weeks away, he was again returned to camp for a court-martial. The court found that, in addition to the two times he had deserted, he had been almost continually drunk for a period of seven months and ordered him to be dismissed from the service.[40]

Most soldiers probably lacked a discriminating palate when it came to the quality of the alcohol they were willing to imbibe. Sutlers and other whiskey sellers were quick to recognize this and were not above "stretching" their supply of whiskey by mixing in liberal amounts of water and tobacco. This lack of sophistication probably reached its height—or depth—during the War with Mexico. A volunteer officer of a scientific bent spent part of his free time in Mexico collecting specimens of local snakes, scorpions, horned frogs, and lizards and preserving them in jars of alcohol. All went well until a couple of his subordinates, desperate for liquor one night, drank this preservative. Of course, the captain quickly discovered the loss and soon lectured the guilty parties. "I don't care a d__n about the liquor," he remonstrated, "but I do protest against your eating my scorpions."[41]

Soldiers stationed near, or passing through, towns and villages had little difficulty finding a place to buy whiskey. A soldier in Santa Fe was convinced that "every House in Town is a Whore House or a Grog Shop." A few years later, a soldier participating in the Mormon campaign was stunned by the number of liquor dispensers he saw.

> Nearly every house that we have passed since we commenced the march has had painted over the door in uncouth, straggling letters, that look as though the artist had been paid for his work in the beverage they announce, and received his recompence [*sic*] before the job was completed, the word *Whiskey*. Whether all the inhabitants of Kansas are dealers in "liquefied strychnine" or not, I cannot say, but certainly I have encountered none who were not.[42]

Just as the cut and fit of military uniforms tended to follow the dictates of civilian fashion, although not very quickly, so too did other aspects of the soldier's life. Various reform movements swept across the nation in the early nineteenth century, and one of these was an antidrinking crusade. And, in spite of all of the opportunities for drink that soldiers might find, temperance societies began to spring up at army posts. In 1830, for example, the very year that the whiskey ration was discontinued, an overwhelming majority of the garrison at Fort McHenry petitioned the commanding officer to stop the whiskey ration and to use the money thus saved on better food. At Fort Brady, Michigan, some soldiers put the money they would formerly have spent on drink into savings accounts, and at Jefferson Barracks almost 400 men signed temperance pledges in 1843. One officer there proudly proclaimed that "we have not now a regular drinker left in the 3rd Infantry, and but few who touch liquor at all." Even though most of these temperance societies were relatively short-lived, the fact that they existed at all is worthy of note, as the loneliness and boredom that was so prevalent at most frontier posts left little else for the soldier to occupy his time with besides liquor. Perhaps the semiliterate scribblings of an Illinois volunteer in Mexico convey a typical attitude toward drink:

> it always was agains my princable to Drink when I was at home though I have altered my notion now for it is a great help to amans helth and also to Dround trouble for when a man is about half Drunk thare is nothing on his mind only good things ... he imagines that Ever button on his Coat is gold.[43]

Soldiers who repeatedly turned up drunk were of little use to themselves or to the Army and faced a variety of disciplinary actions. They might, for instance, feel the sting of the whip. Or they might have to wear a flour barrel like a jacket every day for a week. After repeated offenses, the Army might decide that the best thing would be for the drunkard to return to civil life. One such man was forced, as part of the sentence intended to humiliate him, to wear an empty whiskey bottle tied around his neck as he was being drummed out of camp. The sot, sober now, pointed to the bottle and, with tears running down his cheeks, asked: "Lieutenant dont you think you could put a wee drap in it?" At least one other soldier depended on his superior officers to oust him from the service on account of continued drunkenness. He worked to acquire the reputation of being a habitual drunkard, and in 1825 was released from the service on that count. He then seemed to shed his alcoholic habit along with his blue uniform. As a civilian, he became a complete and instant abstainer and returned to his civilian occupation as a tailor.[44]

Sometimes, incarceration was the tool of punishment, but it did not always have the desired effect. During the Mexican War, twenty members of an Illinois volunteer regiment were arrested and thrown into the guardhouse for drunkenness. Because there were so many of them, military authorities feared they might try to break out, so they posted three sentries at each door. In spite of this precaution, two of the men managed to scale the inside of the chimney and escape, although perhaps "escape" is not the proper word here. These two men each acquired another bottle of whiskey and then sneaked back down the chimney to continue the hilarity with their comrades. Another man used his time in the guardhouse for some self-surgery. In his alcohol-befuddled mind he decided that the source of his problems in life lay in his sexual organs. He therefore borrowed a short, single-bladed folding knife from another inmate and "completely excised the whole of the genital apparatus, close to the body. Flinging them violently into one corner of the room, he very heroically remarked— 'Any d—d fool can cut his throat, but it takes a soldier to cut his privates off.'" A doctor arrived within a few minutes and was able to stop the bleeding. One witness remarked that the soldier sobered up in a hurry after he saw what he had done to himself.[45]

NONALCOHOLIC AMUSEMENTS

Frontier army posts also sometimes provided other amusements for their inhabitants. For the literate soldiers, reading was a popular pastime. At some posts—and as time went on, at most of the major posts—libraries or reading rooms were established for the use of the officers and soldiers. In 1845, the officers at Fort Gibson, for example, budgeted enough money from the post funds to purchase over 200 volumes from *Harper's Family Library* and *Harper's Classical Library* as well as subscriptions to such popular periodicals as *North American Review*, *The United States Service Journal*, *The Southern Literary Messenger*, and various newspapers from different cities around the country. A few years later, troops at Fort Ridgely, Minnesota, were able to while away off-duty hours with an even greater selection that included biographies of famous Americans and periodicals from Europe.[46]

If a post was home to a fairly large number of soldiers, traveling troupes of actors sometimes staged theatrical presentations there. Their offerings included everything from self-written plays to Shakespearean classics. In 1840, a half dozen of these entertainers braved the dangers of Florida to bring some amusement to the soldiers fighting the Seminoles there. Unfortunately, the Indians did not have the level of cultural sophistication that the performers hoped to encounter in their audiences. They ambushed the troubadours, killing half of them, and sending the other three fleeing for the safety of a nearby fort. The Indians then helped themselves to the contents of the eighteen trunks left behind and loaded with costumes and props. In seeking out the murderers, the soldiers later captured several Indians "and as they were robed and decked in the habilments [*sic*] of Othello, Hamlet, and a host of other Shaksperean [*sic*] characters," wrote an observer, "their identity as the murderers was established, and they were hanged."[47]

A few years later, though, there were enough potential patrons in the ranks of Zachary Taylor's Army of Observation, which was camped near Corpus Christi, Texas, for officers to build two theaters. Making maximum use of the available building supplies, these hastily constructed buildings had canvas roofs. To defray the construction costs, the officers staged their own plays and charged admissions, and soon had enough money to purchase more elaborate costumes than those with which they had begun. One officer recalled that as long as they stuck to light comedies they were successful. When they turned to works of a more classic nature, however, they ran into casting difficulties. It seemed that making a believable female character out of an obviously male actor was more difficult than they had imagined. They solved the problem by sending to New Orleans for professional entertainers—some of whom had previously performed for the Florida troops. They played to mixed reviews. One young officer informed his wife that the visiting performers—seven women and four men—left a lot to be desired. They were, he wrote her, nothing more than "a company of strolling actors, who murder tragedy, burlesque comedy, and render farce into buffoonery, in the most approved style."[48]

When not engaged in actual warfare, the army was dispersed to dozens of smaller posts, and that usually meant that professional actors and actresses were less likely to take the time and trouble to put on performances for what would necessarily have been small audiences. In these instances, as in the case of the officers at Corpus Christi in 1846, the men put on their own shows. Most commonly, a mess hall or some other building was commandeered for temporary use as a theater. In the early 1830s, the soldiers at Fort Crawford, Wisconsin, took over a barracks room for their productions. They built a stage, complete with painted backdrops, and arranged tiered seating for their guests. Officers and their families, of course, got the choicest seats near the stage. Behind them the order of preference was: enlisted men, friendly visiting Indians, blacks, and servants. The soldier-actors' well-received repertoire ranged from Cervantes' classic *Don Quixote* to a five-act comedy from the early nineteenth century entitled *Who Wants a Guinea?* Not all attempts ended so successfully. At Monterey, California, in the early 1850s, the garrison staged *Romeo and Juliet.* A soldier's wife—a very large German woman—played the part of Juliet. The audience was amused by her heavy accent and laughed out loud when the balcony collapsed beneath her weight during a crucial scene.[49]

The Army did its best in tending to the soldiers' corporeal requirements, but fell short when it came to their spiritual needs even though the Articles of War contained as its second provision a plea that all officers and soldiers attend divine services. As early as 1791, Congress authorized the appointment of army chaplains, but little seems to have been done to implement the new law until the War of 1812 brought large numbers of volunteers into uniform. For quite some time after that war, the Army's only chaplain was stationed at the Military Academy at West Point, New York. At Fort Snelling, Minnesota, in 1821, the commanding officer's wife and daughter took it upon themselves to help supply the lack of religious instruction by offering a sort of Sunday School in the basement of the colonel's quarters for all the children of soldiers or civilians nearby. The situation did not improve much with the issuance of new regulations in 1825, which only provided for two chaplains, one in the East and one in the West. Soldiers scattered across the frontier had to depend upon civilian preachers ministering to nearby towns or missionaries to the Indians to offer their services occasionally.[50]

In 1838, Congressional legislation provided for the appointment of a total of twenty chaplains and, in 1849, ten more were authorized. By the latter date, the Army was dispersed into dozens of posts, many with only a handful of troops, and that meant that even if all the chaplains' slots were filled, there would still have been a large number of soldiers with no access to regular church services. Most soldiers, indeed, seemed to regard Sunday as nothing more than another day, much like the one that had preceded it and much like the one that would succeed it. A chaplain at Fort Washita commented, in fact, about the lack of religious fervor at that post. "If … the commanding officers will shoot game on Sunday before the Chaplain's door," he complained, "permit men at time of service to walk out of the garrison with their guns to hunt, and the 'nine-pin-alley' to be open, it is impossible for an angel to resist the tide of immorality, and be popular."[51]

In spite of the availability of such civilizing influences as reading rooms and chaplains, army life often seemed only slightly better than peonage. When troops sought ways to alleviate their conditions—perhaps through liquor—they often ran afoul of the military justice system and had to pay the price for their indiscretions.

NOTES

1. *General Regulation for the Army; or, Military Institutes* (Philadelphia: M. Carey and Sons, 1821, 38–43; *General Regulations for the Army of the United States, 1841* (Washington, D.C.: 1841), 63.

2. *Army Regulations for 1821,* 79.

3. Stanley S. Graham, "Routine at Western Cavalry Posts, 1833–1861," *Journal of the West* 15 (July 1976), 52–53.

4. William Wood Thackera, "William Wood Thackera, Volunteer in the War of 1812," edited by Anne Castrodale Golovin, *Pennsylvania Magazine of History and Biography,* 91 (July 1967), 317.

5. Franklin Smith diary, October 13, 1846, Franklin Smith Collection, Mississippi Department of Archives and History.

6. Keith R. Widder, *Reveille Till Taps: Soldier Life at Fort Mackinac, 1780–1895* (Mackinac Island, Michigan: Mackinac Island State Park Commission, 1972), 20; George Croghan, *Army Life on the Western Frontier: Selections from the Official Reports Made Between 1826 and 1845 by Colonel George Croghan,* edited by Francis Paul Prucha (Norman, Oklahoma: University of Oklahoma Press, 1958), 144, 135.

7. Croghan, *Army Life on the Western Frontier,* 5, 38–39.

8. Emanuel Raymond Lewis, *Seacoast Fortifications of the United States: An Introductory History* (Washington, D.C.: Smithsonian Institution Press, 1970), 21–25, 45; John R. Weaver, II, *A Legacy in Brick and Stone: American Coastal Defense Forts of the Third System, 1816–1867,* (Missoula, Montana: Pictorial Histories Publishing Company, 2001), 53, 50.

9. Ebenezer Denny, *Military Journal of Major Ebenezer Denny, An Officer in the Revolutionary and Indian Wars, with an Introductory Memoir* (Philadelphia: J. B. Lippincott and Company, 1859; reprint, New York: Arno Press, 1971), 156, 188.

10. Erasmus D. Keyes, *Fifty Years' Observations of Men and Events Civil and Military,* (New York: Charles Scribner's Sons, 1884), 164–165 (1st quotation); Zenas R. Bliss, "Extracts from the Unpublished Memoirs of Major-General Zenas R. Bliss, U.S.A.," *Journal of the Military Service Institution of the United States,* 38 (1906), 122; Although the event described here occurred in 1867 it aptly illustrates life in such quarters. Ron Field, *Forts of the American Frontier 1820–91: Central and Northern Plains* (Oxford: Osprey, 2005), 35–36 (2d quotation).

11. Croghan, *Army Life on the Western Frontier,* 51; Robert M. Utley, *Frontiersmen in Blue: The United States Army and the Indian, 1848–1865* (1967; reprint, Lincoln and London: University of Nebraska Press, 1981), 37; Percival G. Lowe, *Five Years a Dragoon ('49 to '54) And Other Adventures on the Great Plains,* (Norman, Oklahoma: University of Oklahoma Press, 1965), 107 (1st quotation); "Minnesota as Seen by Travelers: A Dragoon on the March to Pembina in 1849," *Minnesota History,* 8 (1927), 71 (2d quotation); Ethan Allan Hitchcock, *Fifty Years in Camp and Field: Diary of Major General Ethan Allan Hitchcock, U.S.A.,* edited by W. A. Croffut (1909; reprint, Freeport, New York: Books for Libraries Press, 1971), 355 (3d quotation); Dabney Maury, *Recollections of a Virginian in the Mexican, Indian, and Civil Wars* (New York: Charles Scribner's Sons, 1894), 34.

12. James Burn to Charles Jared Ingersoll, July 16, 1813, in "Colonel James Burn and the War of 1812: The Letters of a South Carolina Officer," edited by John C. Fredriksen, *South Carolina Historical Magazine,* 90 (October 1989), 308 (1st quotation); William Duane, "The Letters of William Duane," edited by Worthington C. Ford, *Massachusetts Historical Society Proceedings,* 20 (1906–1907), 363 (2d quotation); [Hildreth], *Dragoon Campaigns,* 180 (3d quotation); Bennet Riley to James H. Hook, February 23, 1823, in " 'Dear Hook': Letters from Bennet Riley, Alphonso Wetmore, and Reuben Holmes, 1822–1833," edited by James S. Hutchins, *Missouri Historical Society Bulletin,* 36 (July 1980), 206–207 (4th quotation).

13. Rufus McIntire, "The War of 1812 in Northern New York: The Observations of Captain Rufus McIntire," edited by John C. Fredriksen, *New York History* (July 1987), 311 (1st quotation), 317 (2d quotation); Diary entry for July 1, 1814, "The Pennsylvania Volunteers in the War of 1812: An Anonymous Journal of Service for the Year 1814," edited by John C. Fredriksen, *The Western Pennsylvania Historical Magazine* 70 (April 1987), 150 (3d quotation); Anonymous, "Reminiscences of Some Incidents in the Career of an United States Dragoon Between the Years 1839 and 1844," *Texas Quarterly* 9, no. 3 (Autumn 1966), 8 (4th quotation); Cave Johnson Couts, *"Hepah, California! The Journal of Cave Johnson Couts from Monterey, Nuevo Leon, Mexico to Los Angeles, California During the Years 1848–1849,* edited by Henry E. Dobyns (Tucson: Arizona Pioneers' Historical Society, 1961), 20 (5th quotation).

14. A. S. Cogswell, "Letters of the War of 1812 in the Champlain Valley," edited by Wilmond W. Parker, *Vermont Quarterly* 12 (1944), 109 (1st quotation); Henry Hollingsworth, "Tennessee Volunteers in the Seminole Campaign of 1836: The Diary of Henry Hollingsworth," edited by Stanley F. Horn, *Tennessee Historical Quarterly* (September 1943), 249 (2d quotation); "Utah" to the *Philadelphia Daily Evening Bulletin,* November 20, 1858, in *To Utah With the Dragoons and Glimpses of Life in Arizona and California 1858–1859,* edited by Harold D. Langley (Salt Lake City: University of Utah Press, 1974), 121, 123 (3d quotation).

15. Diary entry for September 21, 1814, in "Thackera," 310 (1st quotation); Diary entry of Ensign Joseph Hawley for April 9, 1813, in Joseph H. Dwight, "'Plow-Joggers for Generals': The Experiences of a New York Ensign in the War of 1812," edited by John C. Fredriksen, *Indiana Military History Journal,* 11 (1996), 17 (2d quotation); Cogswell, "Letters of the War of 1812," 107 (3d quotation); Robert C. Buchanan, "A Scouting Expedition Along Lake Panasoffkee," edited by Frank F. White, *Florida Historical Quarterly,* 31 (1953), 286

(4th quotation); James D. Elderkin, *Biographical Sketches and Anecdotes of a Soldier of Three Wars, as Written by Himself* (Detroit: James Elderkin, 1899), 23 (5th quotation); Richard S. Ewell to his brother, Ben, February 12, 1847, in R. S. Ewell, *The Making of a Soldier: Letters of General R. S. Ewell,* edited by Percy Gatlin Hamlin, (Richmond, Virginia: Whittet and Shepperson, 1935), 60–61 (6th quotation); Jesse Gove to his wife, October 21, 1857, in Jesse A. Gove, *The Utah Expedition 1857–1858* (Concord, New Hampshire: New Hampshire Historical Society, 1928), 82 (7th quotation).

16. Donald E. Graves, " 'Dry Books of Tactics': U.S. Infantry Manuals of the War of 1812 and After, Part I," *Military Collector and Historian,* 38, no. 2 (Summer 1986), 60n; Samuel E. Chamberlain, *My Confession: The Recollections of a Rogue* (1956; reprint, Lincoln and London: University of Nebraska Press, 1987), 131 (quotation); Grady McWhiney, *Braxton Bragg and Confederate Defeat* (New York and London: Columbia University Press, 1969), 97–98.

17. Charles Fairbanks, "A New Hampshire Volunteer in the War of 1812: The Experiences of Charles Fairbanks," edited by John C. Fredriksen *Historical New Hampshire* 40 (Fall-Winter 1985), 172; Sylvester W. Mason, "With the Third Infantry in New Mexico, 1851–1853: The Lost Diary of Private Sylvester W. Matson," edited by Jerry D. Thompson, *Journal of Arizona History* 31 (Winter 1990), 355.

18. Alan D. Gaff, *Bayonets in the Wilderness: Anthony Wayne's Legion in the Old Northwest* (Norman, Oklahoma: University of Oklahoma Press, 2004), 200, 100–101.

19. J. Henry Carleton, *The Prairie Log Books: Dragoon Campaigns to the Pawnee Villages in 1844, and to the Rocky Mountains in 1845,* edited by Louis Pelzer (Lincoln and London: University of Nebraska Press, 11983), 120–121.

20. Norman W. Caldwell, "The Frontier Army Officer, 1794–1814," *Mid-America: An Historical Review* 37, no. 2 (April 1955), 104n; Dale Richard Steinhauer, " 'Sogers': Enlisted Men in the U.S. Army, 1815–1860" (Ph.D. diss., University of North Carolina at Chapel Hill, 1992), 332; Caldwell, "The Frontier Army Officer," 104n.

21. Caldwell, "The Frontier Army Officer," 104n; Steinhauer, "'Sogers'," 332; Caldwell, "The Frontier Army Officer," 104n; Steinhauer, "'Sogers'," 332.

22. Utley, *Frontiersmen in Blue,* 46.

23. Caldwell, "The Frontier Army Officer," 111–112; Harry C. Myers, ed., "From 'The Crack Post of the Frontier': Letters of Thomas and Charlotte Swords," *Kansas History,* 5 (Autumn 1982), 190n.

24. Jacqueline Dorgan Meketa, "A Soldier in New Mexico, 1847-1848," *New Mexico Historical Review,* 66, no. 1 (January 1991), 21 (1st quotation); Dr. John Dunlap's Journal, John R. Dunlap Collection, Western Historical Manuscript Collection-Columbia, University of Missouri, Columbia, Missouri (2d quotation); A. B. Bender, "The Soldier in the Far West, 1848–1860," *Pacific Historical Review,* 8 (June 1959), 175.

25. Grady McWhiney, "Sex, Women, and the 'Old Army' Officers," *Southerners and Other Americans* (New York: Basic Books, 1973), 48.

26. McWhiney, "Sex, Women, and the 'Old Army' Officers," 53, 52 (1st quotation); Eugene Bandel, *Frontier Life in the Army, 1854–1861,* translated by Olga Bandel and Richard Gente, edited by Ralph P. Bieber, (Glendale, California: Arthur H. Clark, 1932), 95 (2d quotation).

27. McWhiney, "Sex, Women, and the 'Old Army' Officers," 45 (1st quotation); Richard J. Oglesby to H. Prather and J. J. Peddecord, September 9, 1846, Richard J. Oglesby Papers, Illinois State Historical Library, Springfield, Illinois, John P. Brock to his parents, March 24, 1847, Brock Papers, Earl Gregg Swen Library at the College of William and Mary, Williamsburg, Virginia, and T. H. Towner to his mother, March 16, 1847, Benjamin Towner Papers, Duke University Library, Chapel Hill, North Carolina (2d quotation); Diary of Joshua Jackson, December 20, 1846, Illinois State Historical Library, Springfield, Illinois (3d quotation); W. Austine to his cousin, April 23, 1847, William Austine Collection, University of North Carolina Library (4th quotation); Chamberlain, *My Confession,* 71 (5th quotation); George M. Burton to Alex Montgomery, January 16, 1848, George M. Burton Letters, Illinois State Historical Library, Springfield, Illinois (6th quotation); George G. Meade to his wife, May 19, 1846, in George Gordon Meade, *The Life and Letters of George Gordon Meade,* 2 vols. (New York: Scribner's, 1913), I, 86 (7th quotation); Will Wallace to Helen M. Indson, November 16, 1846, Wallace-Dickey Collection, Illinois State Historical Library, Springfield, Illinois (8th quotation); Wiley P. Hale to his mother, August 17, 1846, Letters of Wiley P. Hale, Tennessee State Library and Archives, Nashville, Tennessee (9th quotation); Charles H. Brough to his wife, July 30, 1847, Charles H. Brough Collection, Ohio Historical Society, Columbus, Ohio (10th quotation); Milton Jamieson, *Journal and Notes of a Campaign in Mexico: Containing a History of Company C, of the Second Regiment of Ohio Volunteers* (Cincinnati: 1849), 51 (11th quotation).

28. Frank S. Edwards, A *Campaign in New Mexico,* (Philadelphia: Carey and Hart, 1847; reprint, Ann Arbor, Michigan: University Microfilms, 1966), 50 (1st quotation); George Rutledge Gibson, *Journal of a Soldier Under Kearny and Doniphan, 1846–1847,* edited by Ralph P. Bieber, (Glendale, California: Arthur H. Clarke,1935; reprint, Philadelphia: Porcupine Press, 1974), 210 (2d quotation); John H. Lillard to his brother, September 21, 1846, Lillard Family Papers, Filson Club, Louisville, Kentucky (3d quotation).

29. Osborne Cross, "The Journal of Major Osborne Cross," in *The March of the Mounted Riflemen, First United States Military Expedition to travel the full length of the Oregon Trail from Fort Leavenworth to Fort Vancouver May to October, 1849 as recorded in the journals of Major Osborne Cross and George Gibbs and the official report of Colonel Loring,* edited by Raymond W. Settle (Arthur H. Clark, 1940; reprint, Lincoln and London: University of Nebraska Press, 1989), 188 (1st quotation); Ewell, *The Making of a Soldier,* 40 (2d quotation).

30. Bandel, *Frontier Life in the Army,* 95 (1st quotation), 263 (2d quotation); [Hildreth], *Dragoon Campaigns to the Rocky Mountains,* 210 (3d quotation); Hitchcock, *Fifty Years in Camp and Field,* 71 (4th quotation).

31. W. J. Rorabaugh, *The Alcoholic Republic: An American Tradition,* (New York and Oxford: Oxford University Press, 1979), 96–97; James H. Cassedy, "An Early American Hangover: The Medical Profession and Intemperance 1800–1860," B*ulletin of the History of Medicine* 50 (1976), 405; Rorabaugh, *The Alcoholic Republic,* 20 (quotation); Chamberlain, *My Confession,* 31.

32. Rorabaugh, *The Alcoholic Republic,* 6 (1st quotation), 8, 10; Cassedy, "An Early American Hangover," 405; Rorabaugh, *The Alcoholic Republic,* 96–97 (2d quotation); Reynold M. Wik, "Captain Nathaniel Wyche Hunter and the Florida Indian Campaigns, 1837–1841," *Florida Historical Quarterly*, 39 (1960), 71 (3d quotation).

33. Wilfred W. Black, "The Army Doctor in the Trans-Mississippi West, 1775–1860," *The Southwestern Social Science Quarterly,* 24, no. 2 (1943), 127 (1st quotation); Ulysses S. Grant to Julia Dent, February 7, 1846, in Ulysses S. Grant, *The Papers of Ulysses S. Grant, Vol. I, 1837–1861,* edited by John Y. Simon, (Carbondale, Illinois: Southern Illinois University Press, 1967), 73 (2d quotation); Steinhauer, "'Sogers'," 147, 186; Croghan, *Army Life on the Western* Frontier, 132 (3d quotation).

34. George McFeely, "Chronicle of Valor: The Journal of a Pennsylvania Officer in the War of 1812," edited by John C. Fredriksen, *The Western Pennsylvania Historical Magazine,* 67 (July 1984), 246; John H. Fonda, "Early Wisconsin," *Report and Collections of the State Historical Society of Wisconsin,* 5, part 2 (1868), 283; Abner Doubleday, *My Life in the Old Army: The Reminiscences of Abner Doubleday from the Collections of the New-York Historical Society,* edited by Joseph E. Chance, (Fort Worth: Texas Christian University Press, 1998), 22; Fonda, "Early Wisconsin," 282–283; Henry S. Hamilton, *Reminiscences of a Veteran* (Concord, New Hampshire: Republican Press Association, 1897), 34–35.

35. A. B. Bender, "The Soldier in the Far West, 1848–1860," *Pacific Historical Review*, 8 (June 1959), 174; Cassedy, "An Early American Hangover," 409 (1st quotation); John W. Lowe to his wife, February 18, 1848, John Williamson Lowe Collection, Dayton and Montgomery County Public Library, Dayton, Ohio; Daniel Runyon to his father, May 20, 1848, Runyon Family Papers, Filson Club, Louisville, Kentucky (2d quotation).

36. Edwards, *A Campaign in New Mexico*, 135 (1st quotation); Frances Calderon de la Barca, *Life in Mexico* (1843; reprint, New York: Dutton, 1970), 43 (2d quotation); Thomas E. Breckenridge memoirs, Thomas E. Breckenridge Collection, Western Historical Manuscript Collection-Columbia, University of Missouri, Columbia, Missouri (3d quotation).

37. Stanley S. Graham, "Life of the Enlisted Soldier on the Western Frontier, 1815–1845," (Ph.D. diss., North Texas State University, 1972), 91; Charles W. Ayars, "Some Notes on the Medical Service of the Army, 1812–1839," *The Military Surgeon: Journal of the Association of Military Surgeons of the United States,* 50 (May 1922), 513; Edgar Bruce Wesley, "Life at a Frontier Post," *The Journal of the American Military History Institute,* 3, no. 4 (April 1977), 386.

38. Gaff, *Bayonets in the Wilderness,* 77.

39. LTC R. Mason to Adjutant General, January 7, 1846, Letters Received by the Office of the Adjutant General (Main Series), 1822–1860 (National Archives Microfilm Publication M567 roll 320); Records of the Adjutant General's Office 1780s–1917, Record Group 94; National Archives, Washington, D. C.; Jackson, " 'We Lay There Doing Nothing'," 123.

40. Joseph Gardner Andrews, "A Surgeon's Mate at Fort Defiance: The Journal of Joseph Gardner Andrews For the Year 1795," edited by Richard C. Knopf *The Ohio Historical Quarterly* 66, no. 1 (January 1957), 71–72 (quotation); B. J. Fisher, "Military Justice on the Texas Frontier," *West Texas Historical Association Year Book* 64 (1988), 127.

41. W. N. Davis, Jr., "The Sutler at Fort Bridger," *The Western Historical Quarterly,* 2 (January 1971), 41; Albert G. Brackett, *General Lane's Brigade in Central Mexico* (Cincinnati: H. W. Derby and New York: J. C. Derby, 1854), 166 (quotation).

42. Albert Gay to his parents, August 26, 1847, in Meketa, "A Soldier in New Mexico," 21 (1st quotation); "Utah," *To Utah With the Dragoons,* 25 (2d quotation).

43. Ayars, "Some Notes on the Medical Service of the Army," 513; Richard Dalzell Gamble, "Garrison Life at Frontier Military Posts, 1830–1860," Ph. D. diss. (University of Oklahoma, 1956), 329–330; Hitchcock,

Fifty Years in Camp and Field, 180 (1st quotation); Diary of Joshua Jackson, entry for January 11, 1847, Joshua Jackson Collection, Illinois State Historical Library, Springfield, Illinois (2d quotation).

44. Samuel Newman, "A Picture of the First United States Army: The Journal of Captain Samuel Newman," edited by Milo M. Quaife, *Wisconsin Magazine of History,* 2 (September 1918), 48; Bender, "The Soldier in the Far West," 177; Doubleday, *My Life in the Old Army,* 25 (quotation); Croghan, *Army Life on the Western Frontier,* 152.

45. Adolph Engelmann, "The Second Illinois in the Mexican War: Mexican War Letters of Adolph Engelmann, 1846–1847," translated and edited by Otto B. Engelmann, *Journal of the Illinois State Historical Society* 26, no. 4 (1934), 366; E. W. H. Beck, "Case of Excision of the Whole of the Genital Organs," *Missouri Medical and Surgical Journal*, 3 (1847–1848), 160 (quotation).

46. Gamble, "Garrison Life at Frontier Military Posts," 200–202.

47. Doubleday, *My Life in the Old Army,* 300n.

48. Elderkin, *Biographical Sketches and Anecdotes,* 51; Doubleday, *My Life in the Old Army,* 301n, 300n; Meade, *Life and Letters,* I, 43–44 (quotation).

49. Gamble, "Garrison Life," 206–207; George R. Stewart, *John Phoenix, Esq.: The Veritable Squibob: A Life of Captain George H. Derby, U.S.A.* (New York: Henry Holt and Company, 1937; reprint, New York: Da Capo, 1969), 72–73.

50. Richard D. Gamble, "Army Chaplains at Frontier Posts, 1830–1860," *The Historical Magazine of the Protestant Episcopal Church,* 27, no. 4 (1958), 287–288.

51. Gamble, "Army Chaplains," 294, 296; Gamble, "Garrison Life," 248 (quotation).

4 FOOD, MEDICINE, AND CLOTHING

If, as Napoleon Bonaparte is reputed to have said, an army marches on its stomach, then surely the American army of the early nineteenth century must have made some interesting journeys.

OFFICIAL ARMY RATION

In 1800, the official army ration—the amount of food issued to each soldier per day—consisted of bread and meat. The bread portion of the ration might be in the form of eighteen ounces of baked bread, or an equivalent amount of flour that the soldiers were somehow to bake for themselves. Army regulations specified that the bread must be baked completely through, and that soldiers should not attempt to eat it until it was cold.[1]

Bread

The results of soldier-baked bread were as varied as the soldiers themselves. An army doctor in Texas in the 1850s described his experience with trying to instruct his servant how to make bread. "First," he told him, in terms far from precise, "mix a little flour with some water, then, take some Saleratus [probably sodium bicarbonate] and mix with it." Then, after adding an indeterminate amount of lard, the mixture was placed into a frying pan to bake, but it met with no success. The amalgam of ingredients refused to rise but, as the doctor noted, "there it stayed, sulking and getting flatter and flatter until it settled right down in the pan and turned yellow!!" Undaunted, the officer baked his creation until it "turned black outside, while the yellow within was beautifully variegated with spots! Then I tried to eat it; but couldn't." In lieu of bread, soldiers were authorized to receive a quart of rice or a pound and a half of corn meal.[2]

Meat

The meat portion of the daily ration varied slightly in quantity over the course of years, but remained very limited in quality. The choices were either beef—fresh or salted—or salted pork or bacon. If the day's selection was beef, it was in the amount of a pound to a pound and a quarter, and if it was pork or bacon it was three-quarters of a pound. Army regulations for 1821 also included one gill of whiskey per man and two quarts of salt, four quarts of vinegar, and eight quarts of peas or beans for every 100 rations. The whiskey ration was discontinued in 1830, and changes to the official daily ration soon included the substitution of ten pounds of rice for every 100 men, if peas or beans were not available, and the addition of six pounds of coffee and twelve pounds of sugar per 100 rations. And thus it remained.[3]

Such a menu as this contained enough calories to keep an active man—like a soldier or laborer—from wasting away, but it was sadly lacking in variety. A soldier participating in the Seminole Wars soon found the monotonous bill of fare such that he almost dreaded the next meal. "At first the camp fare of bacon and hard bread washed down morning and evening with coffee without milk, and from a tin cup, was not disagreeable on account of its novelty," he recalled, "but a continued repetition of the same routine of diet awakened feelings of an unpleasant kind whenever the stated hours of replenishing exhausted nature approached."[4]

Of course, as in many cases, what regulations call for and what actually occurs can often be vastly different. So it was when it came to feeding the American soldier. Much of the food the Army provided came from civilian contractors, and it was not unusual for some of these businessmen to enhance their earnings by providing substandard rations. And even when the suppliers conscientiously sought to provide wholesome sustenance to the troops, it was sometimes spoiled in transit due to inefficient packing.

Spoiled or condemned food was often simply thrown away, but there were instances when frustrated soldiers went to considerable lengths to stage mock funerals for the poor food. In the fall of 1814, for example, three or four hundred men joined in such a ceremony to inter four quarters of spoiled beef. The funeral procession included musicians playing funeral dirges and grave diggers solemnly marching in line with their digging implements in place of their muskets. When the graves had been prepared, one of the soldiers intoned a prayer, "reciting," according to a witness, "the virtues of the deceased while living, the barbarity of the men who murdered them, and finally, the beastly act of the *cannibal* who sent them to us to *eat*." The "parson" concluded his remarks by "volunteering to do as much for the contractor as we had done for the beef, that is bury *him* without any expense to his family or the state."[5]

Sometimes, food arrived at military camps in sufficient quantity, but spoiled due to poor packaging. Flour packed in poorly constructed barrels might have as much as twenty pounds of spoilage by the time it reached its intended consumers. Soldiers often received hard bread that had been in storage so long it had attracted large numbers of weevils. Hungry men, however, found that they were not as squeamish about what they ate as they might have been in more comfortable surroundings. One man described the scene of a fellow soldier frying his bread to make it more palatable.

> I looked into the pan, where he had placed a cracker, in the grease fried out of his pickled pork and was amused at seeing a respectable squad of bugs playing on the cracker, and seemingly greatly annoyed by the unceremonious manner in which their winter quarters had been immersed in the hot grease. sometime the bread is literally eaten up

> by the bugs and worms, but we lose nothing by the operation, as I know of no good reason why well-fed bugs should not make as good fresh meat as well-fed hogs.[6]

Similar disregard for the quality of the packaging affected the quality of the pork. Pork, unlike beef, could be fairly well preserved in brine for extended periods of time. But if the barrels were not tight, the brine soon leaked out, and the meat inside was left to rot. An officer on the Mormon Expedition bewailed the lack of salt with which to preserve food, remarking it to be almost a criminal offense.

> Salt! It is but a few days since, that an inspection of the soup in my company kettles, the odor thereof, made up as it is, from the perfectly black and rotting beef of our November slaughter, and with no sign of seasoning—compelled me absolutely to turn aside my head. How the men can partake of such I fail to understand. At any poor-house or jail within the limits of the land at the east, the proffer of any similar soup for human consumption, would bring keeper or superintendent suddenly to indictment.[7]

And, of course, if the only food available to soldiers was food of exceedingly poor quality, they might as well have had no food at all. Such was certainly the case in one of the volunteer camps in the early stages of the Mexican War. "Starvation is the cry here," one officer wrote home to his wife. "I can hardly manage to get enough down to preserve me and am somewhat lean just for want of something good to eat." During the Seminole Wars, another man bemoaned the quality of the coffee, saying that it "could only be made palatable by stirring in a lump of butter and calling it soup." A fresh recruit at an eastern post in 1849 described his breakfast as consisting of "a bowl of fluid resembling coffee, a small piece of fat pork and a piece of bread that would scarcely satisfy a hungry mouse."[8]

Vegetables

After peas and beans were added to the ration, the soldiers' diet improved slightly, but problems of spoilage and lack of adequate quantities still occurred. A New Englander in the Tenth U.S. Infantry described what happened, for example, when he and his messmates attempted to eat some army beans that had been baked for several hours in pork fat. "When … we took them on our plates," he reminisced, "they rattled like shot, and were almost as hard. Each one would take a mouthful and endeavor to chew them, though in every instance the attempt proved a failure."

> One suggested that they be put into the coffee-mill and ground and eaten as porridge; another, that we use them for shot in hunting; while one old Dutchman thought it would be a good idea to use them as a mode of punishment in the guard-house, by making each prisoner eat a certain quantity each day. It was finally settled, that to make them an article of diet for the army it would be necessary for a quartz-crushing machine to accompany each regiment.

Another soldier described the bean soup that was his dinner at an established eastern post. "Why it was called bean soup I could not understand," he recalled, "for I never heard of one being found in it. On one occasion a recruit spilt his soup on the table, and on being censured, gave as a reason that he had been diving in his bowl in search of a bean."[9]

By the 1850s, the Army had begun to make available something called desiccated—or dehydrated—vegetables. These met with mixed reactions from among soldiers on the

Utah Expedition who sampled them. One man characterized them as "indeed very palatable, and undoubtedly very useful as a preventative of the scurvy." Another soldier had quite a different evaluation, likening their taste to that of "hay and straw."[10]

With such almost universal condemnation of army food, it is a wonder that any of the soldiers survived at all. Part of this perception, however, is due to the natural tendency to complain about something that is not up to expectations, but to remain mute if things are satisfactory. Few soldiers, therefore, left written accounts of getting fat on their daily rations. In fact, if troops had been required to eat nothing but what the regulations authorized, they probably would have been in dire straits. There were, however, many ways by which they could supplement their meager provisions. Depending upon their locations, soldiers could often add variety to their daily fare by hunting or fishing.

ALTERNATE SOURCES OF SUSTENANCE

Hunting

Soldiers on the Great Plains early in the nineteenth century found an abundance of wild game—buffalo, deer, elk, bear, and others. One soldier, after having breakfasted on fresh buffalo meat, pronounced: "I think I never had better meat in my life." Another man, less taken with the taste, announced that he "would rather have a piece of good beef." Buffalo were so numerous in the years before the Civil War that many soldiers commented upon the almost infinite availability of their meat. "You are aware that on the prairie you can see at times ten or fifteen miles from the effects of mirage," one officer wrote to his brother in 1843, "but there were points on the trace whence the bare prairie could not be seen, hill after hill covered with buffaloe [*sic*] ad infinitum." Another wrote: "I would see great herds of buffaloes in every direction, as numerous as the stars in the heavens. In all my life I do not believe that I have seen so many cattle as I could then see before me at one glance." These great shaggy beasts were so plentiful that soldiers frequently killed them for sport, leaving their meat to rot under the hot prairie sun. One soldier reported that after killing a buffalo that weighed between eight hundred and a thousand pounds, he might only harvest fifty pounds of meat. The choice cuts were the tongue, liver, heart, and backstrap. "The part most esteemed by hunters," another soldier wrote, "is the small entrails, about a foot in length, and called by the delectable term, 'marrow guts.' These, although highly relished by the old hunters, never looked very inviting to me!" But the buffalo did not exist in infinite numbers, and a dragoon officer—the youngest son of pioneer Daniel Boone—displayed a remarkable level of prescience when he confided to his journal in 1843: "The destruction of these animals yearly and their falling off so rapidly makes it certain, almost, that in a few years they will be known as a rare species."[11]

But buffalo was not the only type of wild game that soldiers enjoyed. Among the other large mammals whose flesh sometimes graced a soldier's kettle were deer, elk, and bear. Deer and elk were rather more plentiful, but at least one soldier thought that elk meat, unlike that of the deer, was too coarse and fibrous. "I think a mule would taste about as well," he thought. A soldier, writing in 1825, mentioned that his comrades seemed to prefer the taste of bear meat to that of either elk or buffalo. He was convinced, however, that it was merely the rarity of bear meat that caused such positive comments from among the men "as the flesh is certainly not as well flavored as either Buffalo or Elk."[12]

During wartime, many soldiers felt justified in stealing food from among the hostile populace. This was particularly true during the Mexican War, when soldiers—and some officers—helped themselves to domestic livestock. In describing such activities in their diaries and letters home, the troops sometimes employed euphemisms for the cattle such as "slow deer" or "short-horned elk." One soldier and his comrades, not restricting themselves just to meat, enjoyed "fat pigs, Chickens, wine, Brandy, and other good things such as we could Draw after knight [*sic*]." Sometimes hungry soldiers, with relaxed scruples against stealing, even victimized American citizens. Near the Canadian border during the War of 1812, some soldiers offered to buy potatoes from a farmer and even to dig them up themselves. The farmer, whose patriotism obviously was not as strong as his desire for profit, informed the men that he was certain that he could harvest them himself and then sell them to British troops across the border for twice as much as the Americans had offered him. "Before the next morning," wrote a drummer boy who was there, "it was decided that he [the farmer] would be spared the trouble and expense of digging his potatoes and transporting them to market."[13]

Smaller game also was utilized when nothing else offered. A soldier stationed in Wisconsin around 1830 made a meal of a porcupine that he had shot. He did not waste much time on preparations, but tossed the animal directly into his campfire. When it appeared to have reached the stage of being well roasted, he dragged it from the flames and only then proceeded to skin it and remove the entrails. "After it had undergone this process," he recorded, "it looked as nice as any roasted pig I ever saw, and with proper seasoning, it tasted better." More common, however, were prairie dogs, which some troops found made rather tasty eating. One soldier described the situation facing him and his comrades on the plains in the early 1850s. "We had not seen a buffalo in more than two months or any fresh meat of any kind except some prairie dogs." "From time to time we killed enough of the little barkers to make a stew, and found them quite as good as the common gray squirrel. Parboiled and then stewed with a little fat bacon made them taste pretty well to the men who had been so long without fresh meat." Other men pronounced the meat of these small creatures "very delicious," or compared the taste of prairie dogs favorably to the taste of rabbits. Some, however, thought the smell too strong and the taste rather less than savory.[14]

Fishing

When troops were stationed adjacent to rivers or other waterways, they often supplemented their rations with various types of seafood. This was especially true for the men in Florida during the Seminole Wars and for those stationed along the south coast of Texas during the Mexican War.

An army doctor in Florida painted a word picture of the endless supply of seafood that was available. "In one hour," he wrote, "one may take as many *Bonetas, Redfish, Groupers, Sheepshead, Bass, Trout,* and myriads of other kinds, unknown elsewhere, of the finest flavour, and of large dimensions, generally from two to three feet in length, as will feast a regiment." He also described a typical meal of oysters as consisting of a half dozen, each of which "after removal from the shell, measure six or seven inches in length, and two or three inches in breadth." A soldier, likewise, described how men in a boat would sortie into Tampa Bay twice a week, and, within an hour each time, harvest enough oysters for all the men in the camp to have their fill. Others baited hooks with salted pork skin (from their regular ration) and routinely hauled in 25- to 30-pound red fish. So plentiful was the supply of sustenance from river and sea that another officer proclaimed: "Turtle steaks are frequently issued instead of fresh beef to the men. Trout, sheepshead, grouper, oysters and crabs go a begging."[15]

A regular, stationed with General Zachary Taylor's Army of Observation along the lower Texas coast in the fall of 1845, painted an idyllic picture.

> We catch, here, every day, with hooks and with Lines, thousands of the finest fish:—among them the Drum—Sheepshead,—red-fish (weighing 50 lbs.) Mullet—Trout &c.; and, on the shoals, at low tides, Crabs,—Oysters, and Turtles in the greatest abundance. The islands are covered with deer, that feed in flocks like sheep, and so tame, that they are killed with hardly an effort ... and Messes, each day, have served up for their dinners, the smoking haunch of a Buck or doe, flanked with huge roast, fried, and boiled red-fish; and with Turtle pies and steaks.

Another soldier seemed satisfied with regular rations, even in the midst of this veritable cornucopia. "There are fish, oysters, venison and fresh beef," he wrote to his sister, "but it is to [*sic*] much trouble to procure and see to the cooking of them, when we have so good a relish for that which is easier obtained, and more substantial."[16]

Food Provided by Sutlers

Soldiers who were unhappy with their prescribed rations—and rare indeed was the man who was satisfied—could explore various avenues toward supplementing them. One of these was by patronizing the post sutler. Sutlers were civilian merchants who had signed exclusive contracts to provide soldiers at a given location, or of specified regiment, with items not issued by the army but which would make life a little more bearable. Sutlers paid fees into the post funds based upon the number of officers and men stationed there. This fee usually ranged from ten to fifteen cents per man per month. Among the food items often stocked were such edible niceties as sausage, cheese, dried fruit, coffee, eggs, tea, raisins, sugar, vermicelli, macaroni, flour, catsup, canned fish, smoked hams, and candies. The prices that sutlers were allowed to charge were set by committees of officers, in order to prevent egregious price gouging of the soldiers. Soldiers' letters, however, are rife with complaints of the high prices, usually comparing them with prices for the same items in more settled areas of the country and not factoring in the added costs of transportation to an often remote army post. A soldier in the War of 1812 was certain that his officers had colluded with the sutler to set prices at twice the normal rate. Troops in Mexico were appalled at some of the prices charged by their sutlers. One of these merchants charged thirsty soldiers twelve-and-a-half cents for a glass of ice water. In the early 1850s, the sutler at Fort Laramie charged soldiers six times as much for a loaf of bread as was the price in Chicago.[17]

Occasionally, unruly soldiers rebelled against this system, which they thought unfairly victimized them. Some Indiana volunteers, awaiting orders to proceed to Mexico in 1846, took matters into their own hands after having fortified themselves with alcohol. They looted and destroyed several sutlers' establishments, apparently in retaliation for what they took to be excessively high prices. Similarly disgruntled Alabamians visited the same sort of vengeance on a sutler in Camargo, Mexico. When the sutler arrived the next morning and discovered the magnitude of damage, according to an observer, "it was not necessary to be close up to hear him 'cuss.' His epithets were long & loud."[18]

Of course, even if a sutler charged the most reasonable prices, it would be of no use to the soldier without any money. So sutlers routinely offered credit to the hungry and thirsty soldiers. Regulations forbade this debt to exceed one-half of the soldier's pay, unless the merchant had received explicit permission from the soldier's commanding officer. Then, on payday, the debt came due. Quite often, the sutler took a seat right next to the paymaster. The paymaster first settled the sutler's bills from the pay of each individual soldier who came up to the table, and paid the rest to the soldier. Sometimes, however, a sutler was too trusting for his own good. During the Seminole Wars, a contingent of volunteers from Alabama feasted on a sutler's supply of fine wines, imported cigars, and other delicacies, instructing him to send the bill to Uncle Sam. It was only after the soldiers had left to return to their homes that the shopkeeper discovered that he had been victimized.[19]

Food Purchased Locally

Soldiers with a little money in their pockets, who decided that the sutler's prices were too steep, sometimes bought food on the local economy. If stationed near a town or village, they might find a ready supply of eggs, vegetables, or dairy products to buy. Such activity usually did not draw much attention in soldiers' letters or diaries, but they often wrote about such things in more exotic locales. Markets in Mexico during the war were full of good things to eat: peas, cabbage, tomatoes, parsnips, asparagus, apricots, peaches, figs, pears, apples, English walnuts, onions, and radishes. Soldiers wrote of buying oranges for ten cents per dozen in Tampico, while in Monterey twelve-and-a-half cents would buy a whole chicken, and a man could buy a dozen large eggs or "a ham of fresh pork" for thirty-seven-and-a-half cents. Alabama volunteers found a ready supply of honey and turkey eggs for sale from civilian vendors and welcomed the addition to their diets. The popularity of these items decreased precipitously, however, when a soldier noticed that the Mexicans transported the honey in bags made of raw cowhide, with the hair on the inside, and when someone else realized that the "turkey" eggs were, instead, the eggs of turkey buzzards.[20]

Soldiers occasionally expanded their culinary horizons by sampling local cuisine. This was especially applicable to troops serving in Mexico during the war with that nation, although some men on the frontier partook of Indian dishes (such as boiled dog meat). A few Americans found Mexican dishes quite tasty, but most found them too highly seasoned to be enjoyable. One man wrote that he found "nothing more palatable" than freshly prepared "thamales" [*sic*] A volunteer officer from Illinois wrote to his sister of his recent forays into Mexican food.

> The peculiarity of the cookery consists of putting a great deal of pepper & garlic in all their dishes. The first course is generally a young kid or lamb, stuffed with rice & raisins & highly seasoned with pepper & garlic. Then a dish of beef alamode with ditto. Then fried eggs & peppers again, & then a dish of real red peppers, stuffed with raisins and pecan nuts & dipped in batter & fried.

It is little wonder that, after having eaten such a meal, he described his throat as being like the crater of a volcano. Not many soldiers were as articulate as this officer, simply stating that only someone with an empty stomach could appreciate Mexican food and "I have not yet drunk a cup of coffee or eaten a tortilla of Mexican preparation without its creating in some degree a sensation of nausea at the stomach."[21]

Most of the trepidation expressed by soldiers when exposed to either Indian or Mexican food centered in the perceived level of hygiene of those who had prepared it. A surgeon's mate in 1795 described the body lice that seemed to infest both the hair and the blanket of an elderly Indian woman, who offered him and his companions a plate of pancakes. For the sake of continued amicable relations between the two peoples, he felt "obliged to partake, not without some disturbance lest there might have been savory additions from the head or blanket. But down it must go." Mexican dairy products also came in for their share of condemnation. One soldier found the taste of Mexican goat milk pleasing, but commented that, because the Mexicans who provided it were "too dirty to suit our taste, we have denied ourselves this luxury, except when hungry enough to eat anything." Another man bought some goat milk but found that he had to strain it through a handkerchief to filter out the dirt and hair before he could bring himself to drink it: "if the old mexican sees a fly or peace [*sic*] of litter of any kind in it," he remembered, "they will souse their fingers in up to their wrist but what they will have it out." At least some American soldiers found the manufacture of Mexican cheese to be wanting as well.

> There is no such thing as a churn there, and they don't exhaust their strength in beating and lashing the milk. They simply put the milk on a fire, in a large vessel, and boil it. The richest part of the milk rises to the top, and is skimmed off, and is worked until they have that which they call butter. And when it is made it is hard to tell which has the predominancy in it—grease or dirt. And its taste is just about as insipid as a piece of an old wool hat, there being not a particle of salt in it.[22]

Soldier Farmers

The unimaginative army diet—notoriously short of vegetables—left the soldiers subject to various problems of poor nutrition. Many post commanders, therefore, had their men put in post gardens to supply the deficiency. And while there can be no doubt that such use of the soil was of considerable benefit to the well being of the troops, the time they spent tending to their crops was necessarily time spent away from military training and patrolling. General James Wilkinson was quite displeased, in 1797, to see so much time taken away from the soldiers' real purpose. He thought such farming was "repugnant to the principles of soldiership, distructive [*sic*] to the service and disgraceful to those who indulge it." An officer, inspecting western posts some thirty years later, shared this opinion. He recognized the value of the supplemental rations, he wrote, but "I would have the soldier point to his garden in proof of the good provision he has made during the short intervals from military exercise, rather than boastingly talk of his proficiency as a farmer." This same officer was equally distressed—and for the same reason—to see the amount of soldier-tended cattle at one of the forts. "Look at Fort Atkinson," he wrote in one of his reports, "and you will see barn yards that would not disgrace a Pennsylvania farmer, herds of cattle that would do credit to a Potomac grazier, yet where is the gain in this, either to the soldier or the government? Ask the individual who boastingly shews you all this," he continued, rather exasperatingly, "why such a provision of hay and corn. His answer will be, to *feed* the *cattle*. But why so many *cattle*? Why—to eat the hay and corn."[23]

By 1851, and in spite of that officer's concerns, Army officials ordered every permanent military post to at least have a garden to supply fresh vegetables for the troops. Depending upon the climate, these gardens turned out quantities of cabbage, cauliflower, peas, beans, squash, pumpkins, cucumbers, lima beans, musk melons, water melons, cantaloupes and tomatoes. The size of these agricultural installations at some of the larger posts were much larger than mere gardens. Some posts were authorized to construct fairly sizable farms, complete with livestock. Unfortunately, although most of the gardens proved fruitful, almost all the farms proved to be dismal failures. The soldier-farmers at one New Mexico fort were unable to harvest enough corn and hay to feed the various mules, horses, milk cows, oxen, and hogs that were resident there. In fact, the fort's commander recommended that the hogs be sold, if they could command any sort of a price at all, or, failing that, they should be given away because it was too expensive to feed them. At other posts, insects virtually destroyed the beans, and parasites destroyed more than half the corn. One commander estimated that four times as much corn could have been purchased on the local market for the amount of money spent trying to grow it. In fact, this experiment in self-sufficiency proved profitable at only a couple of forts. One of them managed to grow a surplus of hay, which it then sold. The "profit" returned by the other fort only came about because officials rented the farm to a civilian.[24]

Soldiers of the antebellum period usually had enough to eat, although perhaps as part of a less-than-imaginative diet. Sometimes, food ran short during campaigns, but this never seemed to have led to any lasting problems. For the most part, the army operated in areas where the men had access to wild game or fish or native supplies if their own commissary ran short. There were instances, however, when a shortage of certain types of food led to health problems. No army can be effective unless its component parts—the soldiers—remain healthy enough to carry out their duties.

MILITARY MEDICINE

A soldier's contact with medical personnel began at the recruiting station, where army doctors were ever on the alert that young men in poor health did not wind up in uniform. Their efforts, generally, were successful. In 1852, for example, barely one of every six potential enlistees passed their physical examinations. Even when a young man was the picture of good health when he entered the service, he usually found himself battling any one of a long list of ailments before very long. Military forts and campsites were fertile grounds for the rapid transmission of many diseases. Measles and mumps, now considered childhood ailments, wrought havoc among the soldiery. Malaria and dysentery were quite common, along with other dreaded diseases, such as yellow fever, smallpox, scurvy, and cholera, which are virtually unheard of today.[25]

Quality of Army Doctors

Army doctors in the first half of the nineteenth century, sometimes came under verbal abuse from their patients—at least the ones who survived their treatments—as well as others. Sometimes, these complaints were simply the result of frustration on the part of a patient whose recovery from a particular malady or wound was slower than he had hoped. The wife of a cavalry officer in Texas, in the 1850s, penned some rather uncomplimentary opinions in her diary about the doctor who had recently treated her husband: "The Dr.," she wrote, "had the sincerity to say well Col I have not the most remote idea what has been the matter with you. This is not the only subject upon which he seems ignorant I have no faith in him. God forbid that any of us should be sick again while he is with us. he certainly knows nothing of his profession." Here was a woman who, perhaps, expected more than contemporary medical science could offer.[26]

Medical schools in the United States were relatively few, and most were clustered in New England and other eastern states. Nor were they all of high caliber. They generally required their students to attend two terms of classes, each of which lasted three to four months. In many of these institutions, the subject matter was identical in each of the two terms, and school officials were not always strict about enforcing attendance at the whole range of lectures. It was not unusual for a man to arrive at the school weeks after the beginning of the term, or to leave well before its completion. The students honed their meager medical knowledge and skills by working alongside practicing physicians, in much the same way as apprentices in other fields. Finally, the school administered an examination—the degree of difficulty varied from school to school—before granting diplomas. A traveler visiting the United States from England in the early 1820s and appalled by the results of this system, wrote:

> Any young man, after an apprenticeship of a year or two in the shop of some ignorant apothecary, or at the most, after a very superficial course of study at some school or college is entitled to cure (or rather kill) all the unhappy Backwoodsmen who may apply to him for advice.... Indeed, to become a doctor in the Backwoods, it is only necessary to have a cabin containing fifty or one hundred dollars' worth of drugs, with a board over the door, affirming that this is Dr. M or N.'s "store."

A prominent doctor in the 1840s thought that none of the medical schools were sufficiently rigorous to weed out incompetent students. "The rejection of candidates," he wrote, "is ... a matter of exceedingly rare occurrence, and almost all who have complied with the most essential requisite of paying their teachers are sure to be honored with the title to which they aspire."[27]

This disparity in the qualifications to practice medicine in civilian life was, of course, mirrored within the military. During the War of 1812, the highest-ranking medical officer in the army disgustedly described one of his underlings as "not only incompetent in medical knowledge, but so sottishly abject in his conduct, as to be unworthy of trust or confidence." He characterized another surgeon as "not only incompetent, but deranged to such a degree as to make it unsafe & improper to trust patients in his charge." A few years later, a different surgeon general described an elderly army doctor as being too old to ever venture forth to join his assigned regiment, "so illiterate that he cannot spell his own name," and so lacking in qualifications as to have previously been pressured into resigning a medical position "to avoid an arrest for incompetence."[28]

Army authorities took steps in 1813 to ensure that only truly qualified doctors earned commissions as military surgeons. After that year, no man could gain an appointment as an army doctor unless he could provide proof of having graduated from a medical school. Of course, at that time, there were many practicing physicians who had learned their profession as apprentices and who had never set foot inside a medical school. Such men as these could still practice military medicine if they were able to pass an examination. These requirements were stiffened again in the early 1830s, when authorities decided that possession of a medical school diploma did not necessarily equate to proficiency, and they required everyone to submit to a rather rigorous examination.[29]

Members of the examining board subjected the prospect to an examination that covered such areas as anatomy, chemistry, physiology, toxicology, clinical medicine, and, perhaps, surgery. The fifty percent failure rate in 1860 was actually a rather respectable mark compared to some earlier years. In 1846, during the war with Mexico, the government decided to authorize another twelve to fifteen physicians for the army. The medical examining board sent invitations to sixty-three civilian doctors, inviting them to sit for the examination. Forty-three showed up, the others perhaps having heard how difficult the exam was to pass. Of this number, three were physically disqualified, and fifteen others had second thoughts and voluntarily removed themselves from consideration. Of the remaining twenty-five stalwarts, five gave up part way through the process, and twelve others failed. From the initial pool of sixty-three physicians, the army wound up with eight men qualified to serve as army surgeons. The following year, the results were even worse. Only eleven men passed from a pool that had originally contained over a hundred.[30]

Those candidates who failed these exams did so for a wide variety of reasons. Several displayed a gross ignorance of the human anatomy, often because some medical schools were so under-financed as to be unable to purchase cadavers for their students to dissect. The report of one examining board rather uncharitably ascribed the lack of practice in dissection to the fact "that dainty fingers might be soiled" in the process. The same board found that several of the candidates they had examined, although possessing diplomas from medical schools, had had absolutely no practical experience, or even instruction, in surgery.[31]

The Navy also set up boards of examination for men seeking medical commissions in that service, but the rate of acceptance does not appear to have been much different. One prospective naval surgeon, asked to discuss the derivation of castor oil, asserted confidently that it was the natural oil secreted by an animal called a castor. Another applicant's grasp of anatomy was shown to have been deficient when he located the solar plexus on the sole of one's foot. Yet a third man was unable to give the respective temperatures at which water froze and boiled, and further indicated that he could see no practical reason why such information should be of any concern to a physician.[32]

The positive aspect of all of this was that these doctors were not going to treat the nation's soldiers. In spite of the low esteem in which some soldier-patients held their caretakers, the filter that the medical boards provided meant that army doctors were, on average, much better than their civilian counterparts. Indeed, the fledgling American Medical Association awarded the military high marks for the manner in which it prevented unqualified men from practicing medicine in the army and navy.[33]

Treatments

In the first half of the nineteenth century, some doctors still subscribed to the notion that removing blood from certain patients was beneficial to their recovery from various ailments, even though others had begun to question the therapeutic value of this practice. A doctor writing near mid-century expressed his opinion that physicians who bled patients should face criminal charges for doing so. The practice was, he wrote, "contrary to common sense, to general experience, to enlightened reason, and to the manifest laws of the Divine Providence." A contemporary soon offered a rebuttal arguing that if blood-letting was harmful, then so was breathing, and he did not advise discontinuing either practice. Some doctors saw bleeding as a panacea which, according to one, would "ameliorate all the symptoms, afford a refreshing sleep, cause the skin to perspire, and the bowels to relax, increase the appetite, and give a feeling of relief and ease which no other remedy or any mode of diet is able to supply."[34]

In actual practice, there were different methods of obtaining blood. Perhaps the simplest method was simply to apply blood-sucking leeches to a patient's body. At other times, the doctor heated up small glass cups and then applied them, open-end down, to the patient's skin, so that, upon cooling, the skin under the cups was raised into blisters. The physician could then cut into the blisters to draw blood. Textbooks that still recommended the practice usually advised limiting the quantity of blood taken at any one time to not more than ten to fourteen ounces, although not every practitioner followed these guidelines. One doctor stated that patients felt cheated if, upon being bled, the doctor took any less than sixteen to twenty-four ounces. In what is assuredly one of the most extreme examples of the use of this technique, a doctor in 1811 bled a patient every day for seven weeks until he had extracted 600 ounces of blood! This patient, somehow, survived, but not all were that fortunate. Another doctor applied this technique to a malaria patient who was shaking violently from the effects of the disease, but later admitted that he "bled the patient till he was too weak to shake, and then the disease and the patient went off together."[35]

Doctors knew that a fair amount of illness arose due to soldiers not wearing proper clothing for the season. Warm woolen socks and adequate shoes were, of course, essential in the winter. Soldiers whose feet were constantly cold or wet were prime candidates for the hospital. Everyone also agreed that wearing woolen clothing would go a long way in staving off various maladies, but not all of them agreed with Benjamin Franklin's ideas on the subject. That elder statesman cautioned that one should wear woolen shirts until the middle of summer, when they could be removed. Renewed wear should then begin the very next day. One prominent military surgeon of the early nineteenth century cautioned that there was equal danger to the health of a soldier who dressed too warmly in summer.[36]

Another causative agent for disease, with which many doctors were concerned, was alcohol. Until 1830, soldiers enjoyed a regular ration of rum (or whiskey), and conventional medical thinking was that excessive use was a "predisponent cause of disease." Some even advocated the removal of alcohol from hospitals because of the danger of men feigning sickness just to get it.

Malaria

Perhaps the greatest continuing health threat facing the American soldier of the early nineteenth century was malaria. Because this disease exhibited different symptoms in different victims—and sometimes different symptoms within the same victim in successive occurrences—it was difficult for doctors to diagnose. Sometimes, the patient's fever would subside temporarily only to recur again and again. This set of symptoms resulted in a diagnosis of intermittent fever. In other cases, the fever would also fluctuate but never quite reach normal. This was identified as remittent fever. It made little difference to the sufferer what name was applied to his illness, and it did not make much difference to the physicians either. Scientists did not yet understand the role played by common mosquitoes in transmitting fevers. They believed that all fevers emanated from the vapors—or miasma—that rose from rotting vegetable and animal matter, and doctors tended to treat all fevers in much the same way.[37]

Accepted treatment for men with fever was to treat the symptom. This might involve bathing the patient in cold water to lower his temperature. Some doctors, at least until the early nineteenth century, bled their feverish patients to achieve the same result. Others kept the patient covered in blankets so he would sweat out the fever. An army doctor, during the War of 1812, commented on an unusual turn of events involving fever patients in the hospital in Buffalo, New York. "Three patients," he wrote, "who had tried most of the remedies with which we were supplied, without effect, cured themselves at once, by taking a pint of brandy undiluted, in which was mixed a large quantity of ground black pepper. . . . This was not followed by inebriation nor any appearance of undue excitement." The record is mute on whether this doctor added this regimen of treatment to his repertoire, but he did increase the dosages of opium that he sometimes prescribed. By mid-century, quinine had supplanted most of the other treatments.[38]

Diarrhea/Dysentery

Diarrhea was a common affliction throughout the nineteenth century. In some cases, as today, it was an isolated incident, and by the day after its initial symptoms, it was gone. Most of the time, however, it was an indication of a more serious affliction—dysentery. Standard treatment for this more serious disease included keeping the patient warm to the point of excessive perspiration.[39]

Scurvy

Scurvy, long the bane of seafarers, is brought about by a prolonged deficiency in Vitamin C and, if left untreated, manifests itself in a most unpleasant death. An army doctor in Nebraska in 1820 described the unfortunate sufferer thus:

> The victim of this dreadful malady is characterized by his extreme feebleness and debility, his pale and bloated complexion; his spongy black and ulcerated gums; by his loosened teeth; his [fetid] urine and offensive breath; by the swelling of his legs; the livid spots on his skin and the universal discolouration of the limbs; by his stiff and swollen joints; his rigid and contracted tendons; his loss of locomotion and by wandering and excruciating [*sic*] pains.[40]

Scurvy did not become a constant threat to the soldiers in the way that such other maladies as malaria and dysentery did, but the year 1820 was particularly severe. Almost 200 soldiers died of scurvy that year, including half of the garrison at a Nebraska post. Ensuring that the men consumed fruits or vegetables that contained the requisite vitamins as a regular part of their diets was the key to both prevention and treatment. Post commanders and doctors accomplished this in different fashions. In the winter of 1792–1793, General Anthony Wayne made an arrangement with farmers near his post by which he traded them his men's whiskey ration for the necessary food items, although some of his men made no secret of the fact that they would gladly risk getting scurvy if it meant the restoration of their alcohol. By this time, too, limes and lemons, in juice form, became regular components of the British Navy's ration. (Hence the nickname "limey.") Army physicians in the Southwest used locally obtained cactus juice to fight off scurvy, although they found they had to add such things as lemon extract, sugar, or whiskey to make it palatable. "Scurvy is pre-eminently a preventable disease," wrote one army doctor, "and its existence in an army is *prima facie* evidence that the medical or military authorities have been neglectful of their duties." Scurvy deaths in the army averaged less than one per year during the 1830s and 1840s.[41]

Cholera

Cholera, although not the constant threat to health that malaria was, produced frightful results when it did descend upon the population. Health officials saw a cholera epidemic in 1832 and another in 1849, the latter seeming to not entirely abate until the mid-1850s. Among the military victims of the 1849 outbreak was Colonel William J. Worth, who had survived combat against the Seminole and the Mexicans. During the 1832 epidemic, soldiers at Rock Island, Illinois, succumbed to the disease so fast that some men were on permanent grave-digging details. They buried the victims in a common trench without the niceties of caskets. At one point, the work detail at Rock Island stopped work. When an officer inquired as to the cause of their inactivity, one of the men told him that the next victim still had life left in him, and they were just waiting for him to breathe his last before they added his body to the mass grave. The 1849 outbreak coincided with the California gold rush and had the same effect on the emigrant trains as it did on the Army outposts. In fact, the gold seekers probably transported the disease to the soldiers as their wagons passed through forts.[42]

The symptoms of cholera, at least in its early stages, were easily confused with other ailments. Diarrhea was usually the first indication, followed by severe vomiting, a feeling of physical exhaustion, uremia, and eventually coma and death—all within a matter of a day or two. An army doctor in Texas during the 1849 outbreak has left a more vivid description.

> The formal onset of the disease was preceded some twenty hours by a diarrhoea, when profuse vomiting and purging of the characteristic discharge (having the appearance of water in which rice has been washed) commenced, attended by painful cramps in the stomach, calves of the legs, thighs, and arms—especially the flexor muscles of the fore-arms. The eyes had a dull, watery, and muddy appearance, with a contracted ill-defined pupil. The features became sharpened, and the entire body was blue, shrunken, shriveled, cold, and clammy. The hands and fingers shrunken and sodden. The tongue gave to the finger a cold and disagreeable sensation. The patient complained of some pain in the stomach, loins and limbs; of insatiable thirst; and a burning heat in the stomach, and distressing heat of the surface of the body; although to the hand it had the cold feeling of a dead body.[43]

Smallpox

There were no vaccines available for most of the ailments that regularly visited army encampments. Smallpox was the exception. The method used throughout most of the eighteenth century was to put an otherwise healthy individual on a regimen of bleeding, purging, and a diet of light, bland food for two weeks. At the end of this preparatory period, the doctor took lymph from an infected person's smallpox sore and injected it, usually in the lower leg. The intent was for this to cause only a minor case of smallpox, one from which the patient would soon recover. Then, having survived it, his body would have developed a certain amount of immunity to recurrences. Of course, some patients developed more virulent cases and died, but the rate of death among inoculated patients was only one-tenth that of patients who acquired the disease through other means. By 1800, another method of immunization had proven to be much more effective. This involved the same basic procedure, but instead of using the serum from smallpox pustules, the vaccination was made from the similar, but less deadly, cowpox. There were two methods of obtaining the serum. The first, and most obvious, was for the physician to remove a cowpox scab and recover the lymph through capillary action into a small tubular glass pipette. He would then quickly melt the ends of the tube over a candle flame to seal in the liquid. This kept the serum viable for an extended period of time, and when he wanted to use it, he simply broke off the ends of the pipette and blew the fluid out onto his vaccinator. Perhaps the more common method was to crush up a cowpox scab on a glass plate and add a small drop of glycerin to give it fluidity. This allowed such scabs to be transported and stored with relative ease until such time as they were needed.[44]

Just before the War of 1812, army doctors received instructions to thus immunize every soldier. Similar orders were routinely issued, so that the incidence of smallpox among troops of the regular army was very low. Medical authorities were not all of one mind on the subject of re-vaccinations. Some believed that an immunization could easily be effective for twenty-five years, while others urged that soldiers be vaccinated at regular intervals. The post surgeon at Fort McKavett, on the Texas frontier, was of the latter persuasion, but found there was a severe shortage of the necessary vaccine when smallpox broke out among the civilian population in San Antonio in 1857. Even though virtually all of the soldiers at the fort had received vaccinations, as per standing orders, the doctor thought it wise to re-vaccinate them. His supply of vaccine, however, was not large enough to cover everybody, so he used what he had to immunize the previously unvaccinated children at the fort. Then, as they developed mild cases of cowpox, he used their lesions to vaccinate the twenty-two members of the post band. He used the scabs from these men to vaccinate half of the remaining soldiers, using them in turn to provide vaccine for the rest of the men.[45]

Shirkers

Sometimes, healthy soldiers appeared at the doctor's quarters asking for treatment. These men were often shirkers, who had grown tired of the soldier's life and wanted to go home. Or they were men who, in time of war, had suddenly come to the realization that continued service posed very real hazards to their health and longevity. If they could just convince the surgeon that they were the victims of some serious malady, perhaps he would order them discharged from the service because of disability. Then they could leave behind whatever irksome tasks awaited their fellows and be on their way home again. Perhaps a healthy man simply wanted to avoid some onerous task, such as accompanying a wood-chopping detail. The surgeons heard all sorts of excuses, and dealt with them in different ways. During the War of 1812, one surgeon had a ready solution for those suffering only from "rascality." If he doubted the sincerity of a patient, he prescribed blistering, a very uncomfortable procedure. He found that this sharply curtailed the incidence of repeat offenders as "rather than submit to the pain of blistering a second time" they "would prefer going to duty." During the War with Mexico, a surgeon in one of the volunteer regiments characterized one of the men in his regiment as being so lazy that all he wanted to do was smoke his pipe and eat. He "would always be on the sick list," this doctor wrote to another physician, "if I did not always stimulate his stomach to action with tartar emetic." One of the most unusual instances of malingering has to have been that of a man who had gone to the surgeon's quarters along with other sick men. The doctor had not previously treated this particular man but noticed he made no effort to approach him. After tending to all the other patients, he asked this man what his complaint was. "Nothing, Sir," he replied, "I just came to learn from the others *what to say when I wanted to get sick.*"[46]

Healthy troops generally looked with disfavor upon the malingerers in their midst, and sometimes went to considerable lengths to expose them to the folks back home. This seems to have been particularly true within the volunteer regiments that were called up for war-time service. The men in these units all tended to come from the same towns or counties, so that both their valor and their misdeeds soon became the gossip of their friends and acquaintances. "There are a great many young gentlemen (query)," one soldier wrote disgustedly from Mexico in 1846, "who are very home-sick & sham sick to keep from duty & and they *do* keep from duty, which, of course makes it harder on those who are willing to do duty." Another man listed the names of a dozen of his comrades who had recently received surgeon's certificates and were even then on their way home. He was certain that they had simply found military life too difficult. "I want you to report these names" to the local newspaper, he confided in a letter home, "many of them are babies and are so badly home sick that they would die if they staid away from home any longer."[47]

It is impossible to determine how many of the these slackers succeeded, but some doctors employed interesting methods to discourage them. In 1849, a soldier presented himself to a surgeon with a complaint that his knee was stiffened such that it was permanently bent. The record is mute on the details, but it is likely that this man sought a medical discharge from the army. To his disappointment, however, an alert surgeon administered a dose of ether, and, when the man was fully anesthetized, easily maneuvered the "paralyzed" limb.[48]

Military hospitals ran the gamut as far as quality of treatment and facilities were concerned. Those built in the more settled areas of the country were usually, but not always, better. During the War of 1812, for example, sick and wounded soldiers had the best of both at the general hospital at Burlington, Vermont. The building that housed the sick was on high ground that drained well. The staff there made sure that the walls and floors were regularly scrubbed down with soap and limewater, that bedpans were emptied immediately after use, that when a patient left the hospital, his bedding was cleaned before the next man used it, and that the windows remained open for ventilation as much as possible. On the other hand, authorities, thirty years later, at Fort Hamilton in New York Harbor designated a couple of casemates within the fort to house the hospital. These rooms were so poorly ventilated that they were uncomfortably warm in the summer months and full of smoke from the chimneys during the winter.[49]

During active campaigning, or at isolated posts on the far frontier, the facilities were often little better than nothing. At the same time that the patients at Burlington were being so well taken care of, other wounded were being put into an old mess hall at Fort Niagara with no roof. An army doctor remembered the abominable conditions at St. Mark's, Florida, in 1822:

> My hospital is very bad and more or less wet at every rain. On the 16th of September the tide rose uncommonly high, which nearly inundated this place and the whole of the adjacent country; the water was a foot deep in the hospital; in fact I visited my sick and went through it in a canoe. The bunks were high, which keep the men out of the water, but this, as well as the wet from the rains, had a very injurious effect on my patients, particularly those laboring under dysenteries and diarrhoea.

The hospital at Fort Davis, in far west Texas, consisted, in 1857, of a large tent and an adjoining structure whose walls were of vertical pickets stuck in the ground and thatched with grass. At the same time, the facility at Fort Walla Walla, in Washington Territory, was a one-room building with four bunks stacked atop one another.[50]

Given the general state of scientific knowledge in the first half of the nineteenth century, military medical treatment was not much different from that offered to the civilian sector. In fact, army doctors were, on average, more knowledgeable than their civilian counterparts, and even though there were sometimes medical shortages and spartan facilities, American soldiers benefited from excellent care.

HYGIENE AND GROOMING

The level of personal hygiene expected of an American soldier in the antebellum era was probably equal to that of society in general, but would cause someone in the twenty-first century to cringe in revulsion. The 1821 Army Regulations, for example, made no mention of bathing, but did enjoin the soldiers to change their underwear three times a week during the summer months, and at least twice a week during the cooler months. As time went by, the Army paid a little more attention to soldiers' cleanliness. Company commanders were ordered to pay especial attention to their men's personal cleanliness, as well as how well the men maintained their weapons, clothing, and living quarters. "Bathing is promotive, both of comfort and health," stated the regulations for 1841, "and … the men should be made to bathe at least once a week. The feet are to be washed at least twice a week." Even this modest frequency of bathing was not always observed, particularly for soldiers on the move. A soldier on the western frontier in 1857 proudly informed his diary: "I had a bath today the first since last season."[51]

The length of a soldier's hair became the subject of specific orders when General James Wilkinson, commanding general of the army, issued a series of orders in 1801 that called for the soldiers to cut their hair short and to shave off their beards, "for the accommodation, comfort and health of the troops." The long hair, complete with queue, fashionable in the late eighteenth century, was slowly going the way of knee breeches. In retrospect, long hair on a soldier might also have been seen as a health issue. Long hair was harder to keep clean with the limited resources available to a soldier on the march. And long hair provided potential nesting sites for all sorts of lice and other small disease-carrying vermin.[52]

Some troops did not embrace this order enthusiastically. They were quite comfortable with things the way they were. Some of the older soldiers had experience dating back to the Revolutionary War and undoubtedly felt that they therefore should be exempt from this attempted change in their tonsorial conditions, but the general did not budge. A captain was so incensed that he preferred to resign his commission rather than comply but, since he was the highest-ranking officer at his post, there was no one to whom he could submit it, and he ultimately complied. Less adaptable was Colonel Richard Butler, commander of the Second U.S. Infantry Regiment. He was adamant. He would not cut his long queue in order to obey this rule. Wilkinson at first allowed Butler his way, but then realized that making exceptions bred discontent among the rest of his troops and ordered Butler to obey. When the colonel refused, he faced a court-martial that ordered him to comply. A second court-martial followed in 1805, in the face of the colonel's continued intransigence. This court sentenced him to a one-year suspension, without pay, from the army. In an effort to overturn the sentence, seventy-five prominent citizens signed a petition on behalf of Colonel Butler and sent it to President Thomas Jefferson. Wilkinson had overstepped his authority, it claimed. Ordering his soldiers to cut their hair in this fashion was, they stated, "unsanctioned by law, without meaning, without utility, capricious and absurd, irrelative to the duties of a soldier, degrading to a man, and destructive of that pride which constitutes the soul of an army." The petition had no effect, but before the sentence could be carried out, Colonel Butler became a victim of yellow fever. As he lay on his deathbed, he asked friends to have a hole bored in the bottom of his coffin, sufficient for his queue to hang down. A final act of defiance.[53]

Regulations through the 1840s generally required soldiers to wear their hair close-cropped. This would have been easy to enforce among the relatively few troops stationed in the permanent forts along the Atlantic coastline, but much more difficult when it came to men on the frontier. Contemporary portraits, however, seldom show a soldier—or an officer—with a regulation haircut. In fact, when an officer on the Utah expedition in 1857 cut his hair very short, it was a cause of great comment among his fellows. "I think you would laugh to see me," he wrote to his wife. "Everyone says it is a decided improvement." Future Confederate General Richard Ewell faced a different problem. "I found not long since," he wrote in 1841, "that all my hair was coming out, and was obliged to shave my head to keep what little I have left from following suit."[54]

And, following civilian trends of the time, soldiers were forbidden to wear beards or moustaches. A young second lieutenant was among many who found these restrictions hard to accept. He had grown a rather wispy moustache and, in 1831, complained all the way to the general commanding the Army when he was ordered to shave it off. He waxed eloquent about the martial appearance that moustaches imparted to army officers, and how his moustache was an "inviolable" part of his persona. He also complained that his moustache was not even as visible as those of some officers who had only recently shaved.[55]

CLOTHING

Uniforms worn by American soldiers underwent considerable change in appearance during the years 1790 to 1860. During the Revolutionary War, soldiers in American units wore uniforms of generally the same cut but of a wide range of colors, depending upon their home state or branch of service. Many infantry regiments wore dark blue coats, trimmed in red, and white trousers, but others chose different trim colors or wore brown or tan trousers. And the men of the Second New Hampshire Regiment sported white coats with light blue trim—looking a lot like French soldiers of the day. The uniforms of mounted troops were, if anything, even more varied. General George Washington specified blue as the dominant color for uniform coats in 1779, but different units continued to use the color and cut of their uniform to express a certain individuality. By 1790, the standard uniform featured a dark blue coat with white lining, which reached almost to the knees, with red collars, cuffs, and lapels, along with white pantaloons. The soldier also wore a black hat, called a round hat, but resembling a more modern top hat. The brim was bound in a color that indicated the soldier's arm of service, and a narrow piece of bearskin was stretched over the top of the hat from front to rear. In 1799, cavalrymen traded in these coats for green ones trimmed in white (and changed again to black in 1800). Although the cut of the coat changed slightly, this was the basic uniform until the War of 1812.[56]

Indigo plants provided the basis of the dyes used to turn the wool broadcloth of military uniforms into the pleasing dark blue color. Care had to be taken to control the dying process or the resulting color could range all the way from a dark blue to a grayish purple. The red dye used for uniform trim came from the bodies of tiny tropical insects—it took 70,000 of them to produce one pound of dye—and could be adjusted to produce a variety of tints.[57]

Active campaigning was, as a matter of course, hard on uniforms, which were supplied on a competitive bidding basis. Some contractors cut corners in quality in order to meet their commitments, and the soldiers thus wound up with clothing and tentage that sometimes lasted mere days or weeks before giving out. One soldier complained about the loose weave of his newly received stockings by confiding to his journal that "they would fit any sized foot; for if too short, the soldier had only to push his toes between the threads." He also grumbled that his blanket only measured three feet by four feet, which was not much protection from the winter cold. General Anthony Wayne recognized the likelihood that his men's uniforms would wear out faster than they should. He therefore requested that the troops of the Legion continue to receive the long uniform coat, so that it would keep them warm during the colder months. When spring arrived, they could cut material from the coat tails to fashion into patches for other pieces of clothing that had deteriorated.[58]

Clothing lasted longer if it was kept clean and, to that end, Army Regulations made specific suggestions. For cleaning white woolens, the soldier was to spread the garment out onto a flat surface and then sprinkle it with very dry bran and Spanish whiting (chalk). He was to work this mixture into the fabric with his hands and then beat it with a mallet or similar tool until that no longer caused dust to rise from it. The last step was to brush it well. Sometimes, however, there were stubborn spots of grease or dirt. In these instances, the soldier was to take a bit of pipe clay in the palm of his hand and moisten it with saliva—but only from an empty stomach—and apply the mixture to the troublesome area. After the application had dried, the soldier was to lightly scratch it and then beat it with his mallet. It this still did not do the trick, he was to moisten it with soap and water and then rinse out the soap. It the stain was caused by tar, there was a different solution. In this case, he was to dissolve the stain with butter, and then scratch and beat it after drying. Lemon juice or vinegar was to be used to remove such blemishes from the red wool trim of the uniform. The regulations did not give guidance as to how a soldier should clean blue wool—the dominant part of the uniform.[59]

A soldier, writing to his sister from Oregon in 1852, offered a method of washing different from that officially recommended. His recipe called for a pint of alcohol, a pint of spirits of turpentine, an ounce of liquid ammonia, and an ounce of gum camphor, all of which were to be stored in a well-corked bottle. "Two tablespoons of this mixture to five gallons of water," were all that was needed, he wrote, "adding about one pound of brown Soap, or more if you choose. Rub the clothes a little if very dirty but this is generally not necessary. After the clothes have soaked one hour in this mixture then boil them in clean water for an hour and wring them dry, which completes the process." And then, lest his correspondent think that he was actually doing his own laundry, he wrote: "My washerwoman uses this in getting up my clothes, with much comfort to herself, great economy of buttons and expletives on my part, and I believe no serious detriment to the linen."[60]

Army Regulations provided for the use of four civilian women as laundresses for each company of troops. They received no salary from the army, but did receive one ration per day and, in most instances, some sort of living quarters on base. The women who did this work were often the wives or widows of enlisted men, and their income came directly from the soldiers and officers who made use of their services. Representative rates from the early 1840s show that enlisted men paid fifty cents per month to have up to a dozen pieces cleaned, and officers paid as much as two dollars for the same service. A decade or so later, these rates had risen to seventy-five cents per month and three dollars per month, respectively. Customers could either pay the women upon completion of the work, or they could have it deducted from their pay.

A typical annual clothing issue of the early nineteenth century might include a hat, a coat, and a vest, along with four pairs of overalls—two each of wool and linen—four pairs of shoes, four pairs of socks, four shirts, a blanket, and a pair of linen trousers and frock for fatigue duty. Loading down the soldier with an entire year's supply would have presented problems with regard to storage and transportation, so clothing reached the men twice during the year. Roughly half of the items, including the woolen overalls, blankets, and vests, were issued in early November for winter use. The other half, including the lighter weight garments, were issued on or about April 1 in the southern states and a month later in the north. Later regulations called for the issue of cold-weather clothing as early as September in the northern climes and a month later elsewhere. Similarly, lighter weight clothing was to be issued in April in the warmer areas and in May in areas where the cool temperatures lingered.[61]

Perhaps the most peculiar piece of clothing specified for military wear was the neck stock. This was nothing more than a snugly fitting collar of leather (or sometimes silk). Its purpose was to force the soldier to keep his head up and not slouched forward. It was not, as might be imagined, a popular piece of apparel among the troops, but some officers continued to insist upon its value as an integral part of the uniform. A young enlisted man in the newly formed Dragoon Regiment appeared on parade one day in 1833 without the required neckwear and faced a severe dressing down by an officer. "Go and put it on, sir," he was told, "and never again come half-dressed upon parade." Twenty-five years later, in Utah, an officer made it known that on parade his men were required to wear their stocks, even though none had been issued.[62]

Evolution of the Uniform

1812

By the eve of the War of 1812, the length of the infantryman's coattails had been reduced by about half, making it more comfortable in warmer weather. This shortened version of the coat was called a coatee. He had white trousers for summer wear and blue for winter. He wore a white shirt and vest, and he was allowed a white linen frock and trousers for fatigue duty. His shoes were black, coming up above the ankle, and he covered the tops of them with short, half gaiters. A black round hat continued to serve as his headgear, although soldiers in other branches wore different head coverings. Artillery and dragoon uniforms generally differed only in matters of trim color, but the members of the Rifle Regiment wore green uniforms with black collars, cuffs, and lapels trimmed in yellow. Musicians, on the other hand, traditionally wore uniform coats that were in reversed colors. That is, while the infantry uniform coat was dark blue with red trim, the infantry musician's coat was red with dark blue trim. This made for interesting situations during the war, because the British line troops wore red coats, and it was easy to mistake an American musician for an enemy soldier. In fact, in 1813, a New England privateer captured a British ship bound for Quebec that was carrying enough red uniforms for the entire British 104th Regiment of Foot stationed there. These 1,100 brand new coats were parceled out to various American bandsmen after simply replacing the British military buttons with American ones.[63]

Disruption of American international trade in the years leading up to the War of 1812 affected the supply of British-produced wool broadcloth to be made into uniforms. Then, of course, with the onset of war, the supply dried up altogether. One result was that the soldiers were now receiving uniforms made of less sturdy fabric than before. And colors other than blue began to be seen among regular army regiments. The men of the Rifle Regiment were soon clad in gray uniforms, a color usually associated with poorly trained and poorly led militia troops. Late in the war, Brigadier General Winfield Scott also resorted to gray uniforms, when he sought to clothe the men in his exhaustively drilled division. As Scott led his command onto the field at the Battle of Chippewa in July 1814, the British officers saw the gray color of their coats and undoubtedly felt relief at the arrival of these undependable militiamen. When, instead, Scott's troops did not waver under heavy enemy fire, British Major General Phineas Riall realized that he faced more than militiamen. "Those are regulars, by God!" he exclaimed to those near him.

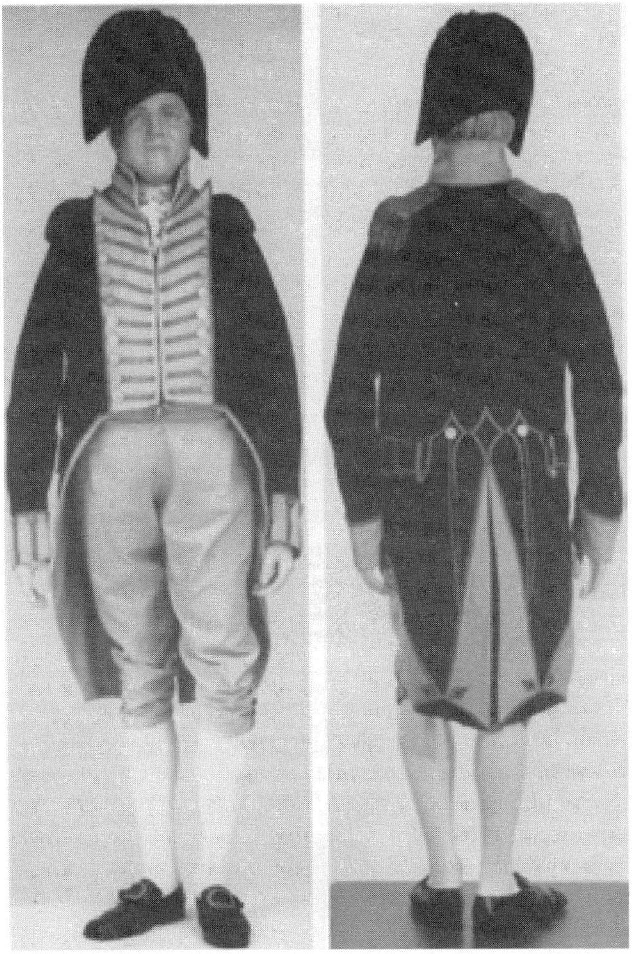

The dress uniform of Brigadier General Peter Gansevoort, ca. 1812. The buff collar, lapels, cuffs, and turnbacks on this blue coat are trimmed in gold lace. Epaulets and buttons are also gold, and the diamonds on the turnbacks are blue with gold lace trim. The breeches are buff. (*Courtesy of the Smithsonian*)

The Army did not issue heavy overcoats, or greatcoats, to the soldiers for winter service. Instead, each regiment received sixty of these coats, which were issued to men on guard duty. When a man came off of such duty, he left the coat for the next man to wear.[64]

Many of the volunteer regiments that marched to war in this second conflict with Great Britain did so in a variety of uniforms. Some New Yorkers wore red uniform coats, not unlike those worn by the enemy, while others turned out resplendent in dark green coatees, with the collars, cuffs, and lapels of black velvet trimmed in gold lace. Along the western frontier, the choice of clothing usually leaned toward function over form. Rare was the carefully tailored coat, with its blind buttonhole trim. Instead, these men tended toward loosely fitting hunting frocks of some sturdy fabric or of buckskin. One contemporary observer described the dress of the "typical" Kentucky volunteer. He wore "a hunting-shirt made of linsey, with a slight fringe border, color either blue, such as obtained from indigo, a pale yellow made from hickory bark, or a dingy brown obtained from black walnut. His pants were Kentucky jeans [a coarse cotton-wool blend], and he walked in shoes or moccasins as was his fancy." Some Ohio troops wore plain, unbleached tow-linen hunting shirts and trousers, while others opted for similar outfits in blue linsey. The common Virginia militiamen wore blue hunting shirts with red fringe and blue overalls with red trim at the seams. The more elite rifle volunteers from that state wore purple linen hunting shirts and trousers. The men of the Orleans Rifle Company of Louisiana, however, took the prize for colorful clothing. They desired a long, caped hunting frock as the basis of their attire, but when it came time to begin manufacture, there was a scarcity of cloth in sufficient quantities. Not wanting to wait until a proper amount could be located they went ahead and had their frocks made of a blue and white checked fabric.[65]

1820s

The Army Regulations for 1821 sought to standardize the variety of uniforms then in service and specified that henceforth dress uniform coats were to be of dark blue "when a different one is not expressly prescribed." The enlisted infantryman's tailcoat was to be single breasted, with ten buttons down the front and wings set into the shoulder seams. The standing collar was four inches wide and had two blind buttonholes of white lace (yellow for artillerymen) on either side. Four buttons spaced an inch apart decorated the upper edges of the three-inch wide cuffs. The members of the Rifle Regiment wore green coats that, with a few exceptions, were cut similarly to those of blue. The most obvious difference was that they sported two additional rows of buttons down the front, giving them a "triple breasted" look. To go along with these coats, most men wore gray, woolen, ankle-length pantaloons during the winter months, and white woolen or cotton garments in the summer. The riflemen wore green pantaloons, the same color as their coats. Grey woolen jackets were specified for all men for fatigue duty. The troops wore black leather, bell-crowned shakoes, or, as they were sometimes derisively termed, "tar buckets" on their heads. Brass spread-winged eagles decorated the fronts of these hats, just below the colorful five-inch tall worsted pompoms. Most artillerymen sported yellow pompoms, although those designated light artillery had white pompoms with red tops. Similarly, infantrymen wore white pompoms, except for those in the light infantry formations, who wore yellow. The riflemen, as might be expected by now, wore green pompoms. All enlisted men wore tall lace-up boots that extended four inches above their ankles.[66]

The only uniform change of note after 1821 was the introduction, four years later, of a more comfortable hat. The shako was still prescribed for dress occasions, but

A blue wool forage cap, ca. 1825–1832. The wool cording radiating from the center of the cap is green, while the other trim is in the branch color. The wide brim is black leather. (*Courtesy of the Smithsonian*)

soldiers now had a cloth fatigue cap to wear while performing less formal duties. Also sometimes known as a forage cap or an undress cap, it was a dark blue cloth cap that sat rather low and flat on top of the head and had a leather bill in front. Twenty dark green cords of twisted worsted binding radiated from a button in the center of the top of the cap, and colored binding around the hatband designated the wearer's branch of service—white for infantry and yellow for artillery.[67]

1830s

Minor changes in uniform regulations ensued over the years, but the next major change occurred in the early 1830s. Gone was the heavy leather bell-crowned shako, replaced by a uniform cap with relatively straight sides approximately seven-and-a-half-inches tall. A new collapsible forage cap made of goatskin made its appearance about 1833. The long woolen tailcoat was still a component of the dress uniform but, for fatigue purposes, the soldier now clothed his upper body in a waist-length jacket, or roundabout. His campaign uniform also underwent a change in color. It was still blue, but not the dark blue of the dress uniform. Instead it was a light, sky blue. In the summer months, some men were lucky enough to have white cotton uniforms of the same cut as those of sky blue. With the exception of the forage cap, which changed again about 1839 to a simple dark blue wool cap with a black leather brim, this was the uniform of the regular U.S. soldier during the Mexican War. At least this was the regulation uniform for those troops.

One army officer, at least, detested the change. Colonel George Croghan urged a return to the uniform of the War of 1812. He thought that the use of the sky blue color for the trousers was a mistake because it was hard to find cloth of that hue on the frontier, in case replacement clothing was sought locally. When inspecting troops at Fort Crawford in 1842, he complained that the soldiers on parade with their dress uniforms, knapsacks, and other accoutrements looked ridiculous. He thought the tails of the coats were too long and that the addition of wings was also wasteful, because they made it difficult for a soldier to put on or take off his knapsack. It is curious that these soldiers were drilling in their dress uniforms instead of the short fatigue jackets they were authorized. He also found fault with the plain white cotton fatigue uniform worn by the dragoons, preferring a darker color. "The present white is so easily soiled," he reported, "that in 10 minutes after the men are mounted, it becomes, by the rubbing of the horses against each other, so stained as to become offensive to the sight."[68]

1840s

At the onset of the war with Mexico, the Army's Quartermaster Department did not have enough uniforms in stock to clothe the thousands of volunteers who rushed to enlist and, therefore, made no effort to do so. Instead, the government added an additional $3.50 per month to the salaries of these instant soldiers in lieu of furnishing them with uniforms. That way, they could wear whatever they wanted to wear. Each company of men was given the latitude to select whatever cut and color of uniform it wanted. This left the way open for a veritable rainbow of raiment.

Since militia companies sometimes enlisted en masse, they simply wore the uniforms they already had on hand. And although some of them wore close approximations of the regular uniform, many others did not. One of the volunteer companies in the Alabama regiment marched off to war wearing green worsted frock suits, and another adopted straw hats in place of the wool cloth caps of the regulars. The men of Colonel Jefferson Davis's Mississippi regiment had traditional dark blue dress uniforms as well as others that were made from striped cloth. The Indiana adjutant general published a set of uniform guidelines that suggested that volunteers from that state select trousers and double-breasted frock coats of light blue or blue-gray material. Since this was only a suggestion, however, Hoosier volunteers were free to choose any uniform that struck their fancy. The men in at least one of the Indiana companies had their distinctive uniforms fashioned from gray cashmere trimmed in black velvet, and the entire Massachusetts regiment also chose gray as its preferred uniform color.[69]

A fair number of volunteer soldiers went off to war, as had some of their predecessors in 1812, in civilian clothing—no uniform at all. In many cases, it was less a rebellion against conformity than it was a situation of not wanting to wait for their chosen uniforms to be manufactured before they began active service. The South Carolina volunteers, for example, contracted with a New York firm to produce their uniforms and deliver them to Charleston before the troops set sail for Mexico. The clothing was duly fabricated and put aboard a ship bound for the South Carolina port. The ship and its cargo, including the uniforms, however, were lost at sea. By this time, the Carolinians were ready to embark for the seat of war, so they ordered a second set of uniforms to be delivered to them in Mexico. This second shipment survived the vagaries of the long sea voyage, only to be stolen by Mexican bandits before it could be delivered. Not to be denied some sense of uniformity, the men decided that their "uniform" would henceforth consist of a long shirt belted at the waist and worn outside the trousers. Each company adopted a different color. One company wore blue-and-white striped shirts, another wore red flannel shirts, and so on throughout the regiment.[70]

Some volunteers, perhaps attempting to "save" the monthly uniform allotment, served their entire one-year enlistment in civilian clothing. The mounted volunteers from Missouri and Texas seem to fall into this category. One of the Show-Me State's volunteers recalled that "in a whole company, no two pair of pantaloons were of the

General Winfield Scott, "Old Fuss and Feathers," so called because he was fastidious about his dress, at about the time of the Mexican War. (*Courtesy of the Library of Congress*)

same hue; and there being few who owned a jacket, the red flannel or checked shirt made up the 'uniform.' Shoes were a luxury, and hats a very doubtful article." With regard to the Texas volunteers, an Illinois volunteer opined that "a more reckless, devil-may-care looking set, it would be impossible to find this side of the Infernal Regions." Another Midwesterner, perhaps subscribing to the maxim that one cannot judge a book by its cover, nevertheless felt that if the Texans' "good qualities at heart were to be judged by the good and fine clothing they wore, they would not make a very favorable impression among moral people. For a more outlandish-looking set of human white beings I never beheld."[71]

Many officers placed little importance on how they, or their troops, were dressed while on the march. Major General Zachary Taylor, who commanded the troops in northern Mexico, seldom wore his uniform, but instead favored comfortable civilian clothes. A civilian, working as a deck hand on a steamboat, was disappointed when he finally got a glimpse of this great man. The general looked "more like an old yankey Farmer than the General in command of the American Army," he observed. A volunteer officer was similarly unimpressed, describing Taylor as looking "more like an old farmer going to market with eggs to sell than anything I can now think of." Major General Winfield Scott was the sartorial antithesis of Taylor. It was no mere accident that Scott's nickname was "Old Fuss and Feathers." Always resplendent, Scott expected the officers on his staff to be equally fastidious when it came to dress. Among his rules was one that stated that officers were always to wear their coats while at his headquarters. And woe to the man who disobeyed! Late one hot night, long past bedtime, an officer in his shirtsleeves appeared at the darkened headquarters looking for a drink of water. He located it and was in the act of raising his cup to his lips, when he heard the gruff old general's voice out of the dark, ordering a nearby sentinel, "Take this man to the guardhouse." [72]

It is not surprising that many of the junior officers, at least among the volunteer regiments in Taylor's army, followed the example of those at the top of the chain of command. A lieutenant described himself on the march as wearing "a white oil silk cap—a blue check shirt—a red handkerchief round my neck—a pair of jeans pants stuffed into a pair of red cow-hide boots … a black leather sword belt in which hang my round-a-bout of jeans, & a Mexican gourd, with a half gallon of water." Although he admitted to wearing the prescribed uniform while on parade, one of his contemporaries said that the only time he wore his uniform was when he went to see his superior officers in town "and even then I may do as I please." Enlisted men likewise forsook uniform regulations and wore whatever clothing pleased them, or whatever they could obtain. A company officer in an Ohio regiment described the dress of the men under his command: "Their jackets are for the most part off, on their heads they have Mexican Hats, old white wool hats and some no hats or caps at all, one is carrying an old umbrella and another a large palm-leaf over him: some with their pantaloons over their boots and some with their boots in their hands and they taking it bare-footed."[73]

Active campaigning was also hard on clothing, even the rugged wool uniforms of the regular troops. The yearly clothing allowance for regulars included five pairs of overalls, two jackets, four shirts, two pairs of drawers, and four pairs of shoes and stockings. If they wore out these items any more frequently, they simply drew more from quartermaster stocks and had the costs deducted from their wages. The volunteers, however, had no such central stock for re-supply but had to rely on shipments from home or had to purchase from sutlers. "The sutlers get all of our money," complained one soldier. "The clothing that they bring out here is the refuse of every slipshop, which they buy at a mere trifle, and sell to the soldiers at an enormous price. Pants that cost them about seventy-five cents, they sell for four, five, and six dollars." Throughout the war, army quartermasters increased production of uniforms until, by mid-1847, there were enough uniforms on hand to start supplying volunteers with replacement clothing. These replacement items were generally of better quality than those provided by civilian sutlers, and cost less as well.[74]

Ironically, the availability of government-issue uniforms did not meet with wholesale acceptance among all the volunteer units. In late 1847, after the fall of Mexico City, a supply of new regulation uniforms arrived for issue to the Massachusetts volunteers stationed at Vera Cruz. The gray uniforms in which these men had proudly bade farewell to the Bay State some nine months earlier had now been reduced to a state of dirty remnants. The men had supplied themselves with a variety of replacement garments, such as straw hats and coats of various colors. In fact, many of them

The much-maligned Model 1851 cap. (*Courtesy of the Smithsonian*)

could hardly be identified as soldiers at all by their dress. General Caleb Cushing ordered new uniforms distributed to them and was surprised to observe considerable resistance among the men. Many of them had grown quite comfortable in their nondescript rags and felt no need to spend some of their uniform allotment on, of all things, new uniforms. Most of the men soon gave in, but one company was obstinate. These men absolutely refused to accept the new uniforms. The general, brooking no insubordination, ordered them disarmed and thrown into the prison in the notorious San Juan de Uloa Castle, on a coral reef just off the coast. After less than a full day on bread and water, even these men gave in.[75]

A regular officer who observed these actions believed that the men's reluctance to accept the new uniforms was because their original uniforms, like those of many of the volunteers, set them apart from the regulars. "This was entirely unnecessary," wrote the officer unsympathetically, "as they were easily to be distinguished from all others … by their 'General rowdy appearance,' and ignorance of a *Soldier's duty*."[76]

By the end of the war, the once-colorful volunteers were, if anything, even more distinctive. A Virginian, for example, once proud of his handsome dark blue frock coat and pants, saw the end of his enlistment with neither. His pants had seen a solid three months of use, and even though he still had two fairly substantial shirts and a pair of shoes, he was entirely bereft of socks and underwear. An Illinoisan, after almost a year of campaigning, noticed similarities within his company. "Nothing is more original," he wrote, "than the present condition of our army … some [men] are wearing hats, others caps, jackets, dress coats, etc. There are no two uniforms alike in the company." Even the civilian clothes in which some men campaigned had undergone a transformation. Meeting some of Colonel Alexander Doniphan's heavily bearded Missouri Volunteers near the end of their service, an observer proclaimed: "If you can imagine a man about six feet two to four and a half inches high, well proportioned, with a deer skin (hair on) hunting shirt and pantaloons, the seams fringed with the same material cut into strings, and a bear skin stretched across his face with nothing but eye holes cut in it, you can see a large portion of Doniphan's Regiment."[77]

1850s

Within a few years of the end of the fighting in Mexico, Army authorities adopted a new uniform. And with the drastic reduction in the size of the army following the end of hostilities, the Office of Army Clothing and Equipage, near Philadelphia, was once again able to keep up with the demand. Dark blue was still considered to be the standard color for uniforms, although soldiers continued to wear sky blue trousers until 1858. One major change in the uniform was that specifications called for the dress coat to be a dark blue, single-breasted frock coat reaching halfway from the soldier's waist to his knees. Gone was the "claw hammer," or tailcoat, of earlier times. For fatigue purposes, the soldier continued to wear a short jacket that was virtually a frock coat without the skirts.

Perhaps the most distinctive new item of apparel authorized in the early 1850s was a new dark blue cloth dress cap, following the lead of the French Army. This cap, or shako, stood about six inches tall and was stiffened by cardboard, or sometimes papier-mâché and was intended to replace the existing uniform cap and the forage cap. The top sloped slightly forward, and it featured a leather bill approximately two inches wide. A leather chinstrap served to hold the cap in place. And even though these caps were often issued with a separate, waterproof cover, they offered little protection against the sun and did not seem very practical for extended field use. One officer, writing to his sister from Oregon, described the new headgear as "rather a preposterous affair," and doubted "whether any of the officers will wear it until they are obliged to do so." Shortly after its introduction, fifty officers at nine different posts responded to questions about the new headgear and only fourteen expressed approval of the new design.[78]

In 1855, when two new cavalry regiments came into existence, the troopers received broad-brimmed hats instead of the shakoes. This followed successful field trials by the Second Dragoons, who found that the shade provided by the brims was of considerable value on the hot dusty plains of Texas. Within a few years, similar headgear was approved for the entire army. Called variously the "Jeff Davis" hat, after the Secretary of War, or the "Hardee" hat, after a dragoon captain who pushed for the new issue, the hat generally had a brim of three inches in width and an approximately six-inch crown with a flat top. One side was looped up and held in place by a brass eagle, and ostrich feathers adorned the opposite side. Worsted hat cords in branch colors—light blue for infantry, yellow for cavalry, and red for artillery—completed the adornments. These hats, as issued, also came in for a share of criticism. Mounted troops generally lamented the lack of chinstraps, while one individual believed that "if the whole earth had been ransacked, it is difficult to tell where a more ungainly piece of furniture could have been found." As actually worn in the field, however, these hats soon lost their parade ground appearance and served as good utilitarian headdress.[79]

The army, as an institution, was slow to embrace change, whether that change was in advanced weaponry or in the clothing its members wore. This may merely have reflected the tendency of officers and soldiers in the army to accept the status quo, to not "rock the boat." There are, however, in every organization a few "boat rockers," and Lieutenant

George Derby may have been one of these. When new uniform regulations were published in the 1850s, Derby took it upon himself to enlighten the readers of a west coast periodical with his own suggestions. Using the pseudonym "Squibob," Derby suggested in great, illustrated detail a new uniform feature that would be of great utility to both soldiers and their officers. It consisted of a hook that was somehow attached to the seat of the trousers. Officers were to be furnished a long pole with a similar hook on the end. Then, when an officer commanded his men to "wheel right" or "wheel left," he could ensure a picture-perfect result by merely sliding his pole through the hooks on the back sides of the front rank of men, keeping them all in alignment with one another. Similarly, if, during a battle, a soldier should attempt to run away, the officer had only to catch the hook on his trousers with the hook on the end of the pole to prevent his escape. A marching column of men could use the hook to hang some of their baggage, such as camp kettles. And Squibob did not forget the cavalrymen. He proposed that a similar hook be affixed to the cantles of the saddles, so that even a poor horseman could retain his seat on a fractious mount. Needless to say, Squibob's suggested modifications never saw the light of day.[80]

Contemporary accounts left by soldiers serving on the western frontier suggest that the wearing of the regulation uniform marked an occurrence of some rarity. It is likely that the men donned their complete uniforms for parade or other such occasions; when on campaign, however, they appear to have had a considerable amount of leeway with regard to their clothing, particularly as uniform articles wore out. "You should see us here in our prairie outfits," wrote an infantryman to his parents in 1857. "Don't imagine a uniform. Every man is wearing a broad-brimmed hat, each of a different color; white trousers of rough material; a woolen shirt of red, green, blue, or brown—in short, of any and every color, usually open in front and worn like a coat." A couple of months later, this same man wrote to his parents:

> By this time you have probably received my photograph. I hope so, for if ever I resembled a white man it must have been last winter. Now no one would recognize me, bearded, sunburnt, long hair, clothes whose original color is unrecognizable, and a hat that any man would call a boot but for the fact that it is worn on the head. Such is the appearance of all who live a few months on these prairies.[81]

Nor were officers immune to the tendency to dress more for comfort than per regulations. A captain on the Texas frontier in 1855 described his dress as consisting of "corduroy pants; a hickory or blue flannel shirt, cut down in front, studded with pockets and worn outside [the trousers]; a slouched hat and long beard, cavalry boots worn over the pants, knife and revolver belted to the side and a double barrel [shot]gun across the pommel." This was, he continued a "costume as truly serviceable as it is unmilitary." Another Texas-based officer chose to wear a black sombrero rather than the regulation head gear and a gray coat instead of a blue one.[82]

Necessity, it is commonly said, is the mother of invention. For soldiers serving on the frontier, when it came to their clothing, necessity was the mother of improvisation. This was never more so than during the frigid winter months of the northern plains. One soldier described what was probably typical winter garb in South Dakota. He wore a headgear made of a wolf skin instead of the regulation cap. His coat was of deerskin, and he wore trousers that were made of the skin of a buffalo calf, worn with the fur to the inside. He wore two pairs of moccasins. The inner pair was of deerskin but, for particularly cold weather, he wore a second pair on top of these. This outer pair, slightly

James D. Elderkin, 4th U.S. Infantry, 1851. His uniform features about twice the number of buttons specified, and his chevrons are also personalized. (*From James D. Elderkin,* Biographical Sketches and Anecdotes of a Solider of Three Wars, as Written by Himself; *Detroit:1899*)

larger in size, was made of tougher buffalo calf hide with the fur turned to the inside for additional warmth. At about the same time, the men of the Utah Expedition were dealing with similarly miserable weather conditions in their winter camp and looking forward to spring. "We are coming to be short of clothing," one officer wrote. "The men go about in pantaloons patched with pieces of cast off coats, of a darker blue, and some bits of blanket. For stockings, many have adopted the sleeves of coats, making an elbow, like a stove-pipe, and sewing up one end for the toe. The shoes worn, many of them, as far past description as mending."[83]

In 1858, the last few changes in the Army's uniform before the Civil War were instituted. The first was in the color of the trousers. In spite of the added cost involved, Congress authorized trousers of dark blue, matching the color of the coats, to be issued to all troops. A new forage cap was also necessary. The one that had first been issued in 1839 was no longer available. Soldiers, instead, had had to make do with the unpopular dress shako after 1855. The new cap, in fact, was similar to the shako in that it shared the same approximate dimensions. The major difference was that only the crown of the new cap was stiffened, the sides being allowed to collapse forward. The biggest uniform change, however, was in the adoption of a new fatigue coat. It followed the fashion of coats long popular in the civilian world. These almost shapeless garments, known as sack coats, were much more comfortable than previous fatigue coats. They were short, coming only to just below the hips, and closed with only four buttons. Instead of the tight, standing collar of the earlier jackets, the sack-coat collars were more like ordinary shirt collars.

In the decades leading up to the Civil War, American soldiers did not experience a tremendous amount of change in their lives with regard to such mundane matters as food, medical care, and clothing. The official army ration, although far from varied, was usually sufficient to keep body and soul together. And most soldiers found ways to supplement their diets, whether it was through hunting and fishing or by purchase from sutlers or other civilian suppliers. Soldiers injured in battle or victims of disease could reasonably expect to receive competent medical care—if they happened to be at a post that included a doctor among its garrison. The clothing issued to soldiers was generally serviceable, even if it was not always the most stylish. Even when changes to the uniform were adopted, it was the policy of the government to issue out all the old style items before beginning to issue the new.

NOTES

1. Norman Caldwell, "Civilian Personnel at the Frontier Military Post (1790–1814)," *Mid-America: An Historical Review*, 38, no. 2 (April 1956), 107n; *General Regulations for the Army of the United States, 1841*,—hereinafter *Army Regulations for 1841*—(Washington, D.C.: J. and G. S. Gideon, 1841), 17.

2. Albert J. Myer to James Walden, March 17 to April 4, 1855, in Albert J. Myer, " 'I Am Already Quite a Texan': Albert J. Myer's Letters From Texas, 1854–1856," edited by David A. Clary, *Southwestern Historical Quarterly,* 82, no. 1 (July 1978), 57.

3. Caldwell, "Civilian Personnel," 107n; *General Regulations for the Army*—hereinafter *Army Regulations* for 1821—(Philadelphia: M. Carey and Sons, 1821), 264; *Army Regulations for 1841,* 261; *Regulations for the Army of the United States, 1857*—hereinafter *Army Regulations for 1857*—(New York: Harper and Brothers, 1857), 207.

4. Jacob Rhett Motte, *Journey Into Wilderness: An Army Surgeon's Account of Life in Camp and Field during the Creek and Seminole Wars,* 1836–1838, edited by James F. Sunderman (Gainesville, Florida: University of Florida Press, 1953), 13.

5. William W. Thackera, "William Wood Thackera, [Pennsylvania] Volunteer in the War of 1812," edited by Anne Castrodale Golovin, *Pennsylvania Magazine of History and Biography,* 91 (July 1967), 316–317.

6. W. M. Albin to George B. Claver, January 15, 1846 [1847], W. M. Albin Collection, Beinecke Library at Yale University, New Haven, Connecticut.

7. George Croghan, *Army Life on the Western Frontier: Selections from the Official Reports Made Between 1826 and 1845 by Colonel George Croghan,* edited by Francis Paul Prucha, (Norman, Oklahoma: University of Oklahoma Press, 1958), 87; Albert Tracy, "The Utah War: Journal of Albert Tracy, 1858–1860," *Utah Historical Journal,* 13 (1945), 1–2 (quotation).

8. James Mahon to his wife, Margaret, September 2, 1846, James Mahon Papers, Illinois State Historical Society Library, Springfield, Illinois (1st quotation); John T. Sprague, "Macomb's Mission to the Seminoles: John T. Sprague's Journal Kept during April and May 1839," edited by Frank T. White, Jr., *Florida Historical Quarterly,* 35, no. 2 (October 1956), 137 (2d quotation); James A. Bennett, *Forts and Forays: A Dragoon in New Mexico, 1850–1856,* edited by Clinton E. Brooks and Frank D. Reeve (Albuquerque: University of New Mexico Press, 1948), 5 (3d quotation).

9. Henry S. Hamilton, *Reminiscences of a Veteran* (Concord, New Hampshire: Republican Press Association, 1897), 72–73 (1st quotation), 33 (2d quotation).

10. John W. Phelps, "Diary of Captain Phelps," *The Utah Expedition 1857–1858: A Documentary Account of the United States Military Movement Under Colonel Albert Sidney Johnston, and the Resistance by Brigham Young and the Mormon Nauvoo Legion,* edited by Leroy R. Hafen and Ann W. Hafen (Glendale, California: Arthur H. Clark, 1958), 110 (1st quotation); Tracy, "The Utah War: Journal of Albert Tracy, 11 (2d quotation).

11. Lindorf Ozburn to his wife Liza N. Ozburn, July 10, 1847, Lindorf Ozburn Letters, Illinois State Historical Library, Springfield, Illinois (1st quotation); Frank S. Edwards, *A Campaign in New Mexico* (Philadelphia: Carey and Hart, 1847; reprint, Ann Arbor, Michigan: University Microfilms, 1966), 29 (2d quotation); R. S. Ewell, *The Making of a Soldier: Letters of General R. S. Ewell,* edited by Percy Gatlin Hamlin (Richmond, Virginia: Whittet and Shepperson, 1935), 45 (3d quotation); Eugene Bandel, *Frontier Life in the Army 1854–1861,* translated by Olga Bandel and Richard Jente, edited by Ralph P. Bieber, (Glendale, California: Arthur H. Clark, 1932), 79 (4th quotation), 202, 198; Edwards, *A Campaign in New Mexico,* 29 (5th quotation); Nathan Boone, "Captain Nathan Boone's Journal," edited by W. Julian Fessler, *Chronicles of Oklahoma,* 7 (1929), 70 (6th quotation).

12. James Allen, "Captain James Allen's Dragoon Expedition From Fort Des Moines, Territory of Iowa, in 1844," *The Iowa Journal of History and Politics,* (January 1913), 94 (1st quotation); "Journal of the Atkinson-O'Fallon Expedition," edited by Russell Reid and Clell G. Gannon, *North Dakota Historical Quarterly,* 4 (October 1929), 40 (2d quotation).

13. John W. Stout to W. H. H. Terrell, September 3, 1847, William Henry Harrison Terrell Collection, Indiana Historical Society Library, Indianapolis, Indiana; George B. McClellan, *The Mexican War Diary of George B. McClellan,* edited by William Starr Myers (Princeton, New Jersey: Princeton University Press, 1917), 57 (1st quotation); DeWitt Clinton Loudon diary, August 15, 1846, DeWitt Clinton Loudon Collection, Ohio Historical Society Library, Columbus, Ohio (2d quotation); Joshua Jackson diary, October 15, 1846, Joshua Jackson Collection, Illinois State Historical Library, Springfield, Illinois (3d quotation); Cromwell Pearce, " 'A Poor But Honest Sodger': Colonel Cromwell Pearce, the 16th U.S. Infantry, and the War of 1812," edited by John C. Fredriksen, *Pennsylvania History,* 52 (July 1985), 158n (4th quotation).

14. John H. Fonda, "Early Wisconsin," *Report and Collections of the State Historical Society of Wisconsin,* 5, part 2 (1868), 251 (1st quotation); Percival G. Lowe, *Five Years a Dragoon ('49 to '54) And Other Adventures on the Great Plains* (Norman, Oklahoma: University of Oklahoma Press, 1965), 107 (2d quotation); Anonymous, "Reminiscences of Some Incidents in the Career of an United States Dragoon Between the Years 1839 and 1844," *Texas Quarterly 9,* no. 3 (Autumn 1966), 12 (3d quotation); Edwards, *A Campaign in New Mexico,* 34; "Journal of the Atkinson-O'Fallon Expedition," edited by Russell Reid and Clell G. Gannon, *North Dakota Historical Quarterly,* 4 (October 1929), 24.

15. Motte, *Journey Into Wilderness,* 177 (1st quotation); James W. Covington, "Life at Fort Brooke, 1824–1836," *The Florida Historical Quarterly,* 36 (1957–1958), 321–322; Reynold M. Wik, "Captain Nathaniel Wyche Hunter and the Florida Indian Campaigns, 1837–1841," *Florida Historical Quarterly,* 39 (1960), 72 (2d quotation).

16. G. H. Crosman to General Dearborn, August 7, 1845, Mexican War Letters, University of Texas Archives, Austin, Texas (1st quotation); Frank Clarke to his sister Caroline M. Clarke, October 10, 1845, Frank Clarke Collection, Beinecke Library at Yale University, New Haven, Connecticut (2d quotation).

17. *Army Regulations for 1821,*71; Richard Dalzell Gamble, "Garrison Life at Frontier Military Posts, 1830–1860," (Ph.D. diss., University of Oklahoma, 1956), 137–138; Charles Fairbanks, "A New Hampshire Volunteer in the War of 1812: The Experiences of Charles Fairbanks," edited by John C. Fredricksen, *Historical New Hampshire,* 40 (Fall-Winter 1985), 177; J. McDougal to *Indiana Democrat,* published August 28, 1846, in Oran Perry, compiler, *Indiana in the Mexican War,* (Indianapolis: William B. Burford, 1908), 86; Alan Culpin, "A Brief History of Social and Domestic Life Among the Military in Wyoming, 1849–1890," *Annals of Wyoming,* 45, no. 1 (Spring 1973), 98.

18. Henry Edwards journal, Henry Edwards Collection, Indiana Historical Society Library, Indianapolis, Indiana; S. F. Nunnelee, "Alabama in Mexico War," *Alabama Historical Quarterly,* 19 (1957), 420 (quotation).

19. *Army Regulations for 1821, 73; Army Regulations for 1841,* 36–37; Motte, *Journey Into Wilderness,* 38.

20. T. H. Towner to his mother, March 25, 1848, Benjamin T. Towner Collection, Special Collections Department, William R. Perkins Library, Duke University; Samuel Steele to William Keller, December 6, 1847, Samuel Steele Collection, Indiana Historical Society Library, Indianapolis, Indiana; Sydenham Moore diary, December 20, 1846, Alabama Department of Archives and History, Montgomery, Alabama; Levi White to his wife, October 10, 1846, Levi White papers, Filson Club, Louisville, Kentucky (quotation); Zo S. Cook, "Mexican War Reminiscences," *Alabama Historical Quarterly,* 19 (1957), 442.

21. "Journal of the Atkinson-O'Fallon Expedition," edited by Russell Reid and Clell G. Gannon, *North Dakota Historical Quarterly,* 4 (October 1929), 27; J. R. McClanahan to his sister, October 25, 1846, McClanahan-Taylor Papers, Southern Historical Collection, Library of the University of North Carolina at Chapel Hill (1st quotation); Will Wallace to Helen M. Indson, November 16, 1846, Wallace-Dickey Collection, Illinois State Historical Library, Springfield, Illinois (2d quotation); Levi Wilson to his wife Sarah, September 12, 1846, Levi White papers,

Filson Club, Louisville, Kentucky; James H. Simpson, *Navaho Expedition: Journal of a Military Reconnaissance from Santa Fe, New Mexico to the Navaho Country Made in 1849 by Lieutenant James H. Simpson,* edited by Frank McNitt (Norman, Oklahoma: University of Oklahoma Press, 1964), 156 (3d quotation).

22. Joseph Gardner Andrews, "A Surgeon's Mate at Fort Defiance: The Journal of Joseph Gardner Andrews For the Year 1795," edited by Richard C. Knopf, *The Ohio Historical Quarterly,* 66, no. 1 (January 1957), 84 (1st quotation); George Rutledge Gibson, *Journal of a Soldier Under Kearny and Doniphan, 1846–1847,* edited by Ralph P. Bieber (Glendale, California: Arthur H. Clarke, 1935; reprint, Philadelphia: Porcupine Press, 1974), 197 (2d quotation); John F. Bouldin to his brother James, May 3, 1847, James O. Bouldin papers, Special Collections Department, William R. Perkins Library, Duke University (3d quotation); Milton Jamieson, *Journal and Notes of a Campaign in Mexico: Containing a History of Company C, of the Second Regiment of Ohio Volunteers* (Cincinnati, 1849), 82–83 (4th quotation).

23. Quoted in Edward M. Coffman, *The Old Army: A Portrait of the American Army in Peacetime, 1784–1898* (New York and Oxford: Oxford University Press, 1986), 19 (1st quotation); Croghan, *Army Life on the Western Frontier,* 6 (2d quotation), 7 (3d quotation).

24. Paul L. Hedren, "On Duty at Fort Ridgely, Minnesota: 1853–1867," *South Dakota History,* 7 (Spring 1977), 178–179; Robert W. Frazer, "Army Agriculture in New Mexico, 1852–1853," *The New Mexico Historical Review,* 50, no. 4 (October 1975), 315, 318, 320, 328, 334.

25. James O. Breeden, "Health of Early Texas: The Military Frontier," *Southwestern Historical Quarterly* 80, no. 4 (April 1977), 370.

26. Eliza Johnston, "The Diary of Eliza (Mrs. Albert Sidney) Johnston: The Second Cavalry Come to Texas," edited by Charles P. Roland and Richard C. Robbins, *Southwestern Historical Quarterly* 60, no. 4 (April 1957), 492–493.

27. William G. Rothstein, *American Physicians in the Nineteenth Century: From Sects to Science* (Baltimore and London: Johns Hopkins University Press, 1972), 88–89; William Newnham Blane, *An Excursion Through the United States and Canada during the Years 1822–1823* (London: 1824), 159–160, as cited in Norman W. Caldwell, "The Frontier Army Officer, 1794–1814," *Mid-America: An Historical Review* 37, no. 2 (April 1955), 123 (1st quotation); F. Campbell Stewart, "An Anniversary Address Delivered before the New York Medical and Surgical Society, on the 3d of January, 1846," in Gert H. Brieger, ed., *Medical America in the Nineteenth Century: Readings from the Literature* (Baltimore and London: Johns Hopkins University Press, 1972), 66 (2d quotation).

28. Mary C. Gillett, *The Army Medical Department, 1775–1818* (Washington, D.C.: Center of Military History, United States Army, 1981), 151 (1st quotation); Mary C. Gillett, *The Army Medical Department, 1818–1865* (Washington, D.C.: Center of Military History, United States Army, 1987), 31 (2d quotation).

29. Gillett, *The Army Medical Department, 1775–1818,* 150; Gillett, *The Army Medical Department, 1818–1865,* 23.

30. Gillett, *The Army Medical Department, 1818–1865,* 23; 29th Congress, 2nd Session, Senate Document No. 1, "Report of the Surgeon General—December 9, 1846," 199; 30th Congress, 1st Session, Senate Ex Doc No. 1—"Report of the Surgeon General, November 23, 1847," 722.

31. Harvey E. Brown, comp. *The Medical Department of the United States Army from 1775 to 1873* (Washington, D.C.: Surgeon General's Office, 1873), 200.

32. John S. Haller, Jr., *American Medicine in Transition, 1840–1910* (Urbana, Chicago, and London: University of Illinois Press, 1981), 213.

33. Brieger, *Medical America in the Nineteenth Century,* 4.

34. Leon S. Bryan, Jr., "Blood-Letting in American Medicine, 1830–1892," *Bulletin of the History of Medicine,* 38 (1964), 519–520 (1st quotation); J. A. Hingeston, "The Neglect of the Use of Bleeding in the Treatment of Some of the Milder Ailments," *Association Medical Journal* 1 (1854), 266, as cited in John S. Haller, Jr., *American Medicine in Transition, 1840–1910* (Urbana, Chicago, and London: University of Illinois Press, 1981), 40 (2d quotation).

35. Henry Burnell Shafer, *The American Medical Profession 1783 to 1850,* (New York: Columbia University Press, 1936), 98; G. S. B. Hempstead, "Reminiscences of the Physicians of the First Quarter of the Present Century…," *Cincinnati Lancet and Clinic,* 40 (1878), 54–55, as cited in Rothstein, *American Physicians in the Nineteenth Century,* 46 (quotation).

36. Gillett, *The Army Medical Department, 1775–1818,* 191–192.

37. Gillett, *The Army Medical Department, 1818–1865,* 8.

38. Peter D. Olch, "Medicine in the Indian-Fighting Army, 1866–1890," *Journal of the West* 21, no. 3 (July 1982), 38; Gillett, *The Army Medical Department, 1818–1865,* 10; W. E. Horner, "A Military Hospital at Buffalo, New York, in the year 1814," *The Medical Examiner and Record of Medical Science,* New Series, No. 97 (January 1853), 10.

39. Gillett, *The Army Medical Department, 1775–1818,* 192.

40. John Gale to Willoughby Morgan, February 16, 1820, in Roger L. Nichols, "Scurvy at Cantonment Missouri, 1819–1820," *Nebraska History* 4 (1968), 340.

41. Gillett, *The Army Medical Department, 1775–1818,* 137; Gillett, *The Army Medical Department, 1818–1865*, 136; William A. Hammond, "Scurvy," *Military Medical and Surgical Essays Prepared for the United States Sanitary Commission,* edited by William A. Hammond, (Philadelphia: J. B. Lippincott, 1864), 175–176 (quotation); Nichols, "Scurvy at Cantonment Missouri, 1819–1820," 343, 346; Wilfred W. Black, "The Army Doctor in the Trans-Mississippi West, 1775–1860," *The Southwestern Social Science Quarterly* 24, no. 2 (1943), 126.

42. Gillett, *The Army Medical Department, 1818–1865,* 52; Black, "The Army Doctor in the Trans-Mississippi West, 1775–1860," 121.

43. Ramon Powers and Gene Younger, "Cholera on the Overland Trails, 1832–1869," *Kansas Quarterly*, 5 (Spring 1973), 32; Breeden, "Health of Early Texas," 380–381(quotation).

44. F. G. Smith and Alfred Stillé, "Vaccination in Armies," *Military Medical and Surgical Essays Prepared for the United States Sanitary Commission,* edited by William A. Hammond (Philadelphia: J. B. Lippincott, 1864), 152–155.

45. Gillett, *The Army Medical Department, 1775–1818,* 14, 191; Gillett, *The Army Medical Department, 1818–1865,* 15, 134–135.

46. Gillett, *The Army Medical Department 1775–1818,* 192 (1st quotation); _________ Massie? to Dr. Thomas Massie, February 28, 1848, Massie Family papers, Virginia Historical Society (2d quotation); Thomas N. Love to Mrs. Cannon, September 1847, Tennessee State Library and Archives (3d quotation).

47. James L. McClaughlin to James McLaughlin, Sr., September 5, 1846, McGlaughlin Family papers, Tennesse State Library and Archives, Nashville, Tennessee (1st quotation); R. H. Milroy to James W. Milroy, October 18, 1846, Mildred Knight Richardson Collection, Indiana State Library, Indianapolis, Indiana (2d quotation).

48. Gillett, *The Army Medical Department, 1818–1865,* 192 (1st quotation); _____ Massie to Thomas Massie, Feburary 28, 1848, Massie Family papers, Virginia Historical Society (2d quotation); Gillett, *The Army Medical Department, 1818–1865,* 18.

49. Gillett, *The Army Medical Department, 1775–1818,* 167; Gillett, *The Army Medical Department, 1818–1865,*8.

50. George McFeely, "Chronicle of Valor: The Journal of a Pennsylvania Officer in the War of 1812," edited by John C. Fredriksen, *The Western Pennsylvania Historical Magazine,* 67 (July 1984), 259; Charles W. Ayars, "Some Notes on the Medical Service of the Army, 1812–1839," *The Military Surgeon, Journal of the Association of Military Surgeons of the United States,* 50 (May 1922), 521–523 (quotation); Paul J. Schieps, "Albert James Myer, an Army Doctor in Texas, 1854–1857," *Southwestern Historical Quarterly,* 82, no. 1 (July 1978), 15; Gillett, *The Army Medical Department, 1818–1865,* 132.

51. *Army Regulation for 1821, 47; Army Regulations for 1841,* 15 (1st quotation); Bandel, *Frontier Life in the Army,* 134 (2d quotation).

52. Robert J. Moore, Jr. and Michael Haynes, *Tailor Made, Trail Worn: Army Life, Clothing & Weapons of the Corps of Discovery* (Helena, Montana: Farcountry Press, 2003), 62.

53. Moore and Haynes, *Tailor Made, Trail Worn,* 63; Donald R. Hickey, "Andrew Jackson and the Army Haircut: Individual Rights vs. Military Discipline," *Tennessee Historical Quarterly* 35 (1976), 368 (quotation); Moore and Haynes, *Tailor Made, Trail Worn,* 63–64.

54. *Army Regulations for 1841,* 393; Jesse A. Gove, *The Utah Expedition 1857–1858,* (Concord, New Hampshire: New Hampshire Historical Society, 1928), 24 (1st quotation); Ewell, *The Making of a Soldier,* 42 (2d quotation).

55. Hamilton Gardner, "Romance at Old Cantonement Leavenworth: The Marriage of 2d Lt. Philip St. George Cooke in 1830," *Kansas Historical Quarterly* 22, no. 2 (Summer 1956), 105.

56. Oscar F. Long, "Changes in the Uniform of the Army 1774–1895," http://www.qmfound.com/changes_in_the_army_uniform_1895.htm, 4, accessed November 21, 2003.

57. Moore and Haynes, *Tailor Made, Trail Worn,* 128.

58. Isaac Roach, "Journal of Major Isaac Roach, 1812–1824," *The Pennsylvania Magazine of History and Biography,* 17, no. 2 (1893), 142 (quotation); Alan D. Gaff, *Bayonets in the Wilderness: Anthony Wayne's Legion in the Old Northwest* (Norman, Oklahoma: University of Oklahoma Press, 2004), 227.

59. *Army Regulations for 1821,* 47.

60. *Army Regulations for 1841, 37; Army Regulations for 1857,* (New York: Harper and Brothers, 1857), 16; Gamble, "Garrison Life at Frontier Military Posts," 175–176; Theodore Talbot, *Soldier in the West: Letters of Theodore Talbot During His Services in California, Mexico and Oregon, 1845–53,* edited by Robert V. Hine and Savoie Lottinville, (Norman, Oklahoma: University of Oklahoma Press, 1972), 174 (quotation).

61. Moore and Haynes, *Tailor Made, Trail Worn, 68; Army Regulations for 1841,* 206.

62. [James Hildreth], *Dragoon Campaigns to the Rocky Mountains,* (New York: Wiley and Long, 1836; reprint, New York: Arno, 1973), 40 (quotation); *To Utah With the Dragoons and Glimpses of Life in Arizona and California 1858–1859,* edited by Harold D. Langley (Salt Lake City: University of Utah Press, 1974), 121.

63. René Chartrand, *Uniforms and Equipment of the United States Forces in the War of 1812* (Youngstown, New York: Old Fort Niagara Association, 1992), 18–19, 35.

64. Chartrand, *Uniforms and Equipment,* 31.

65. Chartrand, *Uniforms and Equipment,* 77–78, 61–62 (quotation), 66–67, 78; John Jackson, "'We Lay There Doing Nothing': John Jackson's Recollection of the War of 1812," edited by Jeff L. Patrick, *Indiana Magazine of History* 88 (June 1992), 116.

66. *Army Regulations for 1821,* 154–161.

67. Edgar M. Howell and Donald E. Klosterman, *United States Army Headgear to 1854: Catalog of United States Army Uniforms in the Collections of the Smithsonian Institution* (Washington, D.C.: Smithsonian Institution Press, 1969), 23.

68. Croghan, *Army Life on the Western* Frontier, 59–61.

69. Nunnelee, "Alabama in Mexico War," 417; Vicksburg (Mississippi) *Whig,* July 30, 1846, Jefferson Davis Papers, Rice University; Joseph Davis Howell to his mother, September 25, 1846, William Burr Howell and Family Papers, Mississippi State Archives; General Orders No. 2, June 4, 1846, in Oran Perry, comp. *Indiana in the Mexican War* (Indianapolis: William B. Burford, 1908), 25, 14; H. C. Duncan, "Monroe County in the Mexican War," *Indiana Magazine of History* 12, no. 4 (December 1916), 291; Romeyn B. Ayres journal, Romeyn Beck Ayres Collection, Southern Historical Collection, University of North Carolina at Chapel Hill; Jamieson, *Journal and Notes of a Campaign in Mexico,* 27–28; Claude M. Fuess, *The Life of Caleb Cushing,* 2 vols. (New York: Harcourt, Brace, 1923), II, 55–56.

70. James Wylie Gettys, Jr., "'To Conquer a Peace': South Carolina and the Mexican War," Ph.D. diss. (University of South Carolina, 1974), 191, 242.

71. Edwards, *A Campaign in New Mexico,* 99 (1st quotation); Samuel Chamberlain, *My Confession: The Recollections of a Rogue* (1956; repr.; Lincoln, Nebraska: University of Nebraska Press, 1987), 39 (2d quotation); Jamieson, *Journal and Notes,* 28 (3d quotation).

72. Allan Peskin, *Winfield Scott and the Profession of Arms* (Kent, Ohio and London: Kent State University Press, 2003), 126 (3d quotation).

73. Will Wallace to Helen M. Indson, August 18, 1846, Illinois State Historical Library; John Campbell to his mother, July 30, 1847, John Campbell letters, University of Virginia Library (1st quotation); John W. Lowe to O. T. Fishback, November 1, 1847, John Williamson Lowe Collection, Dayton and Montgomery County Public Library (2d quotation).

74. *Army Regulations for 1841,* 209; Federal Writers Project, *Military History of Kentucky* (Frankfort: Works Progress Administration, 1939), 132 (quotation).

75. Fuess, *The Life of Caleb Cushing,* II, 55–56.

76. Romeyn B. Ayres journal, Romeyn B. Ayres Collection, Southern Historical Collection, Library of the University of North Carolina at Chapel Hill.

77. T. H. Towner to his father, July 4, 1848, Benjamin T. Towner collection, Duke University; Chamberlain, *My Confession,* 122–123 (1st quotation); Nelson McClanahan to John R. McClanahan, June 19, 1847, Taylor-McClanahan collection, University of North Carolina library (2d quotation).

78. Frederick P. Todd, *American Military Equipage 1851–1872,* Providence, Rhode Island: The Company of Military Historians, 1974, 61; Talbot, *Soldier in the* West, 168 (quotation); Howell and Klosterman, *United States Army Headgear to* 1854, 64.

79. Todd, *American Military Equipage 1851–1872,* 62; Robert M. Utley, *Frontiersmen in Blue: The United States Army and the Indian, 1848–1865* (Lincoln and London: University of Nebraska Press, 1981), 24.

80. Erasmus D. Keyes, *Fifty Years' Observations of Men and Events Civil and Military* (New York: Charles Scribner's Sons, 1884), 199–200.

81. Bandel, *Frontier Life in the Army,* 124 (1st quotation), 127 (2d quotation).

82. Utley, *Frontiersmen in* Blue, 24 (quotation); Albert J. Myer, "'I Am Already Quite a Texan': Albert J. Myer's Letters From Texas, 1854–1856," edited by David A. Clary, *Southwestern Historical Quarterly* 82, no. 1 (July 1978), 63.

83. Bandel, *Frontier Life in the Army,* 125; Albert Tracy, "The Utah War Journal of Albert Tracy 1858–1860," *Utah Historical Journal,* 13 (1945), 1 (quotation).

5 MILITARY DISCIPLINE

Boredom, at least to some degree, was a permanent fixture in a soldier's life except, perhaps, while on an active campaign. For most troops, however, their daily routine of duties left them a fair amount of time to themselves—time that some spent in activities that put them afoul of military laws.

BASIS OF THE MILITARY JUSTICE SYSTEM

Throughout the nineteenth century, and indeed well into the twentieth, the basis of military law was a document called the *Articles of War*. The need for such legal guidance was immediately obvious to the men who sat in the Second Continental Congress, and they wasted no time in setting up a committee to draft such a document. On June 14, 1775, the Congress selected George Washington, a delegate from Virginia and the man it had chosen to lead the fledgling Continental Army, to chair the committee. Using as guides the current code of the British Army and one drawn up a year earlier by Massachusetts, the committee, within two short weeks, produced a list of sixty-nine articles, which detailed a wide range of offenses and punishments likely to be encountered within the military, as well as the desired composition of courts-martial. These articles served to outline the military justice system for the next fifteen months. During that time, however, such a number of instances arose that had not been foreseen by the drafters of the document that Congress took another stab at it. On September 20, 1776, Congress published an expanded, revised *Articles of War,* which contained just over a hundred such articles. Legislative modifications occurred over the next three decades and, in 1806, the much-amended articles were reissued for the last time prior to the Civil War.

PROCEDURE

Of course, every soldier accused of a violation of the *Articles of War* was first to have his day in court. The military judicial system was hierarchical, based upon the gravity of the alleged offense. The commanding general of an army, for example, could call for a general court-martial to hear a particularly serious case. Examples of such crimes included murder, desertion, mutiny, and any other offense that the *Articles of War* specified as meriting the death penalty upon conviction. These courts usually met at large military bases and consisted of thirteen commissioned officers—although as few as five would suffice. For less serious offenses, the accused faced regimental, or garrison, courts-martial, made up of only three relatively lower ranking officers. In 1855, another layer was added, that of summary courts-martial. These courts usually consisted of one officer passing judgment on an enlisted man accused of some minor offense, perhaps not even specifically listed among the *Articles of War*. By that time, too, some company first sergeants had begun to institute legal proceedings whereby three noncommissioned officers heard minor cases within their respective company. Typically, these were minor offenses at small outposts and often resulted in such punishments as having to do an extra turn of guard or fatigue duty. An immediate benefit of these quasi-official proceedings was that convicted wrongdoers quickly served their sentences and returned to duty, rather than waiting in the guardhouse until the necessary number of officers could be rounded up for more formal hearings.[1]

Some officers undoubtedly looked forward to being called for occasional court-martial duty, if it meant traveling from a small frontier post to a larger one. It gave them a break from routine duties and a chance to renew old friendships within the officer corps. On the other hand, when this duty stretched into weeks, as it sometimes could, the novelty probably wore off.

The enlisted man facing a formal court-martial found himself in the midst of a daunting situation. No true jury of his peers would determine his fate because all members of the court were officers. And some officers probably had an inborn prejudice against the lowly, enlisted men. In 1852, for example, a court-martial was being convened in Oregon Territory to try a man who, if guilty, faced the possibility of a death penalty. As officers were being selected for court duty, they were asked if they had "any conscientious scruples as to punishment by death." One prospective jurist admitted that he had no conscience. Another stated very emphatically that he was opposed to the death penalty. (It seems that he was under an indictment for murder at the time.) And a third claimed to have "formed no opinion and had no prejudices," although he did believe that the prisoner before them ought to be hanged.[2]

One of the officers of the court, deemed the judge advocate, had the dual, and seemingly contradictory, responsibilities of serving as the chief prosecutor and as legal counsel for the defendant (although any officer who had preferred charges against the defendant could assume the role of government prosecutor). The judge advocate's legal advice to the accused did not consist of aiding in his defense strategy so much as ensuring a fair proceeding. Realizing that the defendant would likely not have any legal training, the judge advocate protected the rights of the defendant by such actions as registering an objection on his behalf, if one of the members of the court asked a leading question of a witness. He was also on the alert to remind the defendant that he did not have to answer any question if his answer might incriminate him. The accused was allowed to hire an attorney when defending himself against charges, but such help was usually beyond his financial means. In the rare instance where he could obtain such counsel, his lawyer was not allowed to question witnesses or, in fact, to take any actual part in the trying of the case. He was there solely to advise his client. Such a civilian lawyer, according to one contemporary guide to military law, "is not recognised by a court martial, though his presence is tolerated as a friend of the prisoner, to assist him by advice in preparing questions for witnesses, in taking notes and shaping his defence." And most defendants probably needed some assistance, because all questions for witnesses had to be submitted in writing before the trial began.[3]

Serious cases might take several days to resolve, whereas others were relatively open-and-shut and could be conducted in a matter of hours—or even less. The procedure itself could become quite cumbersome, however, particularly when a member of the court held a rather inflated opinion of his own skills as jurist. An officer serving in Texas in the early 1850s has left a description of such an event:

> Ever and anon some member of the court, who thought He was gifted with some superior intuition, would object to one of the questions put by the judge advocate, and the court would look around to see if anyone seconded the objection. If nobody seconded it, the presiding officer would say, "Do you insist upon your objection?" and if the officer said "Yes," then the court would order the accused to be taken out of the room by the guard with the bayonet who had him in charge. Then the door would be closed and an executive session would begin. The officer would fully state, his objection and the objection would be voted upon, the youngest in rank voting first. If it was decided that the question could be put, the accused was brought back, and the question put, and with deliberation answered. The result was that we made slow headway, but the method was in all respects observed. There is generally in every court-martial some simple, meager, vain fellow who wants to show off, and be conspicuous, and take a great deal of a part in the proceedings. He makes a court-martial as irritable and petulant a proceeding as can well be imagined. Every once in a while some member of the court would want to ask a question. So that member would write it down and hand it to the presiding officer. He would then stop the proceedings so he could read the question, and if he did not want to have it put he would ask the member if he insisted. If the member answered "Yes," out went the accused and the question was read and voted on by everyone present. At times every member of the court-martial would be writing questions, and they would be flooded onto the judge advocate. If the presiding officer thought a question all right he would send it down to the judge advocate to be asked. Then somebody on the court would object, having the right to object, then out would go the accused, under guard, and the matter would be discussed.[4]

After the presentation of all the evidence, both for and against the defendant, the judge advocate cleared the courtroom and polled the members of the court. Beginning with the most junior officer, each man registered his vote on whether the accused was guilty or not guilty. A simple majority of votes carried the day. If there were an even number of members in the court, a condition that the officers went to great lengths to avoid, and if their votes resulted in a tied verdict, the defendant stood acquitted.[5]

If the members of the court found the accused guilty, they then had to decide upon a sentence. Each officer, beginning with the most junior, registered his suggestion for a sentence. If the *Articles of War* fixed a specific penalty for the offense in question, the judges had no alternative than to recommend that penalty. In all other instances, however, there was a considerable amount of leeway. Judges who voted for acquittal undoubtedly had a difficult time when it came to the penalty phase because, even though they had not been convinced of the defendant's culpability, they were expected to recommend a punishment that was in keeping with the severity of the crime of which the defendant had been found guilty. The judge advocate recorded the proposed sentences, and if the majority of the court favored any particular one, then that was the sentence imposed. If no particular punishment received a majority vote, the members of the court discussed each recommended penalty, beginning with the mildest, until they found one that most of them agreed upon. The only case in which a simple majority vote for a particular punishment was insufficient was when that punishment was death. A death sentence required the vote of two-thirds of the members of the court.

CRIMES

The sentences that the *Articles of War* prescribed for various offenses were, in most cases, very open-ended. The courts retained a great deal of freedom in determining the appropriate penalties for most offenses. Under the original *Articles,* there was only one infraction that mandated the death penalty, and a couple more that made it an option. "Whatsoever officer or soldier," Article 25 read, "shall shamefully abandon any post committed to his charge, or shall speak words inducing others to do the like, in time of an engagement, *shall suffer death immediately*." [Emphasis added.] If, however, a commanding officer was forced to surrender by those officers and soldiers under his command it was they, not he, who would be punished. In that instance, according to Article 31, they were to "suffer death, *or such other punishment as may be inflicted upon them by the sentence of a court martial*." [Emphasis added.] Likewise, anyone who gave the watch-word (or password) to someone who was not entitled to know it was liable to be executed if that was the judgment of a court-martial. In contrast, the only offense listed in the revised *Articles* that demanded the ultimate penalty was one that, by definition, could only occur while the army was campaigning outside of the United States. In such circumstances, it was quite common for an officer to post guards over various sorts of civilian property. These properties might range from simple dwellings to commercial establishments to churches. If a soldier ignored these sentries and entered into the posted premises—perhaps bent on rape or pillage—he committed the crime of "forcing a safeguard," and the 55th Article left no judicial leeway in arriving at a sentence. A man thus found guilty "shall suffer death."[6]

Mutiny

In addition, courts-martial *could* assign the death penalty for a dozen other offenses—including those in the original document. For example, anyone who caused or participated in a mutiny or who, in the presence of such an event, did not try to stop it could forfeit his life. One problem with this was that there was no clear definition of just what constituted a mutiny, and some officers' interpretations were more than a little liberal. During the later stages of the Mexican War, for example, three Illinois volunteers sent a petition to their colonel asking that the men of their company be allowed to elect replacements for some officers who had left the service. The company commander, however, believed that he should be the one to name replacements and looked upon this petition as an effort on the part of his men to usurp his rightful authority. He promptly arrested them for mutiny! At approximately the same time, a potentially more serious event occurred: an entire company of volunteers from Massachusetts refused to accept new uniforms. Their enlistments were almost over, and they resented being forced to lay out money for clothing that would only be of use to them for a short time. They, too, were charged with mutiny.[7]

The most serious example of mutiny during the antebellum years also occurred during the war with Mexico, and, like the previous examples, involved state volunteers rather than regular soldiers. The men of the North Carolina regiment, who were brigaded with soldiers from Mississippi and Virginia, had grown restive under the authoritarian rule of their colonel, Robert T. Paine. In the summer of 1847, Colonel Paine had had a tall wooden structure resembling a sawhorse erected in his camp as an instrument of punishment for those who committed minor infractions. The unfortunate soldier had to straddle the horizontal beam of this "horse" for varying periods of time, and it was not only quite uncomfortable but a source of ridicule as well.

On the night of August 14, while Colonel Paine was absent from camp, about a hundred men from the other two regiments of the brigade entered the camp of the North Carolinians and destroyed the wooden horse. The next evening, a large group of Virginians strolled through the camp and shouted insults at the colonel as they filed past his tent. The irate colonel followed the men into their own camp, collared two of them, and marched them to the tent of their own commanding officer, Colonel John F. Hamtramck, for him to discipline. He then warned the Virginians to stay out of his camp. This only seemed to add fuel to the fire, however, and, a short time later, Paine was again chasing Virginians out of his camp after they had pelted his tent with rocks. Next, perhaps in an effort to ensure a reasonably peaceful slumber, he ordered an eight-man squad of North Carolinians to set up a protective perimeter around his tent. When two of the eight men refused to comply, he knew that the mutiny had now infected his own regiment. He ordered the arrest of the supposed ringleaders and returned to his tent.

Rocks again rattled off the canvas and, when Colonel Paine emerged, he saw that a large group of Virginians had defied his earlier order and had returned to his camp. He instructed one of his subordinates to order up a twenty-man contingent to escort the visitors back to their camp forcibly. As they began to disperse, however, he changed his mind and ordered them to halt, threatening to shoot if they did not. The mutinous volunteers felt reasonably certain that he would not actually pull the trigger, and one of them yelled at Paine: "Go to hell, God damn you." Another man taunted the colonel: "Shoot and be damned." And he did. The bullet passed through the hand of one of his own men and killed a Virginian. An uneasy peace followed.

The next day, almost all of the officers in the North Carolina regiment presented Colonel Paine with a petition asking him to resign. Brigadier General John Wool, one of the regular army's highest ranking officers, now stepped in and arbitrarily ordered that the first two names on the list of disgruntled officers be immediately dismissed from the service, with the same fate awaiting the rest unless they withdrew their petition. When President James K. Polk heard of this, he instructed that a military court convene and look into the matter. He did not approve of Wool's action, since it denied due process to the recalcitrant officers. After two months of deliberation, during which time the war ended and all of the volunteer officers and men were discharged, the court ruled that a mutiny had indeed occurred and that Colonel Paine's actions in opening fire on the mutineers had been entirely justified.[8]

Desertion

The most common behavior that qualified for the death penalty was desertion in times of war. Even in peacetime, however, if deserters were allowed to gain their freedom from military duties merely by sneaking away from their posts, it would have a very negative effect on the entire army. More men deserting meant fewer men to do the essential day-to-day work of maintaining a military encampment. When soldiers deserted from posts along the Indian frontier, they also potentially endangered their comrades who had been left behind. The editor of an English-language newspaper in Mexico City in early 1848 left no doubt in the minds of his readers about his opinion of deserters. "We can paint no man," he began, "however cursed by conscience and despised by all, so perfectly unmanned, so infamously degraded as the deserter. If all crimes were bundled together," he continued, "and stewed down into one they would not convey the strength of the blackest of all—DESERTER."[9]

The army did not treat lightly the offense of desertion and made significant efforts to apprehend runaway soldiers when it could. The government routinely offered rewards—thirty dollars during most of the nineteenth century—to anyone who captured fugitive soldiers. At posts where there was a reasonable certainty that the only punishment that would be given deserters was time in the guardhouse, soldiers occasionally conspired among themselves to gain these rewards. A soldier would desert, only to have his friend "capture" him and claim the reward. Then, perhaps a few months later, they would reverse roles. Just after the end of the Mexican War, when a volunteer officer and fifteen of his men deserted, a Mexican earned $5,000 when he captured and returned the lieutenant and the six remaining men who were free. In the early 1790s, the territorial governor of Tennessee was so concerned about possible deserters joining forces with the Cherokee that he added an additional incentive to the normal cash rewards. He promised an additional twenty dollars and a keg of whiskey to anyone who brought in a deserter. These rewards constituted significant amounts of money, and therefore invited abuse from unscrupulous civilians living in the environs of military camps and forts. A civilian, for instance, might convince an unhappy soldier to desert, only to then turn him in for the reward. After 1829, in an effort to cut down on this practice, no rewards were paid until after the runaway had been convicted by a court-martial. And in cases of citizens intentionally causing men to desert so they could turn them in for the reward, the citizen was often the only witness to the desertion. This obvious conflict of interest was not lost on the members of courts-martial.[10]

So seriously did army officials regard the crime of desertion that officers often instructed soldiers sent after deserters to either bring them back or kill them. A diarist at Fort Defiance in 1795 described one such instance. The officers at the fort enlisted two friendly Shawnee braves to go after a deserter. The Indians were to receive ten dollars for returning the soldier, or twenty dollars for bringing back his scalp. To probably no one's surprise, the pursuers chose the latter course of action. One of the braves claimed that he tried to convince the soldier to return, but he refused. The Indian then "being wearied with soliciting him [the deserter] to no purpose; shot him in the back as he attempted to fly, & knocked him in the head with a stone: He recd. 10 Dollars from Major Hunt & a like gratuity from Lieut. Pope; besides many compliments from the officers." Similarly, a decade later, after a man deserted from the Lewis and Clark Expedition, four men were dispatched to capture him. "If he did not give up Peaceibly [*sic*]," their orders were "to put him to death." In 1822, the colonel commanding the Sixth U.S. Infantry Regiment was quite blunt when issuing orders about the apprehension of deserters. "Should a deserter be overtaken," he began, "it will be well to take him alive, but better to shoot him than to let him escape. Hence, if he should not stand when hailed, or should attempt to make resistance, the Country will expect the pursuers to do their duty." Violence sometimes visited the deserters even before they were apprehended. In 1852, four soldiers in New Mexico grabbed up one musket and one pistol before heading for what they supposed would be their freedom. After a short time, the men began to argue over who should carry the weapons, whereupon, the man holding the pistol used it to kill one of his comrades. The other two men wrestled the gun away from him, when he tried to use it against them, and killed him with it. Nor did they make good their escape: they were captured and returned to their post to face charges of murder.[11]

Desertion during the antebellum period was a problem for which the Army never found a solution, although it was not due to a lack of effort. It even issued blanket pardons to all deserters in 1807 and again in 1810. A surprising number of men who deserted during peacetime—when the death penalty was not an option—and were later caught, took their punishments and were soon gone again. Some years the number of apprehended deserters who disappeared from the ranks a second time was as high as forty percent. One aspect of the problem that drew a lot of attention from contemporaries was monetary. Early nineteenth-century soldiers received enlistment bonuses. The amount received at the time of enlistment was approximately equal to one month's pay. A like amount was then paid when the soldier reached his first duty station, which could be as soon as a few weeks later. Some enlistees, therefore, saw this as a quick way to acquire cash. They simply signed up for a five-year enlistment, pocketed the bonus, and disappeared back into the civilian sector, perhaps to do the same thing again at a different recruiting location. In 1830, the secretary of war recommended that the bonus be withheld from the new soldier until he had actually been in the service for a period of several months. This, he believed, would discourage opportunists from enlisting with the intention of running away as soon as possible; a few years later, the government did away with the enlistment bonuses altogether.[12]

The other money issue had to do with when, or how often, a soldier received his pay. Military pay was almost always lower than what a working man could have earned in civilian life, but a soldier—at least theoretically—did not have to use part of his pay to buy food, pay rent, or purchase clothing. The Army fed him, housed him, and clothed him. Perhaps more important was the frequency with which the Army paid him. Regulations called for a payday every other month, but it was not at all uncommon for the paymaster to visit some of the more remote posts much less frequently than that. When the men had to wait long periods for their pay, they often went into debt to the company laundresses or the post sutler, each of whom might extend credit to the men. When the soldiers finally received their pay, they found that after they had settled their debts, they were left with almost no money and would become very discouraged with military life. More frugal soldiers might look upon their long overdue pay as windfalls when it finally materialized. Thinking themselves rich, they might wander into the nearest settlement and quickly spend the greater part of it on alcohol, gambling, or loose women. At any rate, civilian sharpers were usually more than willing to separate a soldier from his earnings in record fashion. Sometimes, soldiers in these situations gave in to feelings of frustration and unhappiness, which often accompanies empty pockets, and decided to leave the Army—to desert. One solution, as offered by an army colonel in 1833, was to pay the men every week or two instead of every two (or more) months, and to stop the practice of allowing sutlers to extend credit to soldiers. Being paid more frequently would mean that the soldiers would be less likely to squander all of their money and then face months with no replenishment in sight. Desertion would, therefore, be a less viable option. Implementation of such a program would have been costly, however, and this suggestion went unfulfilled.[13]

Another factor that seemed to play a part in the high percentage of desertion was the wide range of penalties assigned to those convicted of that crime. While regulations

A wooden punishment horse, ca. 1860. (© *Hulton Archive/Getty Images*)

generally permitted a court-martial to impose the death penalty for deserters, at least during wartime, it also gave the courts a tremendous amount of leeway. During the War of 1812, for example, one deserter's sentence was simply to ride the wooden horse for five minutes—certainly the most lenient penalty short of an outright pardon. Several others merely paid $2 fines. Three men had their pay cut by 80 percent, their liquor ration cut off entirely, and were to serve ten years at hard labor with balls and chains attached to their ankles. Yet another man lost four months' pay and was to ride the wooden horse for thirty minutes for three successive days, wearing his coat inside out, a large pair of wooden spurs, and a paper cap with the word "deserter" printed on it.[14]

General Andrew Jackson was a firm believer in corporal punishment and thought it absolutely necessary to prevent desertion. In 1821, the future president recommended that "for the first offense give 39 lashes, the second double them, and the third let them be shot—a few examples will remedy the disease." The same officer who recommended more frequent paydays shared this sentiment. He believed that the sentences for deserters should be more uniform: there should be no doubt in a soldier's mind that if he deserted and was caught, he would pay a price. "The *certainty*," he wrote, "rather than the *severity* of punishments operates as a preventive to crime, and thus with desertion." Nor was he advocating that this *certain* punishment be lenient. He strongly recommended that every convicted deserter should suffer the maximum number of lashes allowed by law, that he spend the rest of his enlistment in chains performing manual labor at military installations, and that he be branded on the shoulder, so that he could never again enlist in the Army. He foresaw that some would find this punishment rather too harsh, since it made no distinction between first-time offenders and recidivists. He answered such concerns by noting that "as for the future I would have no *second* desertions. I have but classed every case that may occur as of the same rank in point of enormity because they must all be of *first* occurrence."[15]

Sleeping on Guard Duty

Sleeping while on guard duty was another offense that had tremendous potential for disaster. An enemy force that came upon a camp, or even a permanent post, that lacked adequate security because one or more of the sentinels were asleep could produce truly calamitous results. For this reason, the sentry who gave in to sleep could earn the death penalty, but he seldom did. One common punishment was for the offender to stand on a tree stump for several hours, perhaps while wearing a placard inscribed with "For sleeping on my post." There were, of course, more severe penalties. During the War of 1812, a sentinel caught sleeping at his post spent the next two months riding the wooden horse twice a day for an hour, while another man spent a month at hard labor with a ball and chain attached to his ankle. A New Hampshire volunteer described what happened to a man in his regiment who committed the double sin of getting drunk and then falling asleep on guard duty. "He was sentenced to wear a ball and chain fastened to his ankle, for a month, and also to dig stumps, although the punishment is death for such a crime." As with other offenses, there was no uniformity with regard to sentences imposed on men found asleep at their posts. In 1803, at Fort Wayne, a soldier convicted of sleeping while on guard duty received a sentence of fifty lashes, but the punishment was never carried out. Barely a week later, another soldier, at the same post, for the same offense, was sentenced to 100 lashes, and this time there was no reprieve.[16]

Disrespect to Superiors

Perhaps the military crime that invited the most draconian punishment —death for the miscreant—was that of striking a superior officer, *or even threatening to do so*. No army, of course, would stay viable if it allowed its soldiers to abuse their superiors. Sometimes, however, the officers or noncommissioned officers (corporals and sergeants), who brought charges for such behavior, had themselves contributed to the situation. During the War of 1812, a sergeant and an enlisted man got into a scuffle. The sergeant repeatedly struck the soldier with a shovel, knocking him down. Only then did the man resort to frontier fighting and try to bite the sergeant's throat and gouge out his eye. In spite of testimony from both an officer and another enlisted man on his behalf, this soldier spent sixty days in solitary confinement for his attack. Courts, however, did not always side with the man of superior rank in instances such as this. A captain serving as officer of the day, apparently having overindulged in spirituous drink, lost his temper at three of his men. After raging at them with considerable venom, he ordered them to their quarters. The men, feeling that they had been unfairly victimized, set upon him and administered a rather sound beating. Because of the officer's actions preceding the attack, the court acquitted all three men.[17]

In late 1847, in northern Mexico, a Prussian-born soldier in an Illinois volunteer regiment violated this particular article of war. He had set up housekeeping with a local Mexican woman and arrived home one day to find his company commander in bed with her. The captain escaped any physical manifestation of the soldier's wrath, but a court-martial convicted the aggrieved immigrant of *threatening* to shoot the officer and sentenced *him* to be shot. One man was selected from each company of the North Carolina and the Virginia regiment to make up the firing party. As the condemned man awaited the volley of musketry, he enjoined his executioners to "Aim well." They did not. Although a score of muskets had fired from point blank range, he was only wounded. It required two more musket shots to the head to end his life.[18]

PUNISHMENTS

Executions

When a man was convicted of desertion, or other serious crime, and sentenced to death, his entire regiment—or maybe even his brigade—was ordered to witness the event. Generally, the spectators formed three sides of a square, facing inward. The offender stood in the open side of the square, perhaps adjacent to a freshly dug grave, and the firing party stood toward the center, just a few yards away from their target. There was no prescribed size of the firing party. It might consist of as few as three or as many as a dozen soldiers. Soldiers often shrank from this duty so, quite often, at least one of the muskets was loaded with a blank before being passed out to the men. That way, each man could believe that he was the one who had fired a harmless load of powder. If the existence of blank loads in one or more of the muskets did not offer enough balm to any one of the executioners, he might intentionally aim at a nonvital part of the condemned man's anatomy, or he might purposely pull his aim entirely off the target. Nevertheless, upon an officer's command, the men fired their muskets at the prisoner. In case the volley did not kill the man outright, a sergeant or an officer administered the *coup de grâce*. In one instance, during the Mexican War, none of the shots took fatal effect, and the man fell to the ground desperately wounded, but still alive. The officer in charge of the firing squad had two more muskets loaded and fired into the wounded man's head at point-blank range. Perhaps the most bizarre example of execution by firing squad took place in General Anthony Wayne's legion in the fall of 1792. Courts-martial found five men guilty of desertion and then handed down an unusual method of applying the sentence. The court ordered four of the men to be shot, *and the fifth man was to carry out the sentences!*[19]

Sometimes reprieves were given, but the condemned men usually did not learn of them until the very last minute. During the War of 1812, General Winfield Scott approved the death sentences of five of his men. Five graves were dug, five coffins provided, and each man knelt next to his own grave. Five separate firing parties of about a dozen men each took position and received loaded muskets from their officers. According to an eyewitness, each prisoner wore a white robe and cap and had a red target affixed to the center of his chest. Unknown to everyone except the officers, Scott had decided to spare one man, a mere boy. After a chaplain offered up a prayer, the men's caps were pulled down over their eyes and the command given to fire. When the combined volley roared forth, all five men fell. Four lay dead of their wounds, the fifth man had fainted with terror. As he regained consciousness, and realized that he had not even been scratched, he remarked, "By God I thought I was dead."[20]

Military courts often made a distinction between simple desertion and desertion to the enemy. The latter crime was much more reprehensible. Soldiers convicted of abandoning friends and country and going over to the other side usually faced hanging, a less honorable form of execution. Like execution by firing squad, however, hangings were also carried out in front of large crowds. During the Mexican War, this method was used on a very wide scale. American soldiers late in the war captured a large number of deserters who had enlisted in the Mexican Army. Fighting for the enemy was especially despicable, and, as one soldier related in a letter home, "We esteemed this capture as one of the best results of the day, for now examples would be made of the perjured villains for the benefit of the wavering."[21]

Courts-martial quickly handed down death sentences for seventy of these men. Commanding General Winfield Scott then faced the daunting task of reviewing each of these cases before allowing the executions to proceed. He pardoned five of them, including a couple of underage recruits and a sixty-year-old. He then reduced the sentences of fifteen more, for various reasons, leaving fifty to face the hangman's noose. Over the course of four days in September 1847, the executions were carried out.

Colonel William S. Harney was in charge of hanging the last thirty, and his behavior at that time probably reflected the feelings of most of the soldiers toward the turncoats. When the prisoners arrived at the execution site, there were only twenty-nine present. Upon inquiring, Harney learned that the other man had lost both of his legs during the battle in which he was captured and would undoubtedly die soon of his wounds. The colonel could not abide the fact that one of these traitors might escape his just deserts and ordered the crippled man brought forward anyway. Teamsters parked open wagons alongside one another, so that, as the condemned men stood in the backs of the wagons, they were all lined up underneath a long scaffold. Nooses were attached to each man, and, upon Harney's order, the draft animals were whipped into action, and the wagons sprang forward, leaving the deserters to strangle to death. (The man with no legs had been propped up in the bed of a wagon.) When all the executions were completed, someone asked Colonel Harney what should be done with the bodies. Should the soldiers at least cut them down from the scaffold? "No," he replied, "I was ordered to have them hanged, and have no orders to *unhang* them."[22]

The purpose of such punishment was twofold—much as it is today in criminal executions. Executions served, obviously, as punishments for the transgressors, and, perhaps more importantly, as examples to others as to what could befall them. Executions did not always have the desired effect, however. In 1813, a soldier of the Fourth U.S. Infantry Regiment named Lord was apprehended about ten miles from his camp while on his way home—without permission. Upon his return to camp, he faced a speedy court-martial that found him guilty of desertion and sentenced him to be shot. He expressed great surprise that his crime should merit such a punishment. "He had not the least suspicions," wrote a fellow soldier, "nor fear of such sentence beforehand." Lord's dismay seems particularly difficult to understand. Desertion, in times of war, was a capital offense. In addition, this soldier had—presumably—witnessed the execution of another deserter only six hours before he left camp. Nevertheless, Lord soon suffered a similar fate. "We should suppose such measures wo'd prevent desertions," mused one observer, "but I was informed two made their escape after Lord was condemned."[23]

Soldiers knew that even during times of peace, they ran the risk of serious punishment if they deserted and were later captured. Still, desertion was almost endemic in the antebellum U.S. Army. In the year 1823, for example, approximately 2,650 men enlisted in the army. At the same time, however, over 650 men deserted. By 1825, the desertion rate exceeded fifty percent of the number of new recruits that year. By the early 1850s, the army was losing one-sixth of its total strength every year through desertion. In the summer of 1850, 274 new recruits left New York City for the training camp at Jefferson Barracks, Missouri. By the time the detachment reached its destination, just outside St. Louis, 104 men were nowhere to be found. A similar expedition, in 1855, saw 41 out of 269 men disappear between New York City and New Orleans. More than half of the men who signed up with the brand new Tenth U. S. Infantry Regiment that year deserted before completing their enlistments.[24]

Convicted deserters did not always suffer the death penalty, even in wartime. Many, maybe most, paid lesser costs. Military courts often assigned other corporal punishments besides execution. One such, at least in the early years of the nineteenth century, was ear cropping. A soldier who had part of an ear cut off carried a permanent reminder of his misdeeds. And all of those with whom he came in contact, for the rest of his life, would know that he was a man with a dark past.

Branding

The same message was also sent when a miscreant soldier was branded. Branding took several forms. In its least permanent mode, it consisted merely of marking, in India ink, a letter somewhere on the face—cheek or forehead—indicating the nature of the man's offense. The letter "D" was used to indicate a deserter; "HD," a habitual drunkard; and, sometimes, "W," for worthless. These marks would eventually fade away, but a more lasting indicator was in the form of a tattoo. Sometimes, when the goal was simply to prevent a deserter from ever entering the military service again, but not to make him a permanent social disgrace, the tattoo was applied to his hip. That way, it was not visible in normal social conditions. If he ever tried to re-enlist, however, an examining physician would see the mark and refuse to allow him back into the army. A lasting, and much more painful, method was to burn the letters into the offender's skin with a hot iron, just as one would brand cattle. Not everyone in the military command structure agreed with such penalties. General Edmund Gaines routinely disapproved of court-martial findings that called for tattooing. He would readily assent to death sentences for chronic deserters, but felt that permanently marking a man with a reminder of past misdeeds was "incompatible with the nature of our public institutions, and is therefore forbidden." General Winfield Scott, with whom Gaines shared command of the army during the early 1820s, had no such compunctions.[25]

Army officials were not the only source of punishment for deserters. In the winter of 1820, an enlisted man deserted from Fort Mackinac, Michigan. By the time he was apprehended and returned to the fort, the bitter weather had frozen both of his feet so badly that the post surgeon had to amputate both of them. A few years later, another soldier at the same post, and one who apparently had not learned from the earlier example, suffered similar injuries when he tried to desert. In his case, he lost all of one foot, most of the other, and both of his ears.[26]

Flogging

Whipping, or flogging, was yet another form of capital punishment often administered to deserters or others guilty of major transgressions. Although officially disallowed by regulations in 1812, it was reinstated for deserters in 1833, and a number of soldiers felt the bite of the cat-o'-nine-tails during the first half of the nineteenth century. The cat typically consisted of a wooden handle about the size of a common drumstick. Attached to this were nine strands of knotted whipcord or, in some cases, leather. Thus every stroke of the cat left a large number of welts, and the knots often tore the flesh. The man chosen to ply the whip was usually a small man, maybe a drummer boy, who, it was felt, would lack the physical strength and stamina to inflict a *fatal* beating. After all, the intent was to injure grievously but not to kill. Such brutal punishment would not be necessary, according to one officer, "were every soldier a proud, high minded citizen." He found this not to be the case, however, and believed that for those men who were "dead to everything like moral feelings and whom nothing can degrade or humiliate, we ought not to withhold from our courts martial the power to

A doctor in a cocked hat supervises an army flogging, ca. 1844. The drummer boys drown the sounds and a soldier on the right has fainted at the spectacle. (© *Hulton Archive/Getty Images*)

inflict upon such subjects either stripes or lashes or such other substituted punishments as may be brief and thus be the most likely to coerce them to a proper performance of their duties."[27]

Army officials hoped that flogging would serve as deterrents to men who saw it, so usually entire garrisons were ordered out to witness the punishment. A dragoon left his impressions of the time, in 1833, when he first saw a fellow soldier thus being whipped. "Could I have retired from the scene," he recalled, "I felt that I would willingly have given all that I possessed." Instead, however, he had to watch as a pair of drummers began plying the whip. "The first six or eight [blows]," noted the reluctant observer, "although applied with force enough to make the blood flow copiously from the lacerated wounds, brought no sign of flinching, but as the subsequent strokes fell upon the wounded flesh, groans, and at length piercing shrieks rent the air, and before the last blow had fallen, the unhappy man had sunk into a swoon." The man carrying out the flogging often did so unwillingly. When one bandsman received an order to do so, he was, as he wrote, "dumfounded." The officer threatened to bring charges against him if he refused, however, so he proceeded to do his duty. "Throughout this punishment," he later remembered, "my sufferings, mentally, were equal to those of the culprit. It was a great shock to me, and I felt both ashamed and disgusted, and sad at the spectacle before me."[28]

Running the Gauntlet

"Running the gauntlet" was another form of punishment for serious offenses, such as desertion. The "gauntlet" was two rows of men facing each other and standing about six feet apart. The prisoner sentenced to run the gauntlet actually had to walk—not run—between the two rows, while each man took a swipe at him with a stick or, perhaps, even the iron ramrod from his musket. To make sure that the man did not move too quickly, a sentry preceded him, walking backwards, with his bayoneted musket at the prisoner's chest. To make sure that the man did not flee, another guard performed a similar function behind him. There was no set number of men forming the gauntlet. At a small frontier post, it might consist only of the men in the transgressor's own company. In a situation like that, where there might only be fifteen or twenty pairs of men lining the way, the sentence might be to run the gauntlet more than once. At a small post in Mississippi Territory in 1799, for example, two captured deserters were sentenced to run the gauntlet eighteen times! "Believe me," wrote a witness, "when I assure you that switches were laid on well, so that they will remember it for some time."[29]

Miscellaneous Physical Punishments

Courts often imposed sentences that combined more than one of these punishments. During the War of 1812, for example, a convicted deserter might have both ears cropped, half his head shaved, and the letter "D" branded on his cheek. In later years, it appears that cropping fell out of favor, but was replaced by flogging. Most of the deserters captured in 1847 in Mexican uniforms were executed, but the rest did not get off lightly. Some, like Sergeant John Riley (sometimes Reilly), escaped the hangman's noose on a technicality. Riley had deserted from Zachary Taylor's army while it was camped near the mouth of the Rio Grande, but before the actual declaration of war. He therefore did not merit hanging, but he was to receive fifty lashes and be branded with the letter "D." General David Twiggs took charge of the punishments and hired experienced Mexican mule drivers to take turns with the whip. He felt that the crimes committed by those about to be punished were too base to be dignified by the use of an American soldier applying the whip. Further, he promised, at least in Riley's case, to pay them a bonus if they could make the whipping fatal. All survived, but not without excruciating pain. To prevent infection of the wounds on their backs, they were thoroughly washed—with salt water! A witness later wrote: "I shall never forget the punishment meted out to those deserters." "Why those thus punished did not die under such punishment," mused another onlooker, "was a marvel to me. Their backs had the appearance of a pounded piece of raw beef, the blood oozing from every stripe."[30]

After the flogging, the men were branded. Most were branded on the cheek, but three received theirs on the hip. Riley, who many saw as a kind of ringleader, was branded twice. Eyewitness accounts differ as to why this happened. Some say that just as the hot iron was about to make contact with Riley's face, he flinched, thus causing the resulting imprint to take on a smeared appearance. Others remarked that the brand was applied without any such facial spasm on Riley's part, but that it was applied upside down. In any case, after the first brand, General Twiggs looked into Riley's face and told him that his sentence called for a letter "D" to be branded on his cheek "and that he would keep on branding him until he made a good plain 'D' if he had to burn his d___ head off." The soldier wielding the iron then branded Riley's other cheek, and this time he got the "good plain 'D' " that Twiggs sought.[31]

Again, however, various punishments other than death were probably much more common, as in the case of an enlisted man in 1812, who went on a verbal tirade. "Making use of profane Oaths and excrations [*sic*] unbecoming a Soldier and a Christian," this man threatened and insulted one of his officers and some of his fellow soldiers. His court-martial assessed him a fine of 16 2/3¢, ordered him handcuffed until his regiment took up the line of march again, and directed that he spend the remaining time of his enlistment wearing a ball and chain. Similarly, an infantryman at Fort Laramie in 1853 had to spend ten days from sunup to sundown carrying a thirty-pound knapsack two hours at a time every two hours.[32]

Probably more common than enlisted men assaulting their officers and noncommissioned officers were officers abusing their authority at the expense of their soldiers. In the mid 1820s, for example, a major, without the benefit of legal proceedings, took a whip to one of his soldiers. He made no effort to conceal his actions, whipping the man in plain sight of all. At his court-martial, two brother officers, the only witnesses called, claimed to have seen nothing. The prosecutor then sought to introduce a copy of a letter in which the major admitted whipping the man. The major objected, saying that the use of his own words to convict him violated his Fifth Amendment rights against self-incrimination. He also complained (in those days before photocopy machines) because the letter was only a copy and not the original document. The court agreed, and the officer went unpunished. A few years later, an enlisted man brought charges against an officer—a surgeon—for having flogged him, again without the benefit of any judicial process. One soldier testified at the trial that he saw the surgeon inflict at least a hundred lashes on the complainant's bare back. Another witness, this one an officer, admitted actually handing the surgeon the whip. Despite this seemingly incontrovertible evidence, however, the court found the officer not guilty.[33]

Even with the long list of *Articles*, there was a lot of room for interpretation as to how military justice should be administered. In 1809, Major Alexander Macomb published *A Treatise on Martial Law and Courts-Martial* and, in 1840, as commanding general of the army, he wrote *The Practice of Courts-Martial*. Macomb's purpose seems to have been to bring about some uniformity to the practice of military law. Within a few years, William DeHart and John O'Brien published similar works. In spite of these helpful books, military justice continued to be administered unevenly. Few, if any, of the men passing judgment in these courts had ever received any formal training in the law, and this often resulted in tremendous disparity in the severity of punishments meted out for similar offenses.[34]

Hard Labor

Most court-martial sentences did not involve capital punishment. Much more common were sentences of incarceration for various lengths of time, and, sometimes, the miscreant spent his confinement at hard labor. When soldiers received sentences that included the provision that they spend a certain amount of time "at hard labor," the type of work assigned to them could be quite varied. The labor might be that of clearing ground for a new post garden, or chopping down trees for firewood, or digging wells. This latter task was the one assigned to a couple of men spending time in the guardhouse at Fort Gibson. It was hard work, and the two men eventually reached a depth of about fifteen feet. At that level, they were out of sight of any casual observer and they discovered that no one was actually monitoring their progress, so they stopped digging. They kept reporting for work every day, however, dutifully climbing down the ladder into the excavation, where they spent the day playing cards. As they climbed out of the hole at the end of the day, they reported some fictitious amount of progress, and no one ever decided to verify it. After a year and a half, the well had reached a reported depth of over 465 feet without striking water. It was only then that the ruse was discovered and the well abandoned.[35]

Some soldiers, it seemed, were always in trouble. Robert Carrey was one of those who seemed to have spent almost as much time in military courtrooms as anywhere else. In the summer of 1802, Carrey reported himself to the camp physician with some ailment. The doctor apparently wrote out an order excusing Carrey from duty for a short while, and the soldier used this opportunity to get drunk. A court-martial met and sentenced him to fifty lashes. A couple of months later, he was absent from a roll call and spent ten days in confinement. Two weeks after being released, he assaulted a sergeant, both verbally and physically, and received seventy-five more lashes. In January 1803, Carrey again tasted the lash, twenty-five strokes this time. And then twenty-five more for "rioting and striking men in his room," and then fifty more for being absent without leave. In June, a court-martial again met to discuss Private Carrey. The charge was sleeping on guard duty, and this time the penalty was one hundred lashes.

Another repeat offender was Philip Warder, who enlisted in the Seventh U.S. Infantry Regiment for five years in 1829. After two years, he decided that a soldier's life was not for him; but, instead of deserting, he hired a substitute to finish out his enlistment for him. After only four months in the civilian world, he realized that perhaps the military life was not so bad, and he enlisted in the Sixth U.S. Infantry Regiment, again for five years. In less than a year he was promoted to sergeant; in July 1834, however, a court-martial reduced him to the ranks. Whatever his crime had been, he quickly won the confidence of his superiors and had regained his rank within three months. His up-and-down cycle continued, however, and, during the next four months, he was court-martialed twice and was again made a private. He finally deserted in 1836, but was recaptured in less than a year. He was allowed to re-enlist, which he did in November 1838, but deserted again and was not again apprehended.[36]

NOTES

1. *U.S.* v. *Robert L. Mitchell*, www.armfor.uscourts.gov/opinions/2003Term/99-0307.htm, accessed November 3, 2004; Percival G. Lowe, *Five Years a Dragoon ('49 to '54) And Other Adventures on the Great Plains* (Norman, Oklahoma: University of Oklahoma Press, 1965), 97–98.

2. Theodore Talbot, *Soldier in the West: Letters of Theodore Talbot During His Services in California, Mexico, and Oregon, 1845–1853*, edited by Robert V. Hine and Savoie Lottinville (Norman, Oklahoma: University of Oklahoma Press, 1972), 138–139.

3. John O'Brien, *A Treatise on American Military Laws, and the Practice of Courts Martial, with Suggestions for Their Improvement* (Philadelphia: Lea and Blanchard, 1846), 260; 69th Article of War (1806) in O'Brien, *American Military Laws*, 345; O'Brien, *American Military Laws*, 258 (quotation), 253.

4. B. J. Fisher, "Military Justice on the Texas Frontier," *West Texas Historical Association Year Book* 64 (1988), 130–131.

5. O'Brien, *American Military Laws*, 269.

6. "The Avalon Project at Yale Law School," http://www.yale.edu/lawweb/avalon/contcong/06-30-75.htm, accessed October 14, 2004 (1st quotation); O'Brien, *American Military Laws*, 343–344 (2d quotation).

7. George M. Burton to a cousin, January 7, 1847 [1848], George M. Burton Collection, Illinois State Historical Library, Springfield, Illinois.

8. Lee A. Wallace, Jr., "The First Regiment of Virginia Volunteers, 1846–1848," *Virginia Magazine of History and Biography* 77, no. 1 (1969): 65–68.

9. *Mexico City North American*, January 6, 1848, as cited in Robert Louis Bodson, "A Description of

the United States Occupation of Mexico as Reported by American Newspapers Published in Vera Cruz, Puebla, and Mexico City, September 14, 1847, to July 31, 1848," Ph.D. diss. (Ball State University, 1971), 63.

10. Mark A. Vargas, "The Military Justice System and the Use of Illegal Punishments as Causes of Desertion in the U.S. Army, 1821–1835," *The Journal of Military History* 55, no. 1 (January 1991), 11; Bill Philpott to Matthew Blue, March 30, 1848, Matthew Potter Blue Papers, Alabama Department of Archives and History, Montgomery, Alabama; Norman Caldwell, "The Enlisted Soldier at the Frontier Post, 1790–1814," *Mid-America: An Historical Review* 37, no. 4 (October 1955), 202n; Vargas, "The Military Justice System," 11.

11. Joseph Gardner Andrews, "A Surgeon's Mate at Fort Defiance: The Journal of Joseph Gardner Andrews For the Year 1795," edited by Richard C. Knopf, *The Ohio Historical Quarterly* 66, no. 3 (1957), 257 (1st quotation); Robert R. Hunt, "Crime and Punishment on the Lewis and Clark Expedition," *Military Collector and Historian* 4, no. 4 (Summer 1989), 60 (2d quotation); Virgil Ney, "Daily Life at Fort Atkinson—on the Missouri—1820–27, Part II," *Military Review* 57 (February 1977), 56 (3d quotation); Leo E. Oliva, *Fort Union and the Frontier Army in the Southwest* (Santa Fe, New Mexico: National Park Service, 1993), 180–181.

12. Caldwell, "The Enlisted Soldier," 202; Graham, "Life of the Enlisted Soldier," 202; Richard Dalzell Gamble, "Garrison Life at Frontier Military Posts, 1830–1860," Ph.D. diss. (University of Oklahoma, 1956), 63; Steinhauer, " 'Sogers'," 203.

13. Croghan, *Army Life on the Western* Frontier, 120.

14. Anonymous, diary entry for May 23, 1814, "The Pennsylvania Volunteers in the War of 1812: An Anonymous Journal of Service for the Year 1814." *Western Pennsylvania Historical Magazine*, 70 (April 1987), 137; Hare, "Military Punishments in the War of 1812," 234, 230.

15. Steinhauer, " 'Sogers'," 254 (1st quotation); Croghan, *Army Life on the Western Frontier*, 120–121 (2d quotation).

16. Hare, "Military Punishments in the War of 1812," 230–232, 234; Charles Fairbanks, "A New Hampshire Volunteer in the War of 1812: The Experiences of Charles Fairbanks," edited by John C. Fredriksen *Historical New Hampshire* 40 (Fall-Winter 1985), 161 (quotation); Robert J. Moore, Jr. and Michael Haynes, *Tailor Made, Trail Worn: Army Life, Clothing & Weapons of the Corps of Discovery* (Helena, Montana: Farcountry Press, 2003), 53–54.

17. O'Brien, *American Military Laws*, 313–330; Hare, "Military Punishments in the War of 1812," 227–228.

18. T. H. Towner to his father, December 29, 1847, Benjamin Towner papers, Duke University; John C. Getsinger to his wife, December 31, 1847, Eastern Carolina University; Edward B. Shelton to his sister, December 24, 1847, Edward B. Shelton papers, Virginia Historical Society; Samuel E. Chamberlain, *My Confession: The Recollections of a Rogue* (1956; reprint Lincoln and London: University of Nebraska Press, 1987), 224–225.

19. James M. McCaffrey, *Army of Manifest Destiny: The American Soldier in the Mexican War, 1846–1848* (New York: New York University Press, 1992), 109; Richard C. Knopf, "Crime and Punishment in the Legion, 1792–1793," *Bulletin: Historical and Philosophical Society of Ohio* 14, no. 3 (July 1956), 237.

20. Jarvis Frary Hanks, "A Drummer Boy in the War of 1812: the Memoir of Jarvis Frary Hanks," edited by Lester W. Smith, *Niagara Frontier* 7 (1960), 55.

21. John S. Hare, "Military Punishments in the War of 1812," *The Journal of the American Military Institute* 4, no. 4 (Winter 1940), 239; W. Austine to his cousin, November 1, 1847, William Austine Collection, Southern Historical Collection, Library of the University of North Carolina at Chapel Hill.

22. W. Austine to his cousin, November 1, 1847, William Austine Collection, Southern Historical Collection, Library of the University of North Carolina at Chapel Hill.

23. A. S. Cogswell, "Letters of the War of 1812 in the Champlain Valley," edited by Wilmond W. Parker, *Vermont Quarterly* 12 (1944), 111–112.

24. Stanley S. Graham, "Life of the Enlisted Soldier on the Western Frontier, 1815-1845," Ph.D. diss., (North Texas State University: 1972), 23n–24n; George Croghan, *Army Life on the Western Frontier: Selections from the Official Reports Made Between 1826 and 1845 by Colonel George Croghan*, edited by Paul Prucha (Norman, Oklahoma: University of Oklahoma Press, 1958), 114n; James A. Bennett, *Forts and Forays: A Dragoon in New Mexico, 1850–1856*, edited by Clinton E. Brooks and Frank D. Reeve (Albuquerque, New Mexico: University of New Mexico Press, 1948), 9–10; John R. Whaley, "A Virginia Soldier in the Frontier Army[:] The Letters of Sergeant John R. Whaley, Second U.S. Artillery, 1854–1859," edited by Robert P. Weittman, Jr., *Military History of the West* 29, no. 1 (Spring 1999), 74; Paul L. Hedren, "On Duty at Fort Ridgely, Minnesota: 1853–1867," *South Dakota History* 7 (Spring 1977), 189.

25. Dale Richard Steinhauer, " 'Sogers': Enlisted Men in the U.S. Army, 1815–1860," Ph.D. diss., (University of North Carolina at Chapel Hill, 1992), 258.

26. Keith R. Widder, *Reveille Till Taps: Soldier Life at Fort Mackinac, 1780–1895* (Mackinac Island, Michigan: Mackinac Island State Park Commission, 1972), 45.

27. Croghan, *Army Life on the Western Frontier,* 112–113.

28. [James Hildreth], *Dragoon Campaigns to the Rocky Mountains* (New York: Wiley and Long, 1836; reprint, New York: Arno, 1973), 50 (1st quotation); Henry S. Hamilton, *Reminiscences of a Veteran*, (Concord, New Hampshire: Republican Press Association, 1897), 45 (2d quotation).

29. Bartholomew Schaumburgh to Thomas Cushing, August 31, 1799, "Fort Stoddard in 1799: Seven Letters of Captain Bartholomew Schaumburgh," edited by Jack D. L. Holmes, *Alabama Historical Quarterly* 26 (Fall-Winter 1964), 238.

30. Hare, "Military Punishments in the War of 1812," 235; Harvey Neville diary, January 9, 1847, Chicago Historical Society; "Mexican War Diary of Augustus Ehinger," January 4, 1847, edited by Charles F. Ward, Rice University Library; A. B. Bender, "The Soldier in the Far West, 1848–1860," *Pacific Historical Review* 8 (June 1959), 177–178; Robert Ryal Miller, *Shamrock and Sword: The Saint Patrick's Battalion in the U.S.-Mexican War* (Norman and London: University of Oklahoma Press, 1989), 103–104 (quotation).

31. Daniel M. Frost, "The Memoirs of Daniel M. Frost," edited by Mrs. Dana O. Jensen, *Missouri Historical Bulletin* 26, no. 3 (1970), 222.

32. John C. Fredriksen, ed., " 'The General is Much Mortified': Orderly Book of General [Adamson] Tennehill's Brigade of Pennsylvania Militia, October to December, 1812," *Journal of Erie Studies* 19 (Spring 1990), 66 (quotation); John Dishon McDermott, "Crime and Punishment in the United States Army: A Phase of Fort Laramie History," *Journal of the West* 7, no. 2 (April 1968), 251.

33. Vargas, "The Military Justice System," 13–14.

34. William C. DeHart, *Observations on Military Law, and the Constitution and Practice of Courts Martial, with a Summary of the Law of Evidence, as Applicable to Military Trials: Adapted to the Laws, Regulations, and Customs of the Army and Navy of the United States*, New York: Wiley and Halsted, 1846, 1850; O'Brien, *A Treatise on American Military Laws*.

35 Carl L. Davis and LeRoy H. Fischer, "Dragoon Life in Indian Territory, 1833–1846," *The Chronicles of Oklahoma*, 48 (1970), 11.

36. Moore and Haynes, *Tailor Made, Trail Worn*, 53–54; Graham, "Life of the Enlisted Soldier," 145–146.

6 ON CAMPAIGN

Living conditions were usually considerably more primitive for soldiers on the march than for those occupying permanent posts. And soldiers of the early nineteenth century were on the march quite a bit. Sometimes they marched to meet an enemy force: British, Indian, Mexican. Sometimes they marched to elude one. Some expeditions were undertaken simply to "show the flag": to let potentially hostile Indians, for example, see that the Army was not sitting idly behind stockade walls somewhere, but was ready and willing to move into their homelands if necessary. Occasionally, soldiers escorted civilian wagon trains along portions of the Santa Fe Trail. Other treks were of an exploratory nature: the Lewis and Clark expedition to the Pacific Coast in 1804 and similar journeys of Zebulon Pike, John Frémont, and other army officers. And, finally, some troops simply marched to relocate from one post to another.

Soldiers on active campaign generally relied on tents to protect them from the weather. Common soldiers' tents were usually of white canvas and intended to provide sleeping quarters for six men. Six men made it very close inside. A British soldier of the late eighteenth century has left a vivid description of sleeping in such a tent, and his experience was no doubt typical for soldiers in the American army of that time. The men lay on the ground side by side with the first, third and fifth man's feet on one side of the tent and the second, fourth, and sixth man's feet on the other. The most senior soldier got to sleep in the back of the tent and the youngest slept nearest the door, which, according to this soldier, "is not a very desirable situation, as every one who goes out or comes in, is likely to tread on you; and what is still worse, as some of the men at night will not go beyond the tent door [to relieve themselves], you often suffer from their evacuations." Oftentimes, however, the soldiers did not even have tents and were forced to find whatever shelter nature offered. This was particularly difficult in snowy weather. It was not uncommon then for three soldiers to cut the limbs from some small saplings and spread them out on top of the snow. They then lay one of their blankets down upon this makeshift mattress and covered themselves with the two remaining blankets while using their knapsacks for pillows.[1]

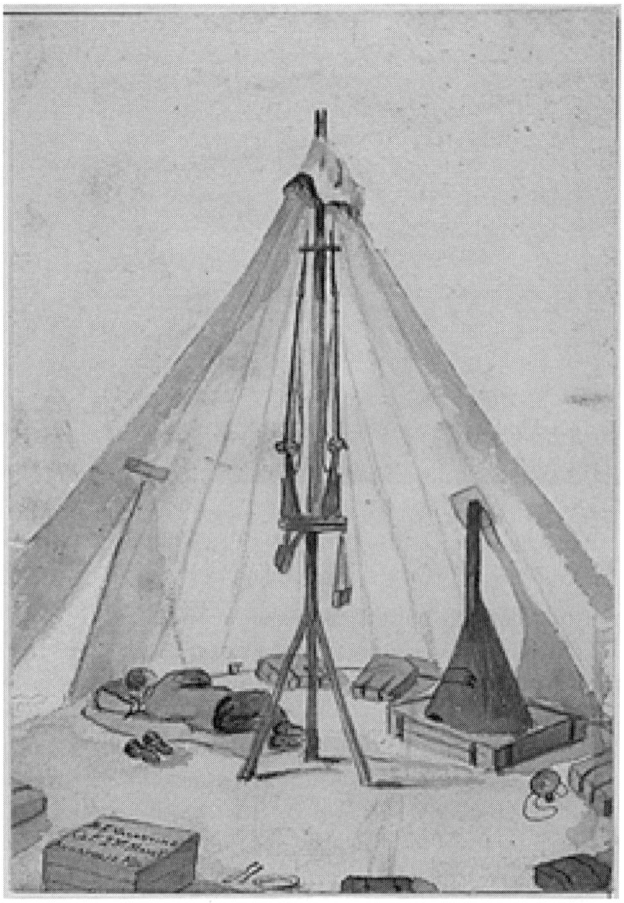

A soldier's sketch of the interior of a Sibley tent. Note that the stove to the right is vented through the canvas wall of the tent and is on a raised platform of dirt or sand. (*Courtesy of the National Archives*)

Rare, indeed, is the soldier's description of comfortable housing, either in a permanent fort or on the march. One such, however, is that of Captain Jesse Gove writing home to his wife while on the Mormon Expedition. His account is such a challenge to credibility that one must wonder whether he was purposely embellishing the truth to put his wife's mind at ease over his safety and comfort. "You do not know," he wrote, "how I take care of myself. Wash as soon as I am in camp all over. My sponge and tub are indispensable. I have not slept but one night without a night gown and clean elegant sheets. I do not, as most of the officers, throw off those little delicacies and luxuries. I maintain the comforts to the last. Everybody remarks, after I get in camp, and Linch [apparently his servant] has made up my bed with the clean sheets turned over, and white pillow case laid above, blankets tucked in all round, 'how comfortable and cool Gove always looks.' I feel so, washed clean with clean clothes on."[2]

Armies of the eighteenth and nineteenth centuries usually put active campaigning on hold during the winter months and settled into winter quarters. Soldiers at these times used whatever scraps of building materials they could find to improve the conditions of their living quarters. Some chopped down small trees and used the logs to erect cabins, complete with fireplaces and wooden floors. Occasionally, however, they had nothing more substantial than tent canvas under which to live. During cold winter nights, soldiers sharing a tent or a small cabin often slept spoon fashion to conserve body heat. Three men, for example, might pool their three blankets, putting one down on the ground and using the other two to cover themselves up. Of course, the only way these two blankets would keep three men warm was if they lay as close together as possible, all facing in the same direction. Then, if sometime during the night one of the men wanted to lie on his other side, all three had to switch. Such sketches of the misery of winter quarters abound, and it almost challenges one's imagination to read another account left by an officer taking part in the Mormon campaign in the winter of 1857–1858. He had not one, but two, large wall tents all to himself, which he erected one over the other for a double canvas thickness to shield him against the weather. This tent, he informed his wife, was to be his sleeping room. He also somehow got possession of one of the Army's new Sibley tents. Named for the inventor, these conical tents very much resembled the Indian tipis from which they derived. They were eighteen feet in diameter and twelve feet high and were intended to house a dozen soldiers. This one, however, served as this officer's sitting room. He then proceeded to use three or four common tents to floor his canvas castle and laid a carpet over them. He assured his wife that "in winter quarters I shall be quite comfortable." The addition of a small stove made his abode "so warm that I can hardly stand it with a small fire." And if he was still cold, this man had two buffalo robes, an elk skin robe and "plenty of blankets."[3]

An army on the move could be a ponderous thing. The expedition, if it was one of much size, might include troops from all three major branches—infantry, cavalry (or dragoons), and artillery. A large body of troops might also be encumbered with supply wagons drawn by horses, oxen, or mules. On certain terrain, where wagons could not be used, the necessary burdens were packed on the backs of beasts of burden. Mules were the most popular animals for this work. An officer in Texas in the middle 1850s tried to describe to a friend how difficult dealing with these often refractory animals could be.

> It was a puzzle to pack the unfortunate animal destined for our transport.... You will readily perceive that stowing tent poles upon horseback is not the easiest matter imaginable. A pack saddle looks like a saw-buck fastened upon the animal like a saddle. To the arms of this saw buck are fastened all those sundry appliances used by "men of war" on their journeys. Imagine—but you can't imagine—a mule buried in tents, blankets, pots, kettles—pans, Pork, Coffee, Hard Bread, Sugar, "Jerked beef" & & something after this plan[:] How "Muley" objects in the most energetic manner to this proceeding; how she elevates her heels toward the skies in deprecation; how she runs side ways[,] bumps her head against the tent poles and how, by skillfull [*sic*] manoeuvre, she often upsets the whole Cargo to the infinite wrath of the packers and the sad demolition of crockery you need not be told.

An officer on an expedition in Arizona at about the same time described a similar event. "The mules," this officer wrote, "packed for the first time scattered in every direction—Some kicking their cargoes off other carried away by the cargoes—Tin pans and camp kettles rattling—mules braying—drunken men singing fighting & swearing—formed a[s] strange a mingling of sweet sounds as one hears generally." The experimental use of camels as pack animals in the Southwest in the 1850s proved of dubious value. These great ships of the desert were able to carry much heavier loads than mules or horses, and they were able to go longer without water than the smaller animals. Their size and demeanor, however, caused other domestic animals to shy away in fright.[4]

Water was more valuable to an army on campaign than even food. Soldiers and their animals can, if they must, get by on little or no food for several days, but a lack of water over this same period can be disastrous. For this reason, every detachment of soldiers, desiring to march from one location to another during hot weather, made it a point to obtain local guides who knew where the natural sources of drinking water were located. And to avoid having to march in the heat of the day, many movements began several hours before daylight and ended at midday. Soldiers sometimes found that the only water available for drinking failed to meet even minimal standards of cleanliness. In the early stages of the Mexican War, a volunteer described to his siblings how he had had to chase hogs out of a pond to get himself a drink. The water, he wrote, was "full of every sort of insects. Some water we came to was very green and we would dip in to it as if it were the best water in the world." Another declared that the water available to him and his companions was so polluted that he would "as soon drink the water out of Father's tan vats after it had been run in there 3 weeks." A soldier, for whom mastery of the written word was clearly a challenge, also commented: "gud water in comparison to the water we had bin useing for we had to use pond water all the wa threw and sum of it thick with mud and perfumed with ded muls."[5]

Campaigning troops often had to face extremes of weather. Soldiers in the Southwest often complained of the dust. "We are beclouded with dust almost without intermission from one day to another," wrote one. "In fact, we cook in dust, eat in dust, sleep in dust, and live in dust." Another man reported that conditions had been so dusty that another soldier had had to consult a doctor about all the sand that he had inhaled. "I say, doctor," the man inquired, "have you any thing that will remove a *sand-bar*?" When the surgeon replied in the negative, the unhappy soldier continued, "Well, then, I am a *gone-sucker*. I've got a sand-bar in my innards, upon which every thing grounds, and I can't get any thing up or down." At the other end of the weather spectrum was rain. "Rain," wrote an officer with a highly developed sense of humor from Oregon in the early 1850s, "is an exceedingly pleasant and gratifying institution in its way, and in moderation; it causes the grass to grow, the blossoms to flourish, and is a positive necessity to the umbrella-maker; but when you get to the country where it rains incessantly twenty-six hours a day, for seventeen months in the year, you cannot resist having the conviction forced upon your mind that the thing is slightly overdone. That's the case in Oregon."[6]

MIXING WITH INDIGENOUS PEOPLES

As the American people gradually flowed westward across the Appalachians, the Mississippi, the Great Plains, and the Rockies, they slowly wiped out or pushed aside all those peoples who stood in the way of this movement. In 1845, newspaperman John L. O'Sullivan finally gave a name to this inexorable process, when he wrote that it was the nation's "manifest destiny to overspread the continent allotted by Providence for the free development of our yearly multiplying millions."[7]

And soldiers played a major part in implementing "manifest destiny." They were the ones, after all, who had to enforce the Indian Removal Act in the 1830s, leading to war against the Indians of Florida. They were the ones who were sent to Mexico in the 1840s to solidify American possession of Texas and to gain the vast areas to the west, all the way to California. They were the ones who had to try to protect the immigrant trains and the gold-seekers as they headed to Oregon and California in the 1850s.

Indians

Soldiers' attitudes toward these "victims" of manifest destiny probably reflected the feelings of the American public in general. Most Americans of the time believed in a racial hierarchy based upon the color of one's skin. The light-skinned Americans of northern European heritage saw themselves as better—more socially advanced—than anyone whose skin was not as white as their own. This belief placed Indians and Mexicans, because of their color, on a lower level of acceptance in the views of most Americans. (Those of African descent, whose skin was darker yet, remained at the bottom of this scale.) Soldiers thus, like almost everyone else, found it easier to accept the subjugation of these "lesser" races.

The relatively small percentage of the army that manned the coastal forts had little opportunity to come into contact with people of other cultures. Soldiers on campaign, however, regularly interacted with Indians—all the way from the Seminoles of Florida to the tribes of the Pacific Northwest—and Mexicans. By most accounts, the American soldiers found little to admire in these alien cultures and much to deprecate. The Cherokee and the Seminole seem to be among the few exceptions. Most—but certainly not all—soldiers who left descriptions of their experiences with these tribes wrote accounts that bordered upon flattery. A dragoon, commenting in 1834 upon some of the earliest of the Cherokees to take up residence west of the Mississippi River, described them as "industrious and enterprising" and that they lived "much in the manner of their civilized [white] neighbors." Another soldier, a quarter century later, met some Cherokees who "seemed to be perfectly civilized." An army doctor, perhaps damning the Cherokee and the Seminole with faint praise, conceded that "it may be possible to civilize" them. The Nez Perce were among the tribes least likely to engender negative comment about any perceived rascality, and other Indians along the Columbia River seemed to be "a harmless and inoffensive race of people."[8]

As far as Indian removal was concerned, some few officers expressed a certain sense of sadness, or regret, at having to impose this upon the "noble savages" of the American Southeast. "We shall…have war to the knife," lamented one such man with a poetical bent. "Every warrior shall be killed, and all the women and children become slaves to the captor! How magnanimous is a civilized and enlightened Republic of the 19th Century! In the catalogue of earth's nations, the name of Seminole shall be erased! They have been weighed in the balance, and found wanting! The edict has gone forth!" Another subaltern, addressing the same issue, came to the conclusion that his government had not dealt fairly with the tribes it was then trying to relocate, and that he could no longer justify his part in the removal process by merely claiming to be a good soldier who followed orders unquestioningly. "Have God and justice no claim upon you," he asked himself, "prior and paramount to a government that incites you to the commission of a crime? Will no compunctions deter you from wringing your hands in innocent blood, even though it be the command of a superior officer?" Near the end of his long-winded diatribe, full of Shakespearian imagery, this officer admitted: "Besides I'm opposed to fighting Indians anyhow." Yet another officer wrote of the Seminoles: "Their sin is patriotism, as true as ever burned in the breast of the most civilized." Even a young Lieutenant William

T. Sherman, who would earn a reputation as being a heartless warrior twenty years later, wrote in 1844: "If ever a curse could fall upon a people or nation for pure and unalloyed villainy towards a part of God's creatures we deserve it for not protecting the Cherokees that lately lived and hunted in peace and plenty" in Georgia. Likewise, another future general praised the Cherokee. "They have among them," he wrote, "many well informed, sensible, orderly industrious and pious people, regardful of everything that contributes to domestic peace, happiness and prosperity, and they exhibit fruits accordingly."[9]

Others were just as adamant in their condemnation of members of the "civilized tribes." One officer, writing in the *Army and Navy Chronicle*, decried such sentiments of "mawkish philanthropy" and recommended that a "few skeletons left to hang and bleach in the wind" would get the message across to the warring Seminoles that their cause was doomed. Another agreed wholeheartedly when he wrote: "There was too much sympathy extended upon these treacherous, murderous savages." The Indians farther west rarely came in for any sympathy from soldiers who left written accounts. An Army doctor in the Southwest in the mid-1850s, for example, was certainly not alone when he sanctioned a war of extermination. "In the worst sense of the word," he informed a friend, "these tribes are savages. They are *devils* and the coldest blood must boil at the narration of the manner in which they have treated prisoners who have fallen into their hands." And when, in 1858, there was talk of peace overtures from the Sioux and Cheyenne, one officer thought that they "should receive a sound thrashing first, & peace afterwards. The Indians of the Plains are all alike," he stated authoritatively, "in, that, they have to be flogged into decency, & flogged out of their predatory & murderous habits."[10]

One soldier, writing in the mid-1830s, exhibited a rare balance of judgment:

> To speak of the Indians as a people, it would be as far from the truth to ascribe to them any peculiar characteristics, as it would be to speak of the likes, and tastes, and motives, and feelings of all the white race of civilized beings under heaven in general terms. To ascribe to them, as a mass, magnanimity, would be perhaps as untrue as it would be, on the other hand, to say that they were all savage and blood-thirsty, and incapable of any noble feelings. Therefore the Indians of almost every tribe differ, in stature, color, habits and temperament, to even a greater degree than the whites; so it may at once be seen how unjustly any epithet or specification of character must be applied to them as a race.[11]

In spite of this reasoned statement, contemporary evaluations of Indian cultures seem to vie with one another over which tribe was the most savage, the most treacherous, the laziest, or the dirtiest. One observer was certain that the Blackfeet were "the most dangerous banditti among all the tribes," while another characterized the Comanches as "arrogant, jealous savages." A military physician in Florida described the Seminoles as "treacherous, murderous savages," and another officer wrote that "a more wicked and demon-like looking set of savages [than the Seminoles] I have never had the fortune to meet with."[12]

The Osage reminded one young dragoon of "wandering Gypsies, hunting and theft being their only means of subsistence." Another soldier was convinced that the "Crows... are the most arrant rascals of the mountains ... never known to do an honorable act or to keep a promise," but they would be hard pressed to compete with the character ascribed to the Navajo. "In the whole nation," reported an officer, "one or two may be found who are reliable men...who would not falsify merely for the sake of falsifying, or steal for the love of stealing." The Sioux, according to a dragoon writing in 1835, "are mostly a dirty thieving race living in the most abominable filthy manner," while a fellow horse soldier, writing a decade later, thought that the Sioux were "prouder of, and more habituated to, lying than truth-telling."[13]

Mexicans

Nor were American soldiers much more tolerant of Mexicans. They did draw a distinction, however, between those Mexicans of obvious European birth—almost invariably labeled Castilians by the soldiers—and those of mixed Spanish/Indian/African heritage. They arbitrarily assigned much higher status to the former than to the latter. What one soldier described as a "mongrel race," another called "a mixture of Indian, negro, and Spanish blood—apparently a great deal below and more ignorant than either race."[14]

Some members of the occupying force, particularly those from the slave states, expressed surprise, and perhaps a little revulsion, at seeing how easily Mexicans of differing hues interacted with one another. "The negroes enjoy the same privileges so far as I could see as the Mexicans do," remarked a Tennessean. One can almost sense his outrage when he continued: "It is quite usual to see a Mexican lady and negro woman walking the streets side by side." An officer from north of the Ohio River made a similar observation about the different classes of Mexican society that he observed in a church in Vera Cruz. He was surprised to see, side by side, "the haughty Castillians [*sic*] in whose veins flowed the pure blood of Cortes, the yellow aztec, the stupid Indian and the decrepid [*sic*] negro." Unlike his fellow soldier, however, this man thought it admirable that people of different skin colors were able to intermingle so comfortably. "I wished that it were so in my own.... native land," he wrote, "where we boast that all men are *free* and *Equal*."[15]

Soldiers campaigning in Mexico were just as parochial in their evaluations of Mexicans as they were of Indians. In fact, they often drew comparisons, seldom flattering to either, between the two peoples. During the early stages of the Mexican War, an Illinois newspaper editorialized that Mexicans were "reptiles in the path of progressive democracy—who, with his bigboots [*sic*] on is bound to travel from Portland to Patagonia—and they must either crawl or be crushed." Most soldier-commentators found fault with Mexicans because they did not seem willing or able to make the maximum use of the good farmland that was available in certain parts of their country. Mexicans had apparently not yet embraced the iron-bladed plow that was in common use in the United States, and many were the comments about the obsolete farming utensils that were still in use south of the Rio Grande. Typical was the observation by a volunteer soldier that the land along the Rio Grande was "very fertile but miserably cultivated; the people are lazy, ignorant & perfidious." "It is an outrage," railed another in his diary, "for the Mexicans to own such a country. They are too lazy to till the soil; they make no improvements whatever in the implements or mode of culture and make but few improvements in the useful or mechanic arts or in cultivation." The agricultural situation in Mexico would be improved immensely, many noted, if the Mexicans would just step aside and allow American farmers, with their superior intellect and technology, to take over. One soldier assured his mother in a letter that the land along the Rio Grande would "rival the coast of Louisiana in the cultivation of Sugar and Cotton whenever the direction of American enterprise shall tend to this country." Another volunteer was a little more direct when he opined that "were Mexico peopled with Americans and blessed with American laws and institutions it would soon become the richest country in the world." A South Carolina volunteer perhaps came closest to using the same words that O'Sullivan did in his newspaper when he discussed the reasons for going to war with Mexico in a letter to his sister. "It really seems to me," he wrote, "that in the present war we are only carrying out the designs of Providence—Mexico is a large and beautiful country now in the possession of a population unworthy to enjoy it. The present war[,] however it may terminate[,] will result not only beneficial to our own country, but a material change for the better I am convinced will be introduced here."[16]

Troops posted to the frontier do not seem to have bestirred themselves to learn to converse with the Indians in their native tongues. Perhaps this was because they were often within a short distance of several different tribes, and it would have been difficult to learn all of the regional languages. Perhaps it was because the soldiers saw little value in Indian culture and, therefore, no compelling reason to ever want to strike up a conversation with a native. Maybe it was because there were usually an adequate number of Indians who were at least nominally fluent in English and could act as translators when the need arose.

There seems to have been much more interest in picking up at least a smattering of Spanish among the soldiers in Mexico. Some tried to pick up at least enough fluency in Spanish to help them converse with the local women. Another man mentioned that he had seen several attractive women at a local fandango. "I could enjoy myself as well with them as with the Americans," he mused, "if I understood their language better. I am at a loss what to say to them." Of course, a little bit of knowledge was probably worse than none at all. A soldier looking for a horse lost in the chaparral met a local man and inquired of him, in his fractured Spanish, if he had seen the animal. "Look here, my man," the American blurted, "have you seen anything of a d__d *caballo*, a *barnosing* about here, with a *cabrista* on his neck?" The Mexican was at a loss as to what the man was asking, and perhaps even what language he was speaking. When he replied, "No entiende, señor," the soldier angrily sputtered: "Don't understand! Why the d__d *fool don't know his own language!*"[17]

The language barrier provided more than a few humorous incidents. When a Mexican messenger arrived at Brigadier General John Wool's headquarters with dispatches, the general wanted to question him further. The problem was that the general spoke no Spanish and the courier spoke no English. Exasperated, the general collared an American soldier passing by and asked him if he could translate. "No, general," he replied, "I am sorry to say I do not." Wool then asked him to find somebody in the camp immediately who could speak Spanish. The soldier quickly grabbed the courier and presented him to the general saying: "Here's a man that cant [*sic*] speak anything else." At other times, even the most well-intentioned attempts to navigate the pitfalls of a foreign language resulted in rather comical situations. In the fall of 1846, one eager linguist brought his sister up to date on the progress he had made up to that point:

> You would be amused, if you could *see* me trying to talk with an old lady & her daughters who keep a boarding house, & sell chocolate &c. *See me*, I say, for the eye has quite as much to do with speaking the Spanish language as the tongue. When at fault for a word I take an English one & give it a Spanish ending & pronunciation & a make a salaam or two with my *fins*, & *look* unutterable things. If that don't go, I throw in a word or two of Latin & French, & occasionally a little German, & conclude with "Señora" or "Señorita". Thus I generally succeed in calling up a smile, & gentle "Si, señor" (yes, sir) then they let loose a torrent of Castillian [*sic*] on me, & I stand & look

knowing, & say "Si Sinorita" when I've no more idea of what they are saying than if Moses was talking to me in his native tongue.[18]

DOING BATTLE

A soldier's *raison d'être* is to fight his nation's battles and, between 1790 and 1860, American soldiers had many opportunities to do just that. There were Indians to fight in the Old Northwest, in Florida, and in multiple locations west of the Mississippi River. There were British to fight from 1812 to 1815, and Mexicans from 1846 to 1848. There were even occasional instances of soldiers being prepared to fight their fellow Americans—in Utah and in Kansas—in the late 1850s.

Tactics

Armies of the late eighteenth century experimented with their battle lines. Some—the French and the Prussians—sent their battle lines forward three ranks deep for additional firepower. In practice, however, only the men in the first two ranks actually fired, while the men in the third rank constantly reloaded muskets for the men in front of them. This formation had the added advantage of allowing the men in the rear to step forward to fill the spaces of killed or wounded companions. One disadvantage, however, was that this formation necessarily constricted the width of the battle line and, theoretically, allowed an enemy to pour converging fire into the sides of the three advancing ranks. Two-rank battle lines, as employed by the British Army after 1801, allowed an army to advance on a wider front against the enemy. The American Army, at various times, used both the two-rank and the three-rank formations.[19]

Until the 1820s, there was no single drill manual specified for use by all units. Consequently, regimental commanders used whatever set of drill regulations they chose, and even though Von Steuben's book called for soldiers to face the enemy in two ranks, some of the other contemporary manuals specified three. The Fifteenth U.S. Infantry used three ranks during the War of 1812, with an added twist. The men comprising the rear, or third rank, in each company formation had had their muskets altered by shortening them some eighteen inches, and these they slung across their backs. Their main weapons were to be pikes eight to ten feet long. The theory was that when the troops were advancing (or even when they were bracing to receive an enemy attack), the men in the rear rank could thrust their pikes forward, so that they reached as far forward or farther than the bayoneted muskets of the men in the front rank and presented a formidable barrier to any attacker. A captain in this regiment expressed his confidence in this arrangement when, in a letter, he wistfully longed to test it against the British army. "I should like to meet with our Regt., as small as it is," he wrote, "the 49th British Regt. on some plain. I think we should have a pretty hard fight or a foot race in a few minutes."[20]

There were various tactics manuals, both official and otherwise, available to the nineteenth-century officer and soldier. These books, despite their titles, did not really educate the reader in battlefield evolutions—or tactics. That is, they informed the reader *how* to accomplish certain types of troop movements, but not *when* to employ them. Precise instructions, with diagrams, showed, for example, how a column of troops moving along a country road could quickly evolve into a battle line perpendicular to their original direction of march. There was nothing in the book, however, to tell a troop commander the circumstances under which such a movement was most beneficial. Likewise, there was very detailed advice on how to effect an orderly retreat; there was no guidance on when this measure should be employed.

All the manuals contained instructions on how to form the defensive formation known as a hollow square—or, simply, a square. When an officer ordered his men to "form square," they quickly arranged themselves in two ranks, so that they all faced outward to repel an enemy from any direction. Their officers took up stations inside the square where they could best direct the ensuing action. The utility of this particular shape was as a defense against rapidly moving enemy cavalry that might simply turn the flank of a simple battle line. The square, therefore, became an island of firepower with, at least theoretically, no single weak point. The men in this formation fastened their bayonets to the ends of their muskets, because if their first volley of fire failed to stop a rapidly approaching enemy there would be no time to load for a second volley, and they would have to rely upon their bayonets to stop the attackers. The Fifth U.S. Infantry Regiment made good use of this formation at the Battle of Palo Alto in 1846, as a defense against Mexican cavalry. The horsemen, undoubtedly recognizing the potential strength of the square, halted some distance away and began a long-distance musketry against the Americans. The defenders soon began to feel the results of this fire, but they were well-trained regulars and held their positions. The Mexicans gained confidence at the lack of return fire and slowly advanced. Then, when they had reached a point about fifty yards from the square, the square erupted into fire. The effect of this fusillade, according on one witness, "emptied upwards of 40 saddles" before the horsemen broke off the attack.[21]

Lines of battle and defensive squares were very useful in situations where the location of the enemy force was known, and there was time to deploy the men under one's command. Fighting Indians, for example, was different from fighting British regulars or Mexican troops. Indians seldom offered battle unless the manpower odds were in their favor. And they refused to present themselves in even rows of battle two or three ranks deep, as European-trained armies did. Thus, they were little hurt by volleys of musketry fired by American soldiers standing shoulder to shoulder, according to contemporary drill manuals. They fought from behind trees, outcroppings of rock, or anything else that offered cover, and moved frequently from one such to another. Some soldiers thought this method was somehow ungentlemanly, and that if the Indians would "only make a fair and stand up fight" they could be easily defeated. Others realized that, in spite of being considered unorthodox, such tactics were of considerable use to white soldiers as well. "Some of our recruits," remembered a veteran of the War of 1812, "did not fight with the regularity of old soldiers, but skulking by companies behind whatever would screen them they kept up a most destructive fire." And even though this particular soldier thought that fighting like this "does no great credit to our discipline," he recognized how effective it was in foiling the tactics of the British. If an American unit fell back before a British attack, it found itself protected by other units behind it. "The enemy boasts that he drove us several hours," recalled an American who was there, "but in all that time he did not get half a mile."[22]

More difficult to implement, of course, were those tactics necessary to repel an Indian ambush while on the march. Baron von Steuben's *Regulations* called for a marching column to form into a square, of sorts, to defend against a cavalry or, one would think, an Indian attack. Later manuals were generally silent on such matters, and none of them gave any guidance to the commander of a force on the move, on how to deploy a part of his men at a distance from the main body to furnish security. Individual leaders implemented march security in a variety of ways. General Josiah Harmar, on his ill-fated march to defeat in 1790, placed his slow-moving and vulnerable baggage wagons in the center of his force, while the infantry marched in two parallel columns some forty yards away on either side. Preceding the column was an advance guard to be on the alert for signs of the enemy, and a similar force followed the column at a short distance to be able to give the alarm in case of an attack from that direction. The following year, General Arthur St. Clair employed similar measures to protect his force. His army, he later related, "was preceded by a small party of riflemen," and

> from that party scouts were sent out to scour the country every way; then followed the road cutters with a party to cover them, then the advanced guard and after them the army in two columns, with one piece of artillery in front, one in the center, and one in the rear of each. In the space between the two columns marched the remaining artillery…then the horses with the tents and provisions, and then the cattle with their proper guards…. Without [outside] the columns, at a distance of about one hundred yards, marched the cavalry in file, and without them, at the same distance, a party of rifleman [*sic*], and scouts without them, then followed the rear guard at a proper distance."

Hostile Indians in the area undoubtedly were aware of these armed incursions, but were smart enough to realize that these marching columns of men were well protected from any surprise attack that they might have had in mind.[23]

Woe to the officer, however, who failed to take such precautions. Vigilant Indians were quick to take advantage of any such lapse. Militia Colonel John Hardin was one who learned this lesson through bitter experience. His 140-man mounted force was intent on finding some Indians to fight and was riding down a trail through a wooded area with no flank security. The Indians prepared a classic ambush to receive him. The men at the head of the column stopped to retrieve a trinket of some sort that the Indians had purposely left on the trail. (Soldiers, after all, are always interested in war trophies.) With all of his troops thus stopped, the Indians opened fire from among the trees only twenty yards to the right of the road. When the startled soldiers fell back to the opposite side of the trail, other Indians began firing from that direction. Hardin's losses were heavy, before he was able to extricate his men from their predicament.[24]

Preparing for Battle

No amount of training could adequately prepare men for the shock and destruction of actual battle, but some commanders had their men engage in mock battles to try to acquaint them with the pace and the noise they might expect to encounter in a real fight. General Anthony Wayne found such training quite helpful, as he prepared his legion to march against the Indians of the Ohio Territory in 1792. In the fall of 1814, troops fired 20,000 blank cartridges at one another in what one observer described as "a beautiful sight." So impressed was the general commanding that he ordered up another "battle" several days later—although rainy weather prevented it from occurring. By this stage of the War of 1812, most of the fighting was over, and these sham battles may have been used more as a way to keep otherwise idle troops busy than for any real training value they might have had.[25]

During the Mexican War, a volunteer colonel tried another method to add realism to his men's training while they were practicing forming squares. Of course, the best method to test the resolve of these men would have been to have friendly cavalry stage a mock attack on the square. This would have given the infantryman some idea of what to expect under actual battle conditions. Since there was no American cavalry unit nearby, the infantry officer tried the next best solution. He mounted his own horse and, from a short distance away, galloped toward his men, waving his sword above his head. As he bore down on them, and just before it would have become necessary for him to rein in his mount, the men in that section of the square broke and fled, allowing him to ride right into the center of the square. Had they been facing a hundred Mexican lancers instead of one friendly officer, the results would have been disastrous, but it was better to have discovered this problem in training. The colonel ordered his men back into their positions and tried again. He was probably fairly certain that his men would give way once again, and made little effort to check his horse until almost too late, because this time they held firm, and the colonel's horse received a rather nasty bayonet wound from one of the defenders. "Well, the horse did his duty," the colonel philosophized, "the rider did his—and the soldier did his—in fact, all did well."[26]

Men about to enter combat reacted as one might expect. Some were contemplative, especially those who had experienced battle before. Some wrote out their wills, or wrote what might have been one last letter to a loved one. Others checked their muskets and other gear to make sure everything they might need was fully functional. Some prayed. Some were jubilant at finally having an opportunity to prove their mettle. For some, the anticipation was harder to deal with than the actual event. "I can hardly describe to you my feeling when I furst [*sic*] began to believe [the enemy] were coming," wrote one man. "It was not fear, & yet it was more like fear than any thing I ever felt during the heat of action, when bullets flew thick as rain around me." Some found themselves completely unable to function due to stark terror, others went about their tasks with workmanlike precision, and still others displayed a coolness under fire that seemed to border on foolishness. At the Battle of New Orleans in 1815, for example, a soldier nicknamed "Sukey" routinely climbed atop the protective breastworks so he would have a better chance of seeing an actual target. He ignored all remonstrance from his comrades to seek a safer spot from which to shoot. Finally, the colonel of his regiment rode along and observed Sukey's actions and ordered him down. "Oh! never mind Colonel," he said, "I don't want to waste my powder, and I'd like to know how I can shoot until I can see something!" During the desperate fighting at Monterrey, in September 1846, one soldier walked away from the firing line and back some two hundred yards to get a light for his pipe from an artilleryman. "He then," according to a witness, "sauntered slowly back puffing away while the Mexican balls flew thick about his ears." A Pennsylvania volunteer in General Winfield Scott's army displayed even more aplomb outside Vera Cruz, during the battle for that important seaport in 1847. When a large Mexican mortar shell landed within a few feet of this soldier, he snatched out the still-burning fuse before it could set off the shell and calmly used it light his pipe.[27]

Young men going to war often had—perhaps subconsciously—a sense of invulnerability. They knew, certainly, that participation in such a dangerous activity as battle could result in their being horribly maimed or even killed, but they usually put that out of their minds in their quest for martial glory. Short-term volunteers, such as those called for service against Mexico, seemed to regard participation in combat as a sort of rite of passage into full manhood. Many expressed fears that the fighting would be over before they could reach the seat of war. A Virginia volunteer, still in his home state while his regiment completed its organization, impatiently wrote to his father: "You can form no idea of the anxiety of the men to be in Mexico, everything here conspires to excite them…. to such a degree that they are continually asking when the ships will arrive in which they are to embark." A few days later, still stuck in the old home state, he wrote: "I am very anxious to get off, fearing that we might not arrive in time for the first great battle, and I believe the last." (He apparently did not assign much credit to the battles already fought at Palo Alto, Resaca de la Palma, and Monterrey.)[28]

When the men of Colonel Stephen Kearny's Army of the West approached Santa Fe, New Mexico, they received word that Mexican troops would be waiting for them in a rocky canyon a dozen miles east of the town. To many of the young untested Missouri volunteers, this was a welcome bit of information. They had, after all, "walked 1,000 miles for this purpose. The battalion appeared to think it hard," wrote one, "we should go back [home] without [a battle] and expressed great anxiety for it to take place." When, later, news arrived that the Mexicans had decided not to dispute the march of the Americans, it threw "rather a gloom over the spirits of the army. They are sadly disappointed," remembered one of their number, "at learning that we shall have no fighting." Not all of Kearny's men were disappointed. One man later admitted: "We all felt well satisfied to pass without being attacked. We had all felt very brave before; but we now saw how difficult it would have been to have forced the pass [in the canyon], and we were glad to be beyond it." It "was better thus to have obtained bloodless victory by the terror of our arms," echoed another, "than to have purchased it with blood and loss of life."[29]

"Seeing the Elephant"

A popular phrase of the mid-nineteenth century, which described having experienced something rare or exotic, was that one had "seen the elephant." The precise origin of the term will perhaps never be known. One account is that it began when a farmer took a wagonload of produce into a town where a traveling circus was about to perform. He had learned that the circus had an elephant, and he wanted to see such an unusual animal for himself. Upon reaching the town, he encountered the circus parade being led by that self same pachyderm, and he was mightily impressed. Not so his horse, which bolted and overturned the wagon, spilling all his wares on the ground. When bystanders rushed to his assistance, he exhibited an unusually jovial mood for someone having just undergone what he had. It was all worth it, he told them, for he had finally seen the elephant.

For soldiers, the phrase "seeing the elephant" first gained currency during the Mexican War and meant participating in combat for the first time. Following his participation in the Battle of Monterrey, an Ohio volunteer proudly informed his father: "I have saw the Elephant and am satisfied." After the Battle of Buena Vista in February 1847, a volunteer officer from Illinois proudly informed a friend: " 'I've seen the eliphant [*sic*]' in every attitude!—walking, running, at bay & fighting!" Some of them found that having survived that first combat experience, they were ready for more. "I came to Mexico to see the 'Elephant,' " wrote one, after the Battle of Buena Vista. "I have seen him," he continued, "& am perfectly willing now to see him again."[30]

One soldier remembered his baptism of fire in 1814. "This, then," he recalled, "was no mere parade—no stage play, for effect—it was a simple and sublime reality—IT WAS

Some people survived being scalped. This man was scalped as a child. (*Courtesy of the Library of Congress*)

WAR." There was no room in this soldier's makeup for false bravado. "I have heard of a Spaniard," he wrote, "who said he never knew what fear was. Such was not the case with me. I should like to have had a strong stone-wall between me and the enemy, for I expected to be either killed or wounded; and I certainly did not want to be either."[31]

American soldiers often seemed confident that they could vanquish any enemy, no matter what disparity in manpower might exist. During the war with Mexico, an Alabama volunteer, who had yet to see combat, was one who expressed extreme confidence. "There would be no use for us," he crowed, "after we had been in one battle for we would so completely annihilate the Mexicans that they would not think of meeting us but once." Another volunteer confided to his father that "we feel fully competent to whip any number of Mexicans from 7 to 15000." At about the same time, a soldier in New Mexico, anticipating an attack by Indians, wrote to his parents that "This is just what I want, for I believe 100 Americans is good for 500 Indians." Ten years later, and a little farther north, a young officer declared: "Our troops are in the best possible fighting condition and only wait for an opportunity to get at the enemy. The ball is fairly opened, and we intend to 'dance all night, till broad daylight', and make the Mormons pay for the music." He was convinced, he later wrote, "I can whip 300 of their best with my company."[32]

Perils of Battle

In spite of such confidence, soldiers facing battle, whether for the first time or not, must have at least considered the possibility of being killed or wounded. And when facing Indian enemies, there was the constant threat of being tortured if they were captured or of having their bodies mutilated if they were killed. Torture was not always simply a means to satisfy some primal lust, as many Americans believed. Sometimes, Indians employed torture, or the threat of torture, to attain some other goals. In early January 1791, for example, a large group of Shawnees approached Dunlap's Station, a small fortification near present-day Cincinnati. When the officer commanding the fort failed to accede to their demand that he surrender, they produced a prisoner, a man who had been captured near the fort the day before. The prisoner, in a desperate bid to save his own life, pleaded with the lieutenant to surrender the fort. The Indians had assured him that if the fort surrendered none of its inhabitants would be harmed. The commander, wisely placing no credence in such an empty promise, continued to refuse to give up his post. The Indians then, within sight and hearing of the fort, stripped the prisoner naked and staked him out spread-eagled on the ground. Then, as the horrified residents of the fort watched, they kindled a fire on his abdomen hoping that the onlookers would give in to their demands in order to save his life. They resolutely refused, however, and the hostage died a horrible death. "His screams of agony were ringing in our ears during the remainder of the night," later remembered one of the fort's inhabitants, "becoming gradually weaker and weaker till toward daylight, when they ceased."[33]

Scalping was a common feature of Indian warfare along the frontier. Possession of an enemy's scalp indicated the bravery and ferocity of the holder of the ghastly souvenir. Different tribes employed different methods of obtaining an enemy's hair. Some satisfied themselves with only a relatively small patch removed from the crown of the head. Others removed as much as they could, sometimes even including the ears. Eastern Indians, according to a colonial-era observer, removed a man's scalp

> as nicely as one would the skin of a rabbit. First they cut the skin to the bone all around the head with a knife. They start in front, in the middle of the forehead, follow around and behind one ear, then in back of the neck and around the other ear and finish in front where they started. Then after pulling a little on the hair to raise the edge of the skin, they throw the head backward...and peel off the scalp as easily as one would a glove from the hand.

Some used their teeth to pull the scalp free after the initial work with the knife. Indians in the Pacific Northwest followed much the same procedure, but their incisions ran down the back of their victim's head all the way to his shoulder blades, and they then ripped the scalp loose from the back instead of the front.[34]

Nor was this macabre practice only performed by the "savages." A Cincinnati newspaper advertised in 1794 that it would pay a bounty for twenty Indians scalps. And to make sure that more than one unscrupulous frontiersman did not try to offer the hair from the same Indian to collect the payment, each scalp was required to include the victim's right ear. The paper offered to pay $100 for the first ten scalps brought in by anyone, but if a subscriber to the paper brought them in, he would receive an additional $36. The sliding scale also applied to the next ten scalps. A subscriber would receive $117, while a nonsubscriber would only be paid $95. Following the Battle of Tippecanoe in 1811, four militiamen divided a single Indian scalp, and each used his portion to decorate his rifle. Some volunteer soldiers, during the short Black Hawk War in 1832, sunk to new depths with regard to scalping. Not content with taking only scalps, these men cut long narrow strips of skin from the backs of dead warriors and used them to make razor strops.[35]

Ritual mutilation was another facet of Indian warfare that was not uncommon. One soldier reported in 1788 on such an occurrence. "The Indians have lately killed a soldier," he wrote, "and not content with scalping him, cut him in four quarters and hung them upon the bushes." The following year, in the same general vicinity, soldiers found the mutilated body of one of their comrades. His body bore the marks of two musket balls and two arrows. The Indians had scalped him, a common practice, and had also cut out his heart and severed his genitals. An army doctor in the Southwest, in the years immediately preceding the Civil War, remarked that it was quite unusual, in light of the time and effort required to craft an arrow, to find a man wounded by only one, or even two, arrows. He reported that three soldiers recently killed by the Navahos were found with a total of forty-two arrows stuck in their bodies.[36]

Battle

Battle in the early nineteenth century—indeed at any time—was an experience that participants were unlikely ever to forget. It was a rite of passage for a soldier, complete with noise, fear, and confusion. A battle between two forces equipped with muskets and artillery could truly be deafening. "The whole heavens were dark with smoke and mad with the continued roar of their mighty pieces of artillery," is how one survivor described it. "The balls whistled through the air like hail in a storm." Another man wrote that a battle was "beyond the power of my pen to describe," but he tried to do so nevertheless. "The discharges [of musketry] were so rapid and incessant," he wrote, "that they sounded like the roll of a drum." "Imagine the most violent hail storm you ever saw," he continued, "attended constantly with the loudest Claps of thunder your ears ever heard and you can form but a faint idea of this battle."[37]

It was during the heat of battle that a soldier's training began to pay dividends. It was then that the countless hours of repetitive drill displayed its value. Men who had had such training were able to perform necessary tasks automatically, without taking the time to think about them. The lack of such training, however, sometimes led to serious problems. The untrained and undisciplined Kentucky militiamen who made up part of General St. Clair's army in 1791 were said to have been so panic stricken when the Indians attacked "that they rushed about from one side of the camp to the other, like a herd of cattle, without the least attempt to fight, or defend themselves." Similarly, an officer noted several instances of unsuitable behavior, possibly stemming from insufficient drill, at a battle in 1813. He saw some men dutifully loading their muskets, but not taking the time to level them at enemy targets before pulling the triggers. Instead, they fired high over the heads of the British. Others did not take the time to ram their cartridges all the way down into the barrels of their muskets, which sometimes resulted in burst barrels. Some dropped their ramrods after loading their muskets and then, in the confusion, were unable to locate them again, thus rendering their muskets useless. Still others rammed home their cartridges, but forgot to extract the ramrod from the barrel before firing, sending the ramrods dozens of yards away and making it impossible for them to use their weapons again.[38]

Officers routinely enjoined their men to aim low to counterbalance an apparently natural tendency to shoot too high. At the Battle of New Orleans, in 1815, a captain, after yelling at his men to keep their shots low, added (perhaps hyperbolically): "They're comin' on their all fours!" It was sound advice. When the battle was over, a soldier looked at a large oak tree that stood just behind the American position and found scarcely a bullet mark on it up to a height of ten or twelve feet. "Above that height," he noted, "it was thickly peppered." Another officer remarked on the same phenomenon at the Battle of Fort George in 1813, when the Americans attacked from the water. The defending British "reserved their fire until our boats were within one hundred and fifty yards when they opened a heavy and galling fire.... As we approached near the shore their firing ought to have been very destructive, but we suffered less owing to their firing too high." He attributed the inaccurate fire to the British soldiers' reluctance to endure the punishing recoil of their muskets when fired from the shoulder. Instead, he claimed, they fired from about waist high, without any semblance of accurate aiming, and the shots flew high.[39]

During the fight for Mexico City in the fall of 1847, an American officer was surprised to feel blood coursing down his face but without any accompanying pain. After waiting a few seconds, and still not experiencing even the slightest of discomfort from his wound, he realized that the "blood" he felt was actually the juice from a nearby cactus that had been destroyed by Mexican cannon fire.[40]

AFTERMATH OF BATTLE

Because of the state of medical knowledge of the time, many of those wounded in battle died of their wounds. Others would require months of convalescence, before being able to resume anything approaching the life they had known before.

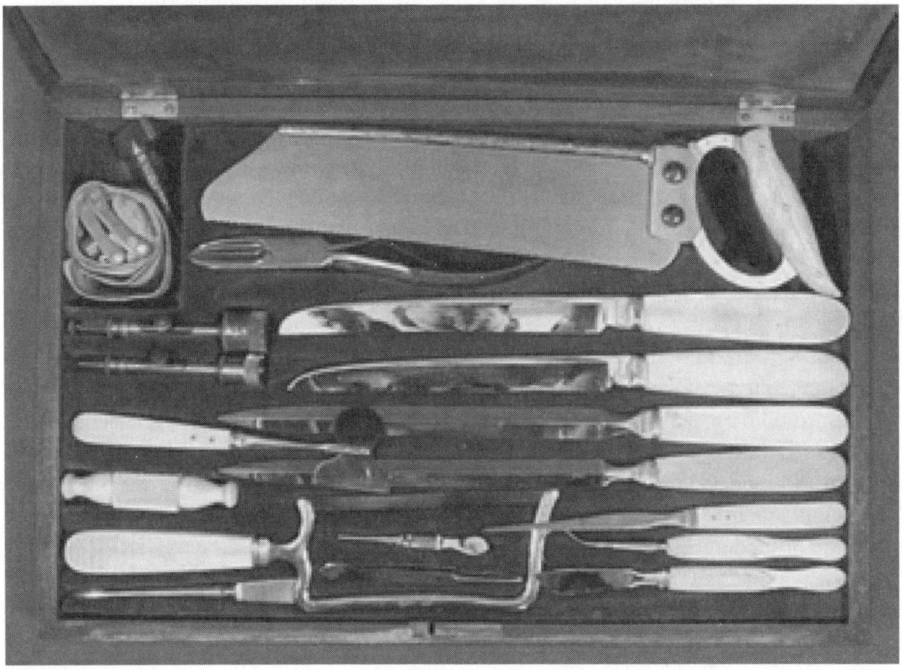

This late eighteenth-century army surgeon's basic field kit contains three different sized amputation knives, two pairs of forceps, and a tenaculum. (*Courtesy of the National Library of Medicine*)

Gunshot Wounds

Up until the Civil War, musket balls inflicted the great majority of wounds on American soldiers. The large, relatively slow-moving lead balls could inflict a considerable amount of damage to the human body. Bullet wounds were of three types: one was where the bullet passed completely through a soldier's limb or body without striking any major bones or organs; the second type occurred when the bullet lodged in the soft tissue of the body; and the third was when the bullet shattered a bone. Doctors treated each differently.

In the first instance, doctors generally allowed the wound to heal itself. They would often pass a probe through the wound and pull a piece of silk completely through it to try to dislodge and remove any foreign matter, such as dirt or a piece of the soldier's clothing. They might then prescribe opium for the soldier's pain until the wound closed up on its own.

When the bullet remained in the patient, it presented different problems for the surgeon. To extract it with a bullet forceps meant that the wound channel had to be enlarged with a scalpel to admit passage of the instrument. When the tip of the forceps reached the ball, the surgeon had to open the jaws of the instrument and pass them around the bullet, further enlarging the original wound. Drawing the bullet out through the narrow wound channel must also have produced excruciating pain for the wounded soldier. Sometimes, when the actual location of the bullet was in doubt, it was left in the patient.

The third type of bullet wound, however, was the most serious. If the bullet shattered a bone, doctors could try to remove the damaged material and leave the patient with a shorter limb than before. This procedure required considerable skill, however, and in battlefield hospitals, where a number of wounded needed attention, surgeons often decided to amputate instead. In cases of compound fracture, amputation was the norm.

There were two major types of amputation. One was the guillotine method and the other was the flap method. The guillotine method was the easier, and quicker, to perform. With the wounded soldier sedated as much as possible with whiskey or opium, and after the mid-1840s with more efficient anesthetics, such as ether and chloroform, the doctor applied a tourniquet above the wound to halt blood flow. Then, with a very sharp knife, he cut quickly through the muscle and other tissues all the way to the bone, completely around the limb. An assistant looped a leather thong around the exposed bone and used it to pull the muscles and other tissues toward the patient's body. This gave the doctor room to saw through the bone. With the limb thus detached, he put down his saw and picked up his tenaculum, a tool with a hook-shaped needle, and gently drew each artery out away from the newly created stump. He then tied these off with an oiled silk suture. The assistant then slowly released the leather thong and allowed the patient's muscles to slide back down and envelope the severed bone. The raw stump was then dressed. A few days after the operation, the doctor tugged loose the arterial sutures and the stump was allowed to continue healing itself. An experienced surgeon could complete the procedure in two to three minutes.

The flap method involved cutting the tissues in such a way as to leave "flaps" that were then brought down to completely cover the stump. This produced a more finished looking stump, but seemed to promote slower healing and sometimes infection. During the War of 1812, a doctor performed a flap amputation of the upper arm of a wounded soldier some thirty-five days after the injury. A few days later, he removed the dressing from the stump to check on the healing process and "was much chagrined at finding that the adhesions of the flap to the muscles had been prevented by a number of maggots finding their way through the dressing into the stump." After a thorough—he supposed—cleansing of the wound, it was again dressed. Monitoring the wound again five days later, he found it again infested with maggots, and the surrounding tissue had so atrophied that the bone stuck out an inch. He cut some more of the bone off, but ten days later the unfortunate soldier died.[41]

A soldier's chance of surviving amputation was variable at best. Statistics indicated that the wounded man's likelihood of a full recovery decreased with the proximity of the amputation to the trunk. For example, the mortality rate for someone having only a foot amputated was about six percent, whereas if the doctor had to take the leg off at mid-thigh, the rate increased to fifty-four percent. The unfortunate man who faced amputation at the hip could expect only a twenty percent survival possibility. Similarly, for the upper extremities, a patient having a hand amputated enjoyed a ninety-seven percent chance for survival, but this dipped to only seventy-six percent if the surgeon had to cut at the upper arm. These statistics are based upon the relatively large number of amputations performed during the Civil War, and these percentages were probably not much lower during the earlier wars.[42]

Whether a wounded soldier lived or died following surgery, it is difficult to imagine that he would ever undergo as much pain as the amputation itself. Yet there are many stories of men bearing up under this pain with immense stoicism. During the War of 1812, a wounded soldier underwent an amputation with seemingly no pain or discomfort, smoking serenely throughout the operation. The Mexican War also provided instances of soldiers reacting to this surgery in unusual ways. Early in this conflict, a soldier, wounded in the leg, begged the surgeons to amputate, but they assured him that he would make a full recovery without the loss of that limb. After the soldier had suffered almost three weeks of pain and misery, the doctors changed their tune and decided that amputation was indeed called for. By now, however, the soldier had also had a change of heart. "I am a poor man," he told a friend, "and have but ten dollars in the world, and…I'le [*sic*] bet all of it, that I outlive the crowd [of surgeons], and furthermore that I'le [*sic*] be d__d, if they shall cut my leg off, neither do I intend to die." And apparently he did not. Later on in the war, a wounded man was undergoing an amputation as the fighting went on nearby. During the course of the procedure, American troops achieved victory and began yelling in triumph. When the patient heard this, he sat up on the operating table, gave three cheers, and then reclined again for the completion of his surgery.[43]

Of course, all surgery performed in the early nineteenth century, military or civilian, was performed by doctors without the least understanding of the principles of antiseptic care. Doctors regularly probed for bullets with their unwashed fingers, only washing their hands when they became too slippery with blood to allow them to pick up their instruments. "We operated in our blood stained and often pus stained coats," one military surgeon remembered. "We used undisinfected instruments from undisinfected plush cases, and still worse used marine sponges which had been used in prior pus cases and had only been washed in tap water. If a sponge or instrument fell on the floor it was washed and squeezed in a basin of tap water and used as if it were clean."[44]

Arrow Wounds

Having an arrow removed, even by an experienced physician, was a very painful experience. The wound channel had to be enlarged with a scalpel to allow room for the doctor to slide a wire loop down the shaft of the arrow to the head. Then the doctor had to maneuver the loop over the head and carefully extricate the arrow. Arrow wounds presented a different set of difficulties in treatment. Probably the most important first step was to leave the arrow in the wound until the injured man reached the doctor. Frontier doctors, civilian and military, soon learned the physical characteristics of the arrows they were likely to encounter. They knew how long they were. The surgeon could then measure the length of shaft extending from the wound and calculate how deep within the victim's body the head of the arrow lay. They knew the orientation of the point with respect to the notch in the feathered end, and this allowed them to orient the wire loop most efficiently.

It was not unusual for a man to be brought to the doctor with more than one arrow in him. During a battle with Pawnees in Nebraska Territory, a soldier suffered eight arrow wounds. A doctor successfully extracted seven of the arrows, but the eighth one proved much more difficult. This arrow had entered the soldier's back on the right side and penetrated his lung. By the time the doctor tried to remove this particular arrow, the man's own bodily fluids had so softened the sinew that held the head to the shaft that all he was able to withdraw was the shaft. In spite of this, the soldier survived. He retired from the army, but he still suffered considerable discomfort from this wound. At times, he found it difficult to swallow or to cough, and it was not unusual for him to spit up blood occasionally. When he applied for a disability pension, he was examined by another army doctor. This man located the arrowhead and was able to remove it surgically. The army then considered his claim for a pension to be groundless and denied it.[45]

The Human Costs of Battle

Battles are not won or lost without human costs. Men died in battle. They suffered horrible wounds in battle. And those who came through without any physical injuries suffered the shock and mental anguish of seeing the human wreckage left behind when a battle finally wore itself out. The same soldiers who had entered battle anxious to "see the elephant" were often sobered by the carnage they saw. "Oh God! what a scene!" wrote a soldier, after the Battle of Chippewa in 1814.

> At every point where the battle raged, were strewn the melancholy vestiges of the recent terrible conflict.... the ground covered with the bodies of the dead and wounded—the former in every stage of mutilation.... The ground was literally *piled* with the dead.... The whole bastion and its immediate neighborhood were heaped with dead, and desperately wounded; while bodies and fragments of bodies were scattered on the ground, in every direction.

Another man described the aftermath of the Battle of New Orleans in 1815:

> When the smoke had cleared away and we could obtain a fair view of the field, it looked, at first glance, like a sea of blood. It was not blood itself which gave it this appearance but the red coats in which the British soldiers were dressed. Straight out before our position, for about the width of a space which we supposed had been occupied by the British column, the field was entirely covered with prostrate bodies. In some places they were lying in piles of several, one on top of the other.

Describing the battlefield of Contreras after the 1847 battle there, a soldier wrote:

> The battlefield was such a sight as I had never seen before, and which I would have been satisfied never to see again. The ground was covered with gore from the wounds of the dying and dead which lay thick upon the field. The sight was horrible—enough to chill the hardest heart. Some had a leg, a foot, an arm or hand mangled to pieces and were lying upon the cold, muddy ground shivering with cold, begging for a bit of bread or a drink of water.

Another soldier, perhaps describing the same battle, wrote: "never can I forget the carnage, the groans of the wounded & dying proceeded from every direction and the horribly mutilated bodies would have moved the heart of any man less familiar with the horrors of battle than ourselves. it is almost incredible how a man can accustom himself to such sights, and look with indifference on the most agonizing spectacle." This man had seen the elephant in its most gruesome aspect. "I have now seen as much of war as I desired," he continued, "and am willing, for the first time, to return to the United States and convert our 'spears into reaping hooks.' "[46]

NOTES

1. Robert J. Moore, Jr. and Michael Haynes, *Tailor Made, Trail Worn: Army Life, Clothing & Weapons of the Corps of Discovery* (Helena, Montana: Farcountry Press, 2003), 29 (quotation); John Jackson, "'We Lay There Doing Nothing': John Jackson's Recollection of the War of 1812," edited by Jeff L. Patrick, *Indiana Magazine of History,* 88 (June 1992), 128.

2. *Jesse A. Gove, The Utah Expedition 1857–1858* (Concord, New Hampshire: New Hampshire Historical Society, 1928), 32.

3. John Jackson, "'We Lay There Doing Nothing': John Jackson's Recollection of the War of 1812," edited by Jeff L. Patrick, *Indiana Magazine of History,* 88 (June 1992), 122; John Scott, "The Letters of Captain John Scott, 15th U.S. Infantry: A New Jersey Officer in the War of 1812,' edited by John C. Fredriksen, *New Jersey History,* 107 (Fall-Winter 1989), 73; [James Hildreth], *Dragoon Campaigns to the Rocky Mountains,* (New York: Wiley and Long, 1836; reprint, New York: Arno, 1973), 85; Jackson, "'We Lay There Doing Nothing,'" 122; Jesse A. Gove, *The Utah Expedition 1857–1858* (Concord, New Hampshire: New Hampshire Historical Society, 1928), 95 (1st quotation), 54 (2d quotation).

4. Albert J. Myer to James Walden, August 13, 1855, in Albert J. Myer, " 'I Am Already Quite a Texan': Albert J. Myer's Letters from Texas, 1854–1856," edited by David A. Clary, *Southwestern Historical Quarterly* 82, no. 1 (July 1978), 62–63 (1st quotation); Leo E. Oliva, *Fort Union and the Frontier Army in the Southwest* (Santa Fe, New Mexico: National Park Service, 1993), 221 (2d quotation).

5. Thomas T. Summers to his brothers and sisters, August 24, 1846, Thomas T. Summers Letters, Filson Club, Louisville, Kentucky (1st quotation); John F. Bouldin to James Bouldin, May 3, 1847, James O. Bouldin Papers, Duke University Library (2d quotation); Miles Morris diary, December 26, 1846, Illinois State Historical Library, Springfield, Illinois (3d quotation).

6. J. R. McClanahan to his sister, October 25, 1846, McClanahan-Taylor Collection, Southern Historical Collection, Library of the University of North Carolina at Chapel Hill (1st quotation); William Seaton Henry, *Campaign Sketches*, 158 (2d quotation); George R. Stewart, *John Phoenix, Esq.: The Veritable Squibob: A Life of Captain George H. Derby, U.S.A.* (New York: Henry Holt and Company, 1937; reprint, New York: Da Capo Press, 1969), 156 (3d quotation).

7. Quoted by Reginald Horsman, in *Race and Manifest Destiny: The Origins of American Racial Anglo-Saxonism* (Cambridge, Massachusetts and London: Harvard University Press, 1981), 87 (quotation).

8. [James Hildreth], *Dragoon Campaigns to the Rocky Mountains* (New York: Wiley and Long, 1836; reprint, New York: Arno, 1973), 141 (1st quotation); Eugene Bandel, *Frontier Life in the Army 1854–1861*, translated by Olga Bandel and Richard Jente, edited by Ralph P. Bieber (Glendale, California: Arthur H. Clark, 1932), 137 (2d quotation); J. H. Bill, "Notes on Arrow Wounds," *The American Journal of the Medical Sciences*, 44 (October 1862), 387 (93d quotation); Osborne Cross, "The Journal of Major Osborne Cross," in *The March of the Mounted Riflemen, First United States Military Expedition to travel the full length of the Oregon Trail from Fort Leavenworth to Fort Vancouver May to October, 1849 as recorded in the journals of Major Osborne Cross and George Gibbs and the official report of Colonel Loring*, edited by Raymond W. Settle (Arthur H. Clark, 1940; reprint, Lincoln and London: University of Nebraska Press, 1989), 189 (4th quotation).

9. Samuel Forry to J. W. Phelps, August 6, 1837, in "Letters of Samuel Forry, Surgeon U.S. Army, 1837–1838," *Florida Historical Quarterly*, 6 (1928), 142 (1st quotation); Reynold M. Wik, "Captain Nathaniel Wyche Hunter and the Florida Indian Campaigns, 1837–1841," *Florida Historical Quarterly*, 39 (1960), 74 (2d quotation); Sprague, "Macomb's Mission to the Seminoles," 178 (3d quotation); Skelton, "Army Officers' Attitudes Toward Indians," 119 (4th quotation), 116 (5th quotation).

10. Skelton, "Army Officers' Attitudes Toward Indians," 121 (1st quotation); Motte, *Journey Into Wilderness*, 141(2d quotation). Albert Myer to James Walden, February 14, 1855, in Myer, " 'I Am Already Quite a Texan'," 42 (3d quotation); Skelton, "Army Officers' Attitudes Toward Indians," 121 (4th quotation).

11. [Hildreth], *Dragoon Campaigns*, 220–221.

12. Lawrence Kip, *Indian War in the Pacific Northwest: The Journal of Lieutenant Lawrence Kip* (Lincoln and London: University of Nebraska Press, 1999), 33 (1st quotation); [Hildreth], *Dragoon Campaigns*, 175 (2d quotation); Jacob Rhett Motte, *Journey Into Wilderness: An Army Surgeon's Account of Life in Camp and Field during the Creek and Seminole Wars, 1836–1838*, edited by James F. Sunderman (Gainesville, Florida: University of Florida Press, 1953), 141 (3d quotation); John T. Sprague, "Macomb's Mission to the Seminoles: John T. Sprague's Journal Kept during April and May 1839," edited by Frank F. White, Jr., *Florida Historical Quarterly*, 35, no. 2 (October 1956), 168 (4th quotation).

13. [Hildreth], *Dragoon Campaigns*, 144 (1st quotation); James A. Bennett, *Forts and Forays: A Dragoon in New Mexico, 1850–1856*, edited by Clinton E. Brooks and Frank D. Reeve (Albuquerque: University of New Mexico Press, 1948), 45 (2d quotation); William B. Skelton, "Army Officers' Attitudes Toward Indians, 1830–1860," *Pacific Northwest Quarterly*, 67, no. 3 (July 1976), 117 (3d quotation); "A Journal of Marches by the First United States Dragoons 1834–1835," edited by Louis Pelzer, *The Iowa Journal of History and Politics*, 7 (July 1909), 372 (4th quotation); James Allen, "Captain James Allen's Dragoon Expedition From Fort Des Moines, Territory of Iowa, in 1844," *The Iowa Journal of History and Politics*, (January 1913), 102 (5th quotation).

14. J. A. Merrifield to Samuel M. Bemis, March 9, 1847, Remiss Family Papers, Virginia Historical Society, Richmond, Virginia (1st quotation); E. Kirby-Smith to ?, May 20, 1846, Edmund Kirby-Smith Papers, University of North Carolina Library (2d quotation).

15. Samuel V. Fulkerson Journal, January 11, 1848, University of Texas Archives, Austin, Texas (1st quotation); John W. Lowe to his wife, October 10, 1847, John Williamson Lowe Letters, Dayton and Montgomery County Public Library, Dayton, Ohio (2d quotation).

16. Horsman, *Race and Manifest Destiny*, 236 (1st quotation); Henry Smith Lane to Samuel Stone, November 5, 1846, Henry Smith Lane Papers, Filson Club, Louisville, Kentucky (2d quotation); Diary of Sydenham Moore, January 11, 1847, Sydenham Moore Collection, Alabama State Archives, Montgomery, Alabama (3d quotation); Frank Hardy to Horace Hardy, October 31, 1846, Frank Hardy Collection, Ohio Historical Society, Columbus, Ohio (4th quotation); John Moragne to Mary E. Dervis, January 24, 1847, Mary Elizabeth Moragne Collection, South Caroliniana Library, University of South Carolina, Columbia, South Carolina (5th quotation).

17. William Austine to his cousin, February 28, 1847, William Austine Collection, University of North Carolina at Chapel Hill; Thomas Barkley to William S. Shulse, May 12, 1847, Joseph K. Johnson Collection, Western Historical Manuscript Collection, University of Missouri Library, Columbia, Missouri; Thomas T. Summers to his brothers, November 15, 1846, Filson Club, Louisville, Kentucky (1st quotation); William Seaton Henry, *Campaign Sketches of the War with Mexico* (New York: Harper and Brothers, 1847; reprint, New York: Arno Press, 1973), 157–158 (2d quotation).

18. Abner Doubleday, *My Life in the Old Army: The Reminiscences of Abner Doubleday*, edited by Joseph E. Chance (Fort Worth, Texas: Texas Christian University Press, 1998), 238 (1st quotation); Will Wallace to Helen M. Indson, November 16, 1846, Wallace-Dickey Collection, Illinois State Historical Library, Springfield, Illinois (2d quotation).

19. Steven T. Ross, *From Flintlock to Rifle: Infantry Tactics, 1740–1866* (London: Frank Cass, 1996), 34–35; Paddy Griffith, *Forward Into Battle: Fighting Tactics from Waterloo to Vietnam* (Chicester, Sussex: Anthony Bird Publications, 1981), 24.

20. John Scott to ?, November 17, 1812, in "The Letters of Captain John Scott, 15th U.S. Infantry: A New Jersey Officer in the War of 1812," edited by John C. Fredriksen, *New Jersey History* 107 (Fall-Winter 1989), 71 (quotation).

21. E. K. Smith to his sister, no date, Smith-Kirby-Webster-Black-Danner Family Collection, U.S. Army Military History Institute, Carlisle, Pennsylvania.

22. William H. Guthman, *March to Massacre: A History of the First Seven Years of the United States Army, 1784–1791* (New York: McGraw-Hill, 1975), 127; Motte, *Journey Into Wilderness*, 143 (1st quotation); Rufus McIntire, "The War of 1812 in Northern New York: The Observations of Captain Rufus McIntire," edited by John C. Fredriksen, *New York History* (July 1987), 303 (2d quotation).

23. Baron von Steuben, *Regulations for the Order and Discipline of the Troops of the United States* (Philadelphia: Styner and Cyst, 1779), as reprinted in Joseph R. Riling, *Baron von Steuben and His Regulations* (Philadelphia: Ray Riling Arms Books, 1966), 52; Guthman, *March to Massacre*, 187, 227–228 (quotation).

24. Guthman, *March to Massacre*, 191.

25. Alan D. Gaff, *Bayonets in the Wilderness: Anthony Wayne's Legion in the Old Northwest* (Norman, Oklahoma: University of Oklahoma Press, 2004), 63; Diary entry for November 11, 1814, "William Wood Thackera, Volunteer in the War of 1812," edited by Anne Castrodale Golovin, *Pennsylvania Magazine of History and Biography*, 91 (July 1967), 314 (quotation).

26. A. G. Blanchard, *Diary and Biography of Capt. A. G. Blanchard Second Louisiana Infantry Volunteers Mexican War, May 2nd, 1846 to July 25, 1848*, Louisiana and Lower Mississippi Valley Collections, Louisiana State University Libraries, Baton Rouge, Louisiana; Albert G. Brackett, *General Lane's Brigade in Central Mexico* (Cincinnati: H. W. Derby; New York, J. C. Derby, 1854), 293, 294 (quotation).

27. Harvey Neville diary entry for January 15, 1847, Chicago Historical Society; Will Wallace to George, March 1, 1847, Wallace-Dickey Collection, Illinois State Historical Library, Springfield, Illinois (1st quotation); "A Contemporary Account of the Battle of New Orleans by a Soldier in the Ranks," *Louisiana Historical Quarterly* 9 (1962), 12 (2d quotation); Doubleday, *My Life in the Old Army*, 93 (3d quotation); Richard Coulter, "The Westmoreland Guards in the War with Mexico, 1846–1848," *Western Pennsylvania Historical Magazine* 24, no. 2 (June 1941), 110.

28. T. H. Towner to his father, February 3, 1847, Benjamin Towner papers, Duke University Library, Durham, North Carolina (1st quotation); T. H. Towner to his father, February 12, 1847, Benjamin Towner papers, Duke University Library, Durham, North Carolina (2d quotation).

29. George Rutledge Gibson, *Journal of a Soldier under Kearny and Doniphan, 1846–1847*, edited by Ralph P. Bieber (Glendale, California: Arthur H. Clarke, 1935; repr. ed. Philadelphia: Porcupine Press, 1974), 186 (1st quotation); Henry S. Turner, "Letters About Mexican War," *Glimpses of the Past* 2, no. 2 (1934–1935), 8 (2d quotation); Jacob S. Robinson, *A Journal of the Santa Fe Expedition under Colonel Doniphan* (Portsmouth, New Hampshire: Portsmouth *Journal* Press, 1848, repr. ed. New York: Da Capo Press, 1972), 24–25 (3d quotation); Kimball Clark, "The Epic March of Doniphan's Missourians," *Missouri Historical Review* 80 (January 1986), 142 (4th quotation).

30. Clinton A. White to his father, September 29, 1846, Carr B. White Collection, Ohio Historical Society, Columbus, Ohio (1st quotation); Will Wallace to George, March 1, 1847, Wallace-Dickey Collection, Illinois State Historical Library, Springfield, Illinois (2d quotation); R. S. Dix to his brother, U.S. Senator John Adams Dix, February 25, 1847, John Adams Dix Papers, Duke University Library, Durham, North Carolina (3d quotation).

31. David Bates Douglass, "An Original Narrative of the Niagara Campaign of 1814," edited by John T. Horton, *Niagara Frontier* 11 (Spring 1964), 5, 12.

32. Stephen Franklin Nunnelee, "Incidents of a Campaign, &c—1846," typescript in Alabama State Archives, Montgomery, Alabama (1st quotation); Will Wallace to his father, January 19, 1847, Wallace-Dickey Collection, Illinois State Library, Springfield, Illinois (2d quotation); Albert Gay to his parents, August 26, 1847, Jacqueline Dorgan Meketa, "A Soldier in New Mexico, 1847–1848," *New Mexico Historical Review* 66, no. 1 (January 1991), 20 (3d quotation); Jesse Gove to his wife, October 9, 1857, Jesse A. Gove, *The Utah Expedition 1857–1858* (Concord, New Hampshire: New Hampshire Historical Society, 1928), 74 (4th quotation); Jesse Gove to his wife, November 19, 1857, Gove, *The Utah Expedition*, 95 (5th quotation).

33. Guthman, *March to Massacre*, 129.

34. Gabriel Nadeau, "Indian Scalping," *Bulletin of the History of Medicine*, 10 (1941), 180, 182 (quotation), 190, 182.

35. Gaff, *Bayonets in the Wilderness*, 228–229; Isaac Naylor, "The Battle of Tippecanoe," *The Indiana Magazine of History*, 2, no. 4 (December 1906), 168; John H. Fonda, "Early Wisconsin," *Report and Collections of the State Historical Society of Wisconsin*, 5, part 2 (1868), 263.

36. Guthman, *March to Massacre*, 129 (quotation); Bill, "Notes on Arrow Wounds," 369.

37. J. Rufus Smith to William M. Stakely (?), October 23, 1847, Atlanta Historical Society (1st quotation); Noah Newton to Brown, April 25, 1847, Ritchie-Harrison Papers, Earl Greg Swen Library, College of William and Mary, Williamsburg, Virginia (2d quotation).

38. Gaff, *Bayonets in the Wilderness*, 4 (quotation); George McFeely, "Chronicle of Valor: The Journal of a Pennsylvania Officer in the War of 1812," edited by John C. Fredriksen, *The Western Pennsylvania Historical Magazine* 67 (July 1984), 263.

39. "A Contemporary Account of the Battle of New Orleans by a Soldier in the Ranks," *Louisiana Historical Quarterly*, 9 (1962), 11 (1st quotation), 12 (2d quotation); McFeely, "Chronicle of Valor," 262 (3d quotation).

40. Edmund B. Alexander to his wife, September 16, 1847, Edmund B. Alexander Collection, United States Military Academy Library, West Point, New York.

41. C. Keith Wilbur, *Revolutionary Medicine, 1700–1800* (Chester, Connecticut: Globe Pequot Press, 1980), 36; Stewart Brooks, *Civil War Medicine* (Springfield, Illinois: Charles C. Thomas, 1966), 100–101; W. E. Horner, "A Military Hospital at Buffalo, New York, in the year 1814," *The Medical Examiner and Record of Medical Science*, New Series, no. 97 (January 1853), 16 (quotation).

42. Brooks, *Civil War Medicine*, 99.

43. Mary C. Gillett, *The Army Medical Department, 1775–1818* (Washington, D.C.: Center of Military History, United States Army, 1981), 96; R. C. Foster to his father, December 10, 1846, Robert C. Foster Papers, University of North Carolina Library (quotation); Robert Hagan diary, September 22, 1847, University of Texas Archives.

44. Peter D. Olch, "Medicine in the Indian-Fighting Army, 1866–1890," *Journal of the West*, 21, no. 3 (July 1982), 38; Volney Steele, "Army Wounds and the Military Surgeon in the West," *Military History of the West*, 30, no. 2 (Fall 2000), 160 (quotation).

45. Steele, "Army Wounds and the Military Surgeon in the West," 166, 168.

46. David Bates Douglass, "An Original Narrative of the Niagara Campaign of 1814," edited by John T. Horton, *Niagara Frontier*, 11 (Spring 1964), 29 (1st quotation); "A Contemporary Account of the Battle of New Orleans", 9 (1962), 14 (2d quotation); J. Rufus Smith to William M. Stakely (?), October 23, 1847, Atlanta Historical Society (3d quotation); G. W. Rains to his brother, August 28, 1847, George Washington Rains papers, University of North Carolina Library (4th quotation).

7 EPILOGUE

There were many men in America who, by 1860, had long since completed their military service, and the federal government was very slow in rewarding such service with pensions—although land grants were more freely distributed. For quite some time, military pensions were given only to officers who had served in the Revolutionary War and had become disabled by wounds, or to the families of officers who had died in service. There was nothing for the disabled enlisted men, or for the families of enlisted men who had given their lives during the war. Pensions were finally made available in 1828—almost fifty years after the guns had fallen silent at Yorktown.[1]

Following the War of 1812, the government offered bounty land warrants to those men who had served for five years or more—which left out most of the volunteer troops. The enabling legislation, furthermore, specified that the veterans had to actually redeem the warrants in land; they could not sell them to speculators or anyone else. In 1850, Congress extended the land warrants to any soldier who had served as little as one month since 1790. By this time, many of the previously neglected veterans of the War of 1812 had reached that stage of their lives when they were unwilling, or in some cases unable, to relocate to the far frontier, where the available land was located. Veterans who had served at least sixty days in that war had to wait until 1871 before receiving service pensions. Such funds were not available, however, to veterans who had subsequently supported the Confederacy in the recent Civil War. A few years later, this restriction was lifted, and the government extended pensions to veterans with as few as fourteen days' service. The last pensioner from the War of 1812 died in 1905.[2]

Mexican War veterans took the hint from their elders and began petitioning Congress in 1874 for a pension bill that would cover them. With the Civil War less than a decade in the past, however, and with the knowledge that hundreds—probably thousands—of Mexican War veterans had fought for the South in that more recent conflict, there was Northern resistance to a pension bill, lest some former Rebels benefit therefrom. An editorial in a veterans' magazine responded rather colorfully to a Vermont congressman's opposition:

> Intense hatred of the whole Southern people has ever been a distinguishing characteristic of a large majority of the inhabitants of that little strip of mountain on the Canadian border, and level-headed Christians usually listen, with a feeling akin to pity, to the inane gabble about their "loy'lty" to the Government, and opposition to "traitors and rebels," because those played out terms of opprobrium so illy conceal the mental infirmity which so largely prevails in the people around the Green Mountains.

The writer went on to suggest that perhaps the government would do well to rid itself entirely of Vermont, perhaps in some sort of a trade with Canada "in payment of some ancient fish indemnity." The Vermonter's fears were only partially assuaged with the passage, in 1887, of a pension bill for disabled Mexican War veterans—except those who had become disabled while aiding the Confederacy—and all other veterans of the earlier war who had reached the age of 62. This pension was extended in 1912 to cover all veterans of this nation's first foreign war, regardless of their physical condition, as long as they had at least sixty days' service and were honorably discharged.[3]

Congress just did not seem willing to appropriate money for all of the nation's aging former soldiers at once. It was not, for example, until 1892 that it provided for men who had fought the Creeks and Seminoles and other Indians between 1832 and 1842. Then, of course, those remaining veterans from both earlier and later Indian conflicts wanted similar benefits and, in 1902, pensions were finally available for those men who had served between 1817 and 1832 and between 1842 and 1858. Perhaps the soldier, writing in 1811 immediately after the Battle of Tippecanoe, was right when he stated: "I am sensable thet it is the opinion of most the people in the U.S. that no honor is to be attached to indian fiteing but I beg leave to disagree with all such, and believe if thay weigh the subject in its proper scale thay would judge different."[4]

The soldiers in the pre–Civil War American Army resembled, in many ways, the American soldiers of later periods. Within their ranks were both heroes and cowards, sinners and saints. They were generally confident that they could defeat any enemy in battle, whether Indian, British, Mexican, or other Americans, even though their actual performance sometimes showed that this feeling of superiority was not always justified.

They enlisted in the army for a variety of reasons. Some did so from a sense of patriotism. Some from a simple need for a steady supply of food and clothing. Others saw army service as a way to escape unpleasant domestic situations. And still others signed up simply for the sheer excitement of it all.

They groused about the quality of their food, the competence of their officers, the drudgery of duty, and many other aspects of military life. Generally, however, the soldiers in antebellum America had enough food, although their diet was often rather unimaginative. Their officers, particularly after the War of 1812, knew their duties well. And as the Military Academy at West Point turned out more and more graduates, the percentage of capable officers went up. There is no denying that their work often resembled that of common laborers more than soldiers, but that was due to the expanding frontier and the need to protect it.

An officer reflecting back on his frontier service perhaps captured the essence of such service when he wrote that Indian fighting was not the hardest part:

> It was the long marches, the fatigue, the exposure, the hunger and thirst, the desolation and loneliness of the stations, and, finally, the loss of health, that made it so very trying

> and so thankless. In addition to this there were the seeming forgetfulness, the indifference, and to all appearances the want of proper appreciation from those from whom praise and commendation should have come, that made frontier service so much worse than it ought to have been.[5]

After 1860, the nature of warfare and the duties and responsibilities of the Army changed. The scale of war increased dramatically. Armies of fifty or sixty thousand men soon faced each other on the fields of battle. The weapons of war also became more sophisticated, dictating a change—albeit a slow change—in both offensive and defensive tactics. The increased industrialization that occurred by the end of the century also led to the use of the Army as a constabulary force to control social unrest during labor strikes. The almost pre-industrial U.S. Army of the first half of the nineteenth century was thus transformed by forces beyond its control. That the Army has continually adapted to such changes is something for which we should be thankful.

NOTES

1. Robert J. Moore, Jr. and Michael Haynes, *Tailor Made, Trail Worn: Army Life, Clothing & Weapons of the Corps of Discovery* (Helena, Montana: Farcountry Press, 2003), 16; James W. Oberly, "Gray-Haired Lobbyists: War of 1812 Veterans and the Politics of Bounty Land Grants," *Journal of the Early Republic*, 5 (Spring 1985), 55; William H. Glasson, *Federal Military Pensions in the United States* (New York: Oxford University Press, 1918), 51.
2. Oberly, "Gray-Haired Lobbyists," 35–37; Glasson, *Federal Military Pensions*, 109–112.
3. Wallace E. Davies, "The Mexican War Veterans as an Organized Group," *Mississippi Valley Historical Review*, 35, no. 2 (September 1948), 233 (quotation), 226; Glasson, *Federal Military Pensions*, 118.
4. Glasson, *Federal Military* Pensions, 114–115; Charles Larrabee to Adam Larrabee, December 11, 1811, near Vincennes, Indiana in Charles Larrabee, "Lieutenant Charles Larrabee's Account of the Battle of Tippecanoe, 1811," edited by Florence G. Watts, *Indiana Magazine of History* 57 (1961), 233 (quotation).
5. William B. Lane, "Frontier Service in the Fifties," The United Service (December 1893), 522, as cited in Leo E. Oliva, *Fort Union and the Frontier Army in the Southwest* (Santa Fe, New Mexico: National Park Service, 1993), 40.

BIBLIOGRAPHY

This bibliography of more than 500 sources is arranged both topically and chronologically in an effort to allow readers to locate sources germane to their particular needs. General sources are listed first, followed next by sources on wars, campaigns, and incidents, and is arranged chronologically. A third group of sources is arranged by topics related to soldiers' lives, such as health or training.

Some sources, however, although only listed once, might just as reasonably have been placed in more than one category. For instance, a particular soldiers' reminiscence might extend across more than one of the time frames used to record sources. Other sources might contain information that could fit into more than one of the topics. For this reason, it is suggested that the interested reader pay close attention to the reference notes for each chapter.

GENERAL SOURCES

The following general sources give a general overview of the U.S. military from 1790 to 1860:

Coffman, Edward M. *The Old Army: A Portrait of the American Army in Peacetime, 1784–1898.* New York and Oxford: Oxford University Press, 1986.

Cunliffe, Marcus. *Soldiers and Civilians: The Martial Spirit in America 1775–1865*. Boston and Toronto: Little, Brown and Company, 1968.

Ekirch, Arthur E., Jr. *The Civilian and the Military.* New York: Oxford University Press, 1956.

Griffith, Paddy. *Forward Into Battle: Fighting Tactics from Waterloo to Vietnam.* Chicester, England: Antony Bird Publications, 1981.

Horsman, Reginald. *Race and Manifest Destiny: The Origins of American Racial Anglo–Saxonism.* Cambridge, Massachusetts and London: Harvard University Press, 1981.

Huidekoper, Frederic. *The Military Unpreparedness of the United States: A History of American Land Forces from Colonial Times until June 1, 1915.* New York: MacMillan, 1916.

Johnson, Richard W. *A Soldier's Reminiscences in Peace and War.* Philadelphia: J. B. Lippincott, 1886.

Keyes, Erasmus D. *Fifty Years' Observation of Men and Events.* New York, 1884.

Kreidberg, Marvin A. and Merton G. Henry. *History of Military Mobilization in the United States Army, 1775–1945.* Washington, D.C.: Department of the Army, 1955.

Millis, Walter. *Arms and Men: A Study of American Military History.* New York: Putnam, 1956.

Richardson, James D., ed. A Compilation of the Messages and Papers of the Presidents, 1789–1897. Washington, D.C.: Government Printing Office, 1897.

Risch, Erna. *Quartermaster Support of the Army: A History of the Corps 1775–1939.* Washington, D.C.: Quartermaster Historian's Office, Office of the Quartermaster General, 1962.

Todd, Frederick P. "Our National Guard." *Military Affairs* 5, no. 2 (Summer and Fall 1941): 73–86.

Urwin, Gregory J. W. *The United States Cavalry: An Illustrated History.* Poole, Dorset: Blandford Press, 1983.

Urwin, Gregory J. W. *The United States Infantry: An Illustrated History 1775–1918.* 1988; reprint Norman, Oklahoma: University of Oklahoma Press, 2000.

U.S. Government. *General Regulations for the Army: or, Military Institutes.* Philadelphia: M. Carey and Sons, 1821.

U.S. Government. *General Regulations for the Army of the United States, 1841.* Washington, D.C., 1841.

U.S. Government. *Regulations for the Army of the United States.* New York: Harper and Brothers, 1857.

SOLDIERS' LIVES: WARS AND CAMPAIGNS

The following sources explore the lives of soldiers, arranged more–or-less chronologically by various wars and campaigns.

The Early Indian Wars until the War of 1812

The following sources immediately below explore the lives of soldiers during the early Indian wars and up until the outbreak of the War of 1812:

Barry, James P. "The Defeats of Harmar and St. Clair." *American History Illustrated* (December 1968): 10–19.

Brown, Alan S. "The Role of the Army in Western Settlement: Josiah Harmar's Command, 1785–1790." *Pennsylvania Magazine of History and Biography* 93 (1969): 161–178.

Burton, C. M. "Anthony Wayne and the Battle of Fallen Timbers." *Michigan Pioneer and Historical Society Collections* 31 (1901): 472–489.

Caldwell, Norman W. "The Frontier Army Officer, 1794–1814." *Mid-America* 37, no. 2 (April 1955): 101–128.

Caldwell, Norman W. "The Enlisted Soldier at the Frontier Post, 1790–1814." *Mid-America* 37, no. 4 (October 1955): 195–204.

Caldwell, Norman W. "Civilian Personnel at the Frontier Military Post (1790–1814)." *Mid-America* 38, no. 2 (April 1956): 101–119.

[Chew, John]. "The Diary of an Officer in the Indian Country in 1794." *American Historical Magazine* 3 (November 1908): 639–643; 4 (January 1909): 69–71.

Clark, William. "William Clark's Journal of General Wayne's Campaign." Edited by R. C. McGrane. *Mississippi Valley Historical Review* 1 (December 1914): 418–444.

Cooke, John. "General Wayne's Campaign in 1794 and 1795: Captain John Cooke's Journal." *American Historical Record* 2 (July 1873): 311–316; (August 1873): 339–345.

Currie, James T. "The First Congressional Investigation: St. Clair's Military Disaster of 1791." *Parameters: Journal of the U.S. Army War College* 20 (December 1990): 95–102.

Denny, Ebenezer. *Military Journal of Major Ebenezer Denny, An Officer in the Revolutionary* and Indian Wars, with an Introductory Memoir. Philadelphia, J. B. Lippincott, 1859; reprint New York: Arno, 1971.

Eid, Leroy V. "American Indian Military Leadership: St. Clair's 1791 Defeat." *Journal of Military History* 57, no. 1 (June 1993): 71–88.

Flores, Dan L., ed. *Jefferson and Southwestern Exploration: The Freeman and Custis Accounts of the Red River Expedition of 1806.* Norman, Oklahoma: University of Oklahoma Press, 1984.

Forman, Sidney. "Why the United States Military Academy Was Established in 1802." *Military Affairs* 29, no. 1 (Spring 1965): 16–28.

Gaff, Alan D. *Bayonets in the Wilderness: Anthony Wayne's Legion in the Old Northwest.* Norman, Oklahoma: University of Oklahoma Press, 2004.

Guthman, William H. *March to Massacre: A History of the First Seven Years of the United States Army, 1784–1791.* New York: McGraw-Hill, 1974.

Hasbrouck, Alfred. "Our Undeclared War With Spain." *Journal of the American Military History Foundation* 2, no. 3 (Autumn 1938): 115–125.

Jacobs, James Ripley. *The Beginnings of the U.S. Army, 1783–1812.* Princeton, New Jersey: Princeton University Press, 1947.

Knopf, Richard C., ed. "Two Journals of the Kentucky Volunteers, 1793 and 1794." *The Filson Club History Quarterly* 27 (July 1953): 247–281.

Knopf, Richard C., ed. "A Precise Journal of General Wayne's Last Campaign in the year 1794." *American Antiquarian Society Proceedings* 44: 273–302.

Mahon, John K. "Pennsylvania and the Beginnings of the Regular Army." *Pennsylvania History* 21, no. 1 (January 1954): 33–44.

Mahon, John K. "Anglo-American Method of Indian Warfare, 1674–1794." *Mississippi Valley Historical Review* 45 (September 1958): 254–275.

Malone, Patrick M. *The Skulking Way of War: Technology and Tactics Among the New England Indians.* Baltimore and London: Johns Hopkins University Press, 1993.

Martin, James Kirby and Mark Edward Lender. *A Respectable Army: The Military Origins of the Republic, 1763–1789.* Wheeling, Illinois: Harlan Davidson, 1982.

McGrane, Reginald C., ed. "Journal of General Wayne's Campaign Against the Shawnee Indians in Ohio, 1794–1795 (Clark)." *Mississippi Valley Historical Record* 1, no. 3 (December 1914): 418–444.

Nadeau, Gabriel. "Indian Scalping." *Bulletin of the History of Medicine* 10, no. 2 (1941): ??

Newman, Samuel. "A Picture of the First United States Army: The Journal of Captain Samuel Newman." Edited by Milo M. Quaife. *Wisconsin Magazine of History* 2 (September 1918): 40–73.

Palmer, Dave Richard and James W. Stryker. *Early American Wars and Military Institutions.* The West Point Military History Series. Thomas E. Griess, Series Editor. Wayne, New Jersey: Avery Publishing Group, 1986.

Pitcavage, Mark. "Ropes of Sand: Territorial Militias, 1801–1812." *Journal of the Early Republic* 13 (Winter 1993): 481–500.

Sargent, Winthrop. Diary of Col. Winthrop Sargent, Adjutant General of the United States' Army, During the Campaign of MDCCXCI [1791]. Wormsloe, Georgia, 1851. Reprinted as "Winthrop Sargent's Diary While With General Arthur St. Clair's Expedition against the Indians." *Ohio Archaeological and Historical Quarterly* 33 (July 1924): 237–273.

Schaumburgh, Bartholomew. "Fort Stoddart in 1799: Seven Letters of Captain Bartholomew Schaumburgh." Edited by Jack D. L. Holmes. *Alabama Historical Quarterly* 26 (Fall-Winter 1964): 231–252.

Skelton, William B. "The Confederation's Regulars: A Social Profile of Enlisted Service in America's First Standing Army." *William and Mary Quarterly* 3rd series, 46, no. 4 (October 1989): 770–785.

Skelton, William B. "Social Roots of the American Military Profession: The Officer Corps of America's First Peacetime Army, 1784–1789." *Journal of Military History* 54, no. 4 (October 1990): 435–452.

Smith, James. *A Treatise on the Mode and Manner of Indian War.* Paris, Kentucky: Joel R. Lyle, 1812.

Stagg, J. C. A. "Soldiers in Peace and War: Comparative Perspectives on the Recruitment of the United States Army, 1802–1815." *William and Mary Quarterly* 57, no. 1 (January 2000): 79–120.

Steinle, John. "Unlucky Soldier: Josiah Harmar's Frontier Struggle." *Timeline: A Publication of the Ohio Historical Society* 8 (April/May 1991): 2–17.

Twiggs, John. "The Creek Troubles of 1793." Edited by E. Merton Coulter. *Georgia Historical Quarterly* 11 (September 1927): 274–280.

Ward, Harry M. *The Department of War, 1781–1795.* Pittsburgh: University of Pittsburg Press, 1962.

Warner, Michael S. "General Josiah Harmar's Campaign Reconsidered: How Americans Lost the Battle of Kekionga." *Indiana Magazine of History* 83 (March 1987): 43–64.

Wilkinson, James. "General James Wilkinson's Narrative of the Fallen Timbers Campaign." Edited by Milo M. Quaife. *Mississippi Valley Historical Review* 16 (June 1921): 81–90.

Winder, C. S. "Captain C. S. Winder's Account of a Battle with the Indians." *Maryland Historical Magazine* 35 (1940): 56–59.

The War of 1812

The following sources explore the lives of soldiers during the War of 1812:

A Soldier's Life on the Western Frontier in 1813. Fort Wayne: Fort Wayne and Allen County Public Library, 1953.

Anderson, Fanny J. "Medical Practices in Detroit During the War of 1812." *Bulletin of the History of Medicine* 16 (1944): 261–275.

Archer, Mary Roach. "Journal of Major Isaac Roach, 1812–1824." *Pennsylvania Magazine of History and Biography* 17 (1893): 129–158.

Askin, Charles. "The Fort Dearborn Massacre." Edited by Milo M. Quaife. *Mississippi Valley Historical Review* 1, no. 4 (March 1915): 561–573.

Beall, William K. "Journal of William K. Beall, July–August, 1812." *American Historical Review* 17 (1912): 783–808.

Blackman, Learner. "The Diary of a Chaplain in Andrew Jackson's Army: The Journal of Mr. Learner Blackman." Edited by Dawson A. Phelps. *Tennessee Historical Quarterly* 12 (1953): 265–281.

Callaway, James. "James Callaway in the War of 1812, Diary." Edited by Edgar Wesley. *Missouri Historical Society Collections* 5 (1927): 38–81.

Cassell, Frank A. "Baltimore in 1813: A Study of Urban Defense in the War of 1812." *Military Affairs* 33, no. 3 (December 1969): 349–361.

Clift, G. Glenn. "War of 1812 Diary of William B. Northcutt." *Register of the Kentucky Historical Society* 56 (1958): 325–344; 56 (1958): 253–270.

Coffee, John. "Letters of General John Coffee to His Wife, 1813–1815." Edited by John H. DeWitt. *Tennessee Historical Magazine* 2 (December 1916): 264–295.

Cogswell, A. S. "Letters of the War of 1812 in the Champlain Valley." Edited by Wilmond W. Parker. *Vermont Quarterly* 12 (1944): 104–124.

"A Contemporary Account of the Battle of New Orleans by a Soldier in the Ranks." *Louisiana Historical Quarterly* 9 (1926): 11–15.

Corbin, James. "The Story of James Corbin, A Soldier at Fort Dearborn." Edited by M. M. Quaife. *Mississippi Valley Historical Review* 3, no. 2 (September 1916): 219–228.

Crombie, John W. "The Twenty-Second United States Infantry: A Forgotten Regiment in a Forgotten War, 1812–1815." *Western Pennsylvania Historical Magazine* 50, no. 2 (April 1967): 133–148; 50, no. 3 (July 1967): 221–238.

Cutrer, Thomas W. " 'The Tallapoosa Might Truly be Called the River of Blood': Major Alexander McCulloch and the Battle of Horseshoe Bend, March 27, 1813." *Alabama Review* 43 (January 1990): 35–39.

Darlington, William. "William Darlington's Diary of Service in the War of 1812." *Western Pennsylvania Historical Magazine* 20 (1937): 189–214.

Davis, Andrew McFarland. "The Employment of Indian Auxiliaries in the American War." *English Historical Review* 2 (1887): 709–728.

Douglass, David Bates. "An Original Narrative of the Niagara Campaign of 1814." Edited by John T. Horton. *Niagara Frontier* 11 (Spring 1964): 1–36.

Duane, William. "The Letters of William Duane." Edited by Worthington C. Ford. *Massachusetts Historical Society Proceedings* 20 (1906–1907): ??

Floyd, John. "Letters of John Floyd, 1813–1818." *Georgia Historical Quarterly* 33 (September 1949): 228–269.

Fredriksen, John C. *Free Trade and Sailors' Rights: A Bibliography of the War of 1812.* Westport, Connecticut: Greenwood Press, 1985.

Fredriksen, John C. "Memoirs of Captain Ephraim Shaler: A Connecticut Yankee in the War of 1812." *New England Quarterly,* 57 (September 1984): 411–420.

Fredriksen, John C. "Reynold M. Kirby and His Race to Join the Regiment: A Connecticut Yankee in the War of 1812." *Connecticut History* 32 (November 1991): 51–82.

Fredriksen, John C., ed. "Chronicle of Valor: The Journal of a Pennsylvania Officer in the War of 1812." *Western Pennsylvania Historical Magazine* 67 (July 1984): 243–284.

Fredriksen, John C. " 'A Poor but Honest Sodger': Colonel Cromwell Pearce, the 16th U.S. Infantry, and the War of 1812." *Pennsylvania History* 52 (July 1985): 131–161.

Fredriksen, John C. "Kentucky at the Thames, 1813: A Rediscovered Narrative by William Greathouse." *Register of the Kentucky Historical Society* 83 (Spring 1985): 93–117.

Fredriksen, John C. "A New Hampshire Volunteer in the War of 1812: The Experiences of Charles Fairbanks." *Historical New Hampshire* 40 (Fall-Winter 1985): 156–178.

Fredriksen, John C. "A Georgia Officer in the War of 1812: The Letters of Colonel William Clay Cumming." *Georgia Historical Quarterly* 71 (Winter 1987): 668–691.

Fredriksen, John C. "The War of 1812 in Northern New York: The Observations of Captain Rufus McIntire." *New York History* 68 (July 1987): 297–324.

Fredriksen, John C. "The Pennsylvania Volunteers in the War of 1812: An Anonymous Journal of Service for the Year 1814." *Western Pennsylvania Historical Magazine* 70 (April 1987): 123–157.

Fredriksen, John C. "Colonel James Burn and the War of 1812: The Letters of a South Carolina Officer." *South Carolina History Magazine* 90 (October 1989): 299–312.

Fredriksen, John C. " 'The General is Much Mortified': Orderly Book of General Tannehill's Brigade of Pennsylvania Militia, October to December 1812." *Journal of Erie Studies* 19 (Spring 1990): 50–88.

Fredriksen, John C. "The Letters of Captain John Scott, 15th U.S. Infantry: A New Jersey Officer in the War of 1812." *New Jersey History* 107 (Fall-Winter 1989): 60–81.

Fredriksen, John C. "The Pittsburgh Blues and The War of 1812: The Memoir of Private Nathaniel Vernon." *Pennsylvania History* 56 (July 1989): 197–212.

Fredriksen, John C. "The War of 1812 in Northern New York: General George Izard's Journal of the Chateauguay Campaign." *New York History* 76 (April 1995): 173–200.

Fredriksen, John C. "Lawyer, Soldier, Judge: Incidents in the Life of Joseph Lee Smith." *Connecticut Historical Society Bulletin* 51 (1986): 103–121.

Fredriksen, John C. "Plow-joggers for Generals: The Experience of a New York Ensign in the War of 1812." *Indiana Military History Journal* 11 (1986): 16–27.

Golovin, Anne C. "William Wood Thackera, Volunteer in the War of 1812." *Pennsylvania Magazine of History and Biography* 91 (1967): 299–325.

Greene, Jerome A. 'Historic Resource Study: Chalmette Unit: Jean Lafitte National Historical Park and Preserve." United States Department of the Interior. National Park Service, 1985, http://www.cr.nps.gov/history/online_books/jela/hrs.htm, accessed December 8, 2004.

Greenhous, Brereton. "A Note on Western Logistics in the War of 1812." *Military Affairs* 34 (1970): 41–44.

Hamilton, Robert. "The Expedition of General Samuel Hopkins Up the Wabash, 1812: The Letters of Captain Robert Hamilton." *Indiana Magazine of History* 43 (1947): 393–402.

Hanks, Jarvis Frary. "A Drummerboy in the War of 1812: The Memoirs of Jarvis Frary Hanks." Edited by Lester W. Smith. *Niagara Frontier* 7 (1960): 53–62.

Hitsman, J. Mackay. "David Parrish and the War of 1812." *Military Affairs* 26 (Winter 1962–1963): 171–177.

Holden, Horace. "Reminiscences of the War of 1812." *New Jersey Historical Society Proceedings* 2 (1917): 20–26.

Horton, John T. "An Original Narrative of the Niagara Campaign of 1814." *Niagara Frontier* 11 (Spring 1964): 1–36.

Jackson, John. " 'We Lay There Doing Nothing': John Jackson's Recollections of the War of 1812." Edited by Jeff L. Patrick. *Indiana Magazine of History* 88 (June 1992): 111–131.

Jarvis, James. "The British Invasion of Hampton in 1813: The Reminiscences of James Jarvis." Edited by Parke Rouse, Jr. *Virginia Magazine of History and Biography* 76 (July 1968): 318–336.

Kerby, Robert L. "The Militia System and the States' Militia in the War of 1812." *Indiana Magazine of History* 73 (1977): 104–124.

Kimball, Jeffery. "The Battle of Chippawa: Infantry Tactics in the War of 1812." *Military Affairs* 32 (1968): 169–186.

Latour, A. Lacarriere. "Historical Memoir of the War in West Florida and Louisiana, 1814–1815." *Louisiana Historical Quarterly* 2 (1919): 143–153.

Mahon, John K. "The Principle Causes for the Failure of the United States Militia System During the War of 1812." *Indiana Military History Journal* 4 (1979): 15–21.

Mahon, John K. "Letters From Virginia Camps in 1814." *West Virginia History* 12 (1951): 280–284.

Patterson, John. "The Letters of John Patterson, 1812–1813." *Western Pennsylvania Historical Magazine* 23 (1940): 99–109.

Peckham, Howard. "An Eyewitness Account of the Siege of Fort Wayne." *Indiana Magazine of History* 44 (1948): 409–418.

Pitcavage, Mark. " 'Burthened in Defence of our Rights': Opposition to Military Service in Ohio During the War of 1812." *Ohio History* 104 (Summer/Autumn 1995): 142–162.

Quaife, Milo M. "A Diary of the War of 1812." *Mississippi Valley Historical Review* 1 (1914): 272–278.

Raynaud, L. M. "Officers and Soldiers, 1814–1815." *Southern Historical Society Papers* 36 (1908): 133–140.

Schillinger, William. "Journal of Ensign William Schillinger, A Soldier in the War of 1812." *Ohio Archaeological and Historical Society Quarterly* 41 (1932): 51–82.

Sholes, Stanton. "Narrative of the Northwestern Campaign of 1813." *Mississippi Valley Historical Review* 15, no. 4 (1929): 519–525.

Shriver, Phillip R. "Broken Locks and Rusty Barrels: A New York Militia Company on the Eve of the War of 1812." *New York History* 67 (July 1986): 353–357.

Sibert, Daniel. "Daniel Sibert's Reminiscences of the War of 1812: Letters to His Brother, Jeremiah Siebert." *Register of the Kentucky Historical Society* 36 (1938): 66–71.

Smyth, Alexander. "Reminiscences of the Late War." *Army and Navy Chronicle* 1 (1835): 59–60.

Stagg, J. C. A. "Enlisted Men in the United States Army, 1812–1815: A Preliminary Survey." *William and Mary Quarterly* 43, no. 4 (October 1986): 615–643.

Towle, Edward L. "The Militia Myth: Letters from Lt. William B. Rochester on the Niagara Frontier, 1813." *University of Rochester Library Bulletin* 19 (1964): 33–41.

Walker, Joseph E., ed. "A Soldier's Diary for 1814." *Pennsylvania History* 12 (October 1945): 292–304.

Wilkinson, W. C. "Private John Jones in the War of 1812." *Indiana Military History Journal* 7 (1982): 4–11.

The End of the War of 1812, the Seminole Wars, and the Mexican War

The following sources explore the lives of soldiers from the end of the War of 1812 until the Mexican War, including the Seminole Wars:

Allen, James. "Captain James Allen's Dragoon Expedition From Fort Des Moines, Territory of Iowa, in 1844." Edited by Jacob Van der Zee. *Iowa Journal of History and Politics* 11 (January 1913): 68–108.

Allen, James. "The Dragoons in the Iowa Territory, 1845." Edited by Robert Rutland. *Iowa Journal of History* 51 (April 1953): 156–182.

Anderson, Robert. "Reminiscences of the Black Hawk War." *Wisconsin Historical Collections* 10 (1888): 167–176.

"Arrival of American Troops at Green Bay, in 1816." *Wisconsin Historical Collections* 13 (1895): 441–447.

Beers, Henry P. *The Western Military Frontier, 1815–1846.* Philadelphia, 1935.

Beers, Henry P. "Military Protection of the Santa Fe Trail to 1843." *New Mexico Historical Review* 12 (April 1937): 113–133.

Bemrose, John. "Bemrose's Medical Case Notes From the Second Seminole War." Edited by E. A. Hammond. *Florida Historical Quarterly* 47 (1969): 401–413.

Bemrose, John. *Reminiscences of the Florida Seminole War.* Edited by John K. Mahon. Gainesville, Florida: University of Florida Press, 1966.

Boone, Nathan. "Captain Nathan Boone's Journal." Edited by W. Julian Fessler. *Chronicles of Oklahoma* 7 (March 1929): 58–105.

Buchanan, Robert C. "A Journal of Lt. Robert C. Buchanan during the Seminole War." Edited by Frank F. White, Jr. *Florida Historical Quarterly* 29 (October 1950): 132–151.

Buchanan, Robert C., "A Scouting Expedition Along Lake Panasoffkee." Edited by Frank F. White, Jr. *Florida Historical Quarterly* 31 (April 1953): 282–289.

Carleton, James Henry. *The Prairie Logbooks: Dragoon Campaigns to the Pawnee Village in 1844, and to the Rocky Mountains in 1845.* Edited by Louis Pelzer. Chicago, 1943; Lincoln, Nebraska: University of Nebraska Press, 1988.

Chapman, William Warren. "A West Point Graduate in the Second Seminole War: William Warren Chapman and the View from Fort Foster." Edited by Edward C. Coker and Daniel L. Schafer. *Florida Historical Quarterly* 68 (April 1990): 447–475.

Covington, James W., ed. "Life at Fort Brooke, 1824–1836." *Florida Historical Quarterly* 36 (1957–58): 319–330.

Crane, Charles. "Our Military Policy from the End of the War of 1812–1815 to the Beginning of the Civil War." *Journal of the United States Infantry Association* 4: 677–709.

Croghan, George. *Army Life on the Western Frontier: Selections from the Official Reports Made Between 1826 and 1845 by Colonel George Croghan.* Edited by Francis P. Prucha. Norman, Oklahoma: University of Oklahoma Press, 1958.

Dallam, James B. "A Soldier's View of the Seminole War." Edited by William D. Hoyt, Jr. *Florida Historical Quarterly* 25 (1947): 356–362.

Davis, Carl L. and LeRoy H. Fischer. "Dragoon Life in Indian Territory, 1833–1845." *Chronicles of Oklahoma* 48 (1970): 2–24.

Davis, David Brion, ed. *Antebellum American Culture: An Interpretive Anthology.* Lexington, Massachusetts and Toronto: D. C. Heath, 1979.

Davis, Jefferson. "Jefferson Davis Ponders His Future, 1829." Edited by Lynda J. Lasswell. *Journal of Southern History* 41, no. 4 (November 1975): 507–522.

Evans, Hugh. "Hugh Evans' Journal of Colonel Henry Dodge's Expedition to the Rocky Mountains in 1835." Edited by Fred S. Perrine. *Mississippi Valley Historical Review* 14, no. 2 (September 1927): 192–214.

Evans, Hugh. "The Journal of Hugh Evans, Covering the First and Second Campaigns of the United States Dragoon Regiment in 1834 and 1835: Campaign of 1834." Edited by Fred S. Perrine and Grant Foreman. *Chronicles of Oklahoma* 3 (September 1925): 175–215.

[Flynn, John]. "Reminiscences of Some Incidents in the Career of a United States Dragoon Between the Years 1839 and 1844." *Texas Quarterly* 9 (Autumn 1966): 7–20.

Fonda, John H. "Early Wisconsin." *Report and Collections of the State Historical Society of Wisconsin* 5, part 2 (1868).: ??

Ford, Lemuel. "Captain Ford's Journal of an Expedition to the Rocky Mountains, 29 May to 16 September 1835." Edited by Louis Pelzer. *Mississippi Valley Historical Review* 12, no. 4 (March 1926): 550–579.

Forry, Samuel. "Letters of Samuel Forry, Surgeon, U.S. Army 1837, '38." *Florida Historical Quarterly* 6 (January 1928): 133–148; (April 1928): 206–219; 7 (July 1928): 88–105.

Forsyth, Thomas. "Journal of a Voyage from St. Louis to the Falls of St. Anthony, in 1819." *Wisconsin Historical Collections* 6 (1872): 188–219.

Gale, John. *The Missouri Expedition, 1818–1820: The Journal of Surgeon John Gale, with Related Documents.* Edited by Roger L. Nichols. Norman, Oklahoma: University of Oklahoma Press, 1969.

Gardner, Hamilton. "The March of the First Dragoons From Jefferson Barracks to Fort Gibson, 1833–1834." *Chronicles of Oklahoma* 31 (1953): 22–36.

Gardner, Hamilton. "A Young West Pointer Reports for Duty at Jefferson Barracks in 1827." *Missouri Historical Society Bulletin* 9 (1952–53): 124–138.

Goetzmann, William H. *Army Exploration in the American West, 1803–1863.* New Haven and London: Yale University Press, 1959.

Gratiot, Henry. "Journals and Reports of the Black Hawk War." Edited by M. M. Quaife. *Mississippi Valley Historical Review* 12, no. 3 (December 1925): 392–409.

Hagan, William T. "General Henry Atkinson and the Militia." *Military Affairs* 23, no. 4 (Winter 1959–1960): 194–197.

Hayne, Arthur P. "Report of Inspection of the Ninth Military Department, 1819." Edited by L.B.S. *Mississippi Valley Historical Review* 7, no. 3 (December 1920): 261–274.

[Hildreth, James]. *Dragoon Campaigns to the Rocky Mountains: Being a History of the Enlistment, Organization and first Campaigns of the Regiment of United States Dragoons, Together with Incidents of a Soldier's Life, and Sketches of Scenery and Indian Character.* New York, 1836; reprint New York: Arno, 1973.

Hollingsworth, Henry. "Tennessee Volunteers in the Seminole Campaign: The Diary of Henry Hollingsworth." Edited by Stanley F. Horn. *Tennessee Historical Quarterly* 1 (September 1942): 269–274; (December 1942) 344–366; 2 (March 1943): 61–73; (June 1943) 163–178; (September 1943) 236–256.

Hoyt, William D., Jr. "A Soldier's View of the Seminole War, 1838–1839." *Florida Historical Quarterly* 25 (April 1947): 356–362.

Hughes, Willis B. "The First Dragoons on the Western Frontier, 1834–1846." *Arizona and the West* 12 (Summer 1970): 115–138.

Hunter, Nathaniel W. "Captain Nathaniel Wyche Hunter and the Florida Indian Campaigns, 1837–1841." Edited by Reynold M. Wik. *Florida Historical Quarterly* 39 (1960): 62–75.

Jamison, Isabel. "Independent Military Companies of Sangamon County in the 30's." *Journal of the Illinois State Historical Society* 3 (January 1911): 22–48.

Jones, Roger. "Gen. Brown's Inspection Tour Up the Lakes in 1819." *Publications of the Buffalo Historical Society* 24 (1920): 295–323.

Kearny, Stephen Watts. "An Expedition Across Iowa in 1820." *Annals of Iowa* 3rd Series, 10 (1912): 345–371.

Kellogg, Louise Phelps. "Old Fort Howard." *Wisconsin Magazine of History* 18 (December 1934): 125–140.

Kennerly, James. "Diary of James Kennerly, 1823–1826." Edited by Edgar B. Wesley. *Missouri Historical Society Collections* 6, no. 1 (October 1928): 41–97.

Larabbe, Charles. "Lieut. Charles Larabbe's Account of the Battle of Tippecanoe." Edited by Florence G. Watts. *Indiana Magazine of History* 57 (1961): 225–247.

Lea, A. M. Briggs. "The Expedition of 1835." Edited by John Ely. *Palimpsest* 16 (April 1935): 105–136.

Mahon, John K. *History of the Second Seminole War, 1835–1842.* Gainesville, Florida: University of Florida Press, 1967.

Mahon, John K. "A Board of Officers Considers the Condition of the Militia in 1826." *Military Affairs* 15, no. 2 (Summer 1951): 85–94.

McPhail, Leonard. "Notes and Documents: The Diary of Assistant Surgeon Leonard McPhail on His Journey to the Southwest in 1835." Edited by Harold W. Jones. *Chronicles of Oklahoma* 18 (1940): 281–292.

Meek, A. B. "The Journal of A. B. Meek and the Second Seminole War, 1836." Edited by John K. Mahon. *Florida Historical Quarterly* 38 (1960): 102–318.

Miller, John. "The Military Occupation of Green Bay." *Mississippi Valley Historical Review* 13, no. 4 (March 1927): 549–553.

Motte, Jacob Rhett. *Journey Into Wilderness: An Army Surgeon's Account of Life in Camp and Field during the Creek and Seminole Wars, 1836–1838.* Edited by James F. Sunderman. Gainesville, Florida: University of Florida Press, 1953.

Myers, Harry C., ed. "From the 'Crack Post of the Frontier': Letters of Thomas and Charlotte Swords." *Kansas History* 5 (Autumn 1982): 184–213.

Nelson, Harold L. "Military Roads for War and Peace—1791–1836." *Military Affairs* 19, no. 1 (Spring 1955): 1–14.

Nichols, Roger L. "Soldiers as Farmers: Army Agriculture in the Missouri Valley, 1818–1827." *Agricultural History* 44, no. 2 (April 1970): 213–222.

Nichols, Roger L. "The Army and the Indians, 1800–1830—A Reappraisal: The Missouri Valley Example." *Pacific Historical Review* 41 (May 1972): 151–168.

Palmer, Dave R. *1794: America, Its Army, and the Birth of the Nation.* Novato, California: Presidio Press, 1994.

Pelzer, Louis. "A Frontier Officer's Military Order Book." *Mississippi Valley Historical Review* 6, no. 2 (September 1919): 260–267.

Pelzer, Louis, ed. "A Journal of Marches by the First United States Dragoons, 1834–1835." *Iowa Journal of History and Politics* 7 (July 1909): 331–378.

Peters, George P. "George P. Peters' Version of the Battle of Tippecanoe (November 7, 1811)." Edited by Richard G. Carlson. *Vermont History* 45 (Winter 1977): 38–43.

Phelps, John W. "Letters of Lieutenant John W. Phelps, U.S.A., 1837–1838." *Florida Historical Quarterly* 6 (October 1927):

Pickell, John. "The Journals of Lieutenant John Pickell, 1836, 1837." Edited by Frank F. White, Jr. *Florida Historical Quarterly* 38 (1959): 143–171.

Prucha, Francis P. *Broadax and Bayonet: The Role of the United States Army in the Development of the Northwest, 1815–1860.* Madison, Wisconsin: State Historical Society of Wisconsin, 1953.

Prucha, Francis Paul. *The Sword of the Republic: The United States Army on the Frontier, 1783–1846.* New York: Macmillan, 1969.

Prucha, Francis Paul. "The United States Army as Viewed by British Travelers, 1825–1860." *Military Affairs* 7, no. 3 (Fall 1953): 113–124.

Quaife, Milo M., ed. "Journals and Reports of the Black Hawk War." *Mississippi Valley Historical Review* 12 (December 1925): 392–409.

Reid, Russell, and Clell G. Gannon, eds. "Journal of the Atkinson-O'Fallon Expedition." *North Dakota Historical Quarterly* 4 (October 1929): 5–56.

"Reminiscences of Some Incidents in the Career of a United States Dragoon Between the Years 1839 and 1844." *Texas Quarterly* 9, no. 3 (Autumn 1966).

Riley, Bennet, Alphonso Wetmore and Reuben Holmes. "'Dear Hook': Letter from Bennet Riley, Alphonso Wetmore, and Reuben Holmes, 1822–1833." Edited by James S. Hutchins. *Bulletin of the Missouri Historical Society* 36 (pt. 1, July 1980): 203–220.

Rutland, Robert, ed. "A Journal of the First Dragoons in the Iowa Territory, 1844." *Iowa Journal of History* 51 (1953): 57–78.

Skelton, William B. "Army Officers' Attitudes Toward Indians, 1830–1860." *Pacific Northwest Quarterly* 67, no. 3 (July 1976): 113–124.

Skelton, William B. "The Commanding General and the Problem of Command in the United States Army, 1821–1841." *Military Affairs* 34, no. 4 (December 1970): 117–122.

Smith, Joseph R. "Letters From the Second Seminole War." Edited by John K. Mahon. *Florida Historical Quarterly* 36 (April 1958): 331–353.

[Snelling, William J.] "Early Days at Prairie du Chien and Winnebago Outbreak of 1827." *Wisconsin Historical Collections* 5 (1868): 123–153.

Sprague, John T. "Macomb's Mission to the Seminoles: John T. Sprague's Journal Kept during April and May, 1839." Edited by Frank F. White, Jr. *Florida Historical Quarterly* 35 (October 1956): 130–193.

Talbot, Theodore. *The Journals of Theodore Talbot 1843 and 1849–1852—With the Fremont Expedition of 1843 and With the First Military Company in Oregon Territory, 1849–1852.* Edited by Charles H. Carey. Portland, Oregon: Metropolitan Press, 1931.

Tipton, John. "John Tipton's Tippecanoe Journal." *Indiana Magazine of History* 2 (1906): 170–184.

Trowbridge, Charles C. "With Cass in the Northwest in 1820: The Journal of Charles C. Trowbridge." Edited by Ralph H. Brown. *Minnesota History* 23 (June 1942): 126–148; (September 1942): 233–252; (December 1942): 328–348.

Wesley, Edgar Bruce. "Life at a Frontier Post: Fort Atkinson, 1823–1826." *Journal of the American Military Institute* 3 (1939): 203–209.

Wesley, Edgar Bruce. "Life at Fort Atkinson." *Nebraska History* 30 (December 1949): 348–358.

Young, C. R., ed. *Westward Into Kentucky: The Narrative of Daniel Trabue,* Lexington, Kentucky: University of Kentucky Press, 1981.

Young, Otis E. "The United States Mounted Ranger Battalion, 1832–1833." *Mississippi Valley Historical Review* 41, no. 3 (December 1954): 453–470.

Young, Tommy R. "The United States Army in the South, 1789–1835." Ph. D. diss., Louisiana State University, 1973.

The Mexican War

The following sources explore the lives of soldiers during the Mexican War:

Anderson, Robert. *An Artillery Officer in the Mexican War, 1846–1847.* New York and London: G. P. Putnam's Sons, 1911.

Archer, J. J. "A Marylander in the Mexican War: Some Letters of J. J. Archer." Edited by C. A. Porter Hopkins. *Maryland Historical Magazine* 54, no. 4 (1959): 408–422.

Backus, Electus. "A Brief Sketch of the Battle of Monterey, with details of that portion of it, which took place at the eastern extremity of the city." *Historical Magazine* 10, no. 7 (July 1866): 207–213.

Backus, Electus. "Details of the Controversy Between the Regulars and Volunteers, in relation to the part taken by each in the capture of Battery No. 1 and other works at the east end of the City of Monterey, on the 21st of September, 1846." *Historical Magazine* 10, no. 8 (August 1866): 255–257.

Bailey, Thomas. "Diary of the Mexican War." *Indiana Magazine of History* 14, no. 2 (1918): 134–147.

[Ballentine, George.] *Autobiography of an English Soldier in the United States Army, Comprising Observations and Adventures in the States and Mexico.* New York: Stringer and Townshend, 1853.

Baylies, Francis. "The March of the United States Troops, Under the Command of General John E. Wool, from San Antonio, Texas, to Saltillo, Mexico, in the Year 1846." *Stryker's American Register and Magazine* 4 (July 1850): 297–312.

Beauregard, P. G. T. *With Beauregard in Mexico: The Mexican War Reminiscences of P. G. T. Beauregard.* Edited by T. Harry Williams. [Baton Rouge]: Louisiana State University Press, 1956.

Beck. E. W. H. "Case of Excision of the Whole of the Genital Organs." *Missouri Medical and Surgical Journal* 3 (1847–1848): 160.

Bigler, Henry W. "Extracts from the Journal of Henry W. Bigler." *Utah Historical Quarterly* 5, no. 2 (April 1932): 34–64.

Bliss, Robert S. "The Journal of Robert S. Bliss, with the Mormon Battalion." *Utah Historical Quarterly* 4, no. 3 (July 1931): 67–96; 4, no. 4 (October 1931): 110–128.

Bodson, Robert Louis. "A Description of the United States Occupation of Mexico as Reported by American Newspapers Published in Vera Cruz, Puebla, and Mexico City, September 14, 1847, to July 31, 1848." Ed.D. diss., Ball State University, 1971.

Brackett, Albert G. *General Lane's Brigade in Central Mexico.* Cincinnati: H. W. Derby; New York: J. C. Derby, 1854.

Brydolph, Fabian. "An Iowan in the Mexican War." Edited by George S. May. *Iowa Journal of History* 3, no. 2 (1955): 167–174.

Campbell, William Bowen. "Mexican War Letters of Col. William Bowen Campbell, of Tennessee, Written to Governor David Campbell, of Virginia, 1846–1847." Edited by St. George L. Sioussat. Tennessee Historical Magazine 1, no. 2 (1915): 129–167.

Chamberlain, Samuel E. *My Confession: The Recollections of a Rogue.* 1956. Reprint. Lincoln and London: University of Nebraska Press, 1987.

Chapman, William. "Letters from the Seat of War—Mexico." *Green Bay Historical Bulletin* 4, no. 4 (July–August 1928): 1–24.

Clark, Kimball. "The Epic March of Doniphan's Missourians." *Missouri Historical Review* 80 (January 1986): 134–155.

Clutter, George Washington. "George Washington Clutter in the Mexican War." Edited by Florence Johnson Scott. *Texas Military History* 4, no. 2 (1964): 119–131.

Coffey, Chesley Sheldon. "The Mexican War Letters of Chesley Sheldon Coffey." Edited by Mary Ellen Rowe. *Journal of Mississippi History* 44, no. 3 (August 1982): 235–252.

Collins, Francis. "Journal of Francis Collins: An Artillery Officer in the Mexican War." Edited by Maria Clinton Collins. *Quarterly Publication of the Historical and Philosophical Society of Ohio* 10, no. 2 and 3 (April and July 1915): 37–109.

Cook, Zo. S. "Mexican War Reminiscences." *Alabama Historical Quarterly* 19 (1957): 435–465.

Cooke, P. St. George. "Report of Lieut. Col. P. St. George Cooke of His March from Santa Fe, New Mexico, to San Diego, Upper California." Edited by Hamilton Gardner. *Utah Historical Quarterly* 22, no. 1 (January 1954): 15–40.

Cooke, Philip St. George. *The Conquest of New Mexico and California; An Historical and Personal Narrative.* New York: G. P. Putnam's Sons, 1878, Reprint. New York: Arno Press, 1976.

Coulter, Richard, and Barclay, Thomas. *Volunteers: The Mexican War Journals of Private Richard Coulter and Sergeant Thomas Barclay, Company E, Second Pennsylvania Infantry.* Kent, Ohio: Kent State University Press, 1991.

Cox, Leander M. "Mexican War Journal of Leander M. Cox." Edited by Charles F. Hinds. *Register of the Kentucky Historical Society* 55, no. 1 (1957): 29–52; 55, no. 3 (1957): 213–36; 56, no. 1 (1958): 47–69.

Crockett, John M. "Letter of John M. Crockett, 1846." *Register of the Kentucky Historical Society* 52, no. 178 (January 1954): 305–309.

Dana, N. J. T. *Monterrey Is Ours!: The Mexican War Letters of Lieutenant Dana, 1845–1847.* Edited by Robert H. Ferrell. Lexington, Kentucky: University Press of Kentucky, 1990.

Deas, George. "Reminiscences of the Campaign on the Rio Grande." *Dawson's Historical Magazine* 17, no. 1 (January 1870): 19–22; 17, no. 2 (1870): 99–103; 17, no. 4 (April 1870): 236–238; 17, no. 5 (May 1870): 311–316.

De Leon, Arnoldo. *They Called Them Greasers: Anglo Attitudes toward Mexicans in Texas, 1821–1900.* Austin, Texas: University of Texas Press, 1983.

Doubleday, Abner. *My Life in the Old Army: The Reminiscences of Abner Doubleday.* Edited by Joseph E. Chance. Fort Worthj, Texas: Texas Christian University Press, 1998.

Duncan Louis C. "The Days Gone By: A Volunteer Regiment in 1846–1847." *Military Surgeon: Journal of the Association of Military Surgeons of the United States* 56, no. 5 (1929): 709–713.

Edwards, Frank S. *A Campaign in New Mexico.* Philadelphia: Carey and Hart, 1847, Reprint. Ann Arbor, Mich.: University Microfilms, 1966.

Elderkin, James D. *Biographical Sketches and Anecdotes of a Soldier of Three Wars as Written by Himself.* Detroit: Record Printing, 1899.

Emory, William H. "New Mexico Diary—1846." Edited by Irving F. Hand. *New Mexico* 26, no. 10 (October 1948): 24, 47.

Engelmann, Adolph. "The Second Illinois in the Mexican War: Mexican War Letters of Adolph Engelmann, 1846–1847." Translated and edited by Otto B. Engelmann. *Journal of the Illinois State Historical Society* 26, no. 4 (1934): 357–452.

Eubank, Damon. "Kentuckians in Mexico: Kentucky Volunteers and Their Attitudes toward the War, Mexico, and the Mexicans." *Kentucky Review* 14 (Summer 1998): 38–50.

Evans, Joseph. "Around Cape Horn with Colonel Stevenson's Regiment in 1846." *Quarterly of the Society of California Pioneers* 7, no. 4 (1930): 244–254.

Ewell, Richard S. *The Making of a Soldier: Letters of General R. S. Ewell.* Edited by Percy C. Hamlin. Richmond, Virginia: Whittet and Shepperson, 1935.

Fleming, Thomas. "From the Hudson to the Halls of Montezuma," *MHQ: The Quarterly Journal of Military History* 11 (Spring 1999): 62–77.

Frost, Daniel M. "The Memoirs of Daniel M. Frost." Edited by Mrs. Dana O. Jensen. *Missouri Historical Society Bulletin* 26, no. 3 (1970): 200–226.

Fuess, Claude M. *The Life of Caleb Cushing.* 2 vols. New York: Harcourt, Brace, 1923.

Fuller, Claud E. *The Rifled Musket.* New York: Bonanza Books, 1958.

"A General's Orderly in Mexico." *The United Service Magazine* 78, no. 318 (1855): 78–85.

Gibson, George Rutledge. *Journal of a Soldier under Kearny and Doniphan, 1846–1847.* Edited by Ralph P. Bieber. Glendale, Calif.: Arthur H. Clarke, 1935, Reprint. Philadelphia: Porcupine Press, 1974.

Gordon, George H. "The Battle of Contreras and Churubusco." *Papers of the Military Historical Society of Massachusetts* 13 (1913): 561–598.

Gordon, George H. "Battles of Molino del Rey and Chapultepec." *Papers of the Military Historical Society of Massachusetts* 13 (1913): 601–613.

Grant, Ulysses S. *The Papers of Ulysses S. Grant, Vol. 1, 1837–1861.* Edited by John Y. Simon. Carbondale: Southern Illinois University Press, 1967.

Hamilton, Charles S. "Memoirs of the Mexican War." *Wisconsin Magazine of History* 14, no. 1 (1930): 63–92.

Hartman, George W. *A Private's Own Journal: Giving an Account of the Battles in Mexico, under Gen'l. Scott.* Greencastle, Pennsylvania.: E. Robinson, 1849.

Henry, William Seaton. *Campaign Sketches of the War with Mexico.* New York: Harper and Brothers, 1847, Reprint. New York: Arno Press, 1973.

Hess, John W. "John W. Hess, with the Mormon Battalion." *Utah Historical Quarterly* 4, no. 2 (1931): 47–55.

Heyer, Charles H. "A Mexican War Letter." *Magazine of History* 17, no. 6 (1913): 238–241.

H. [Hill, D. H.] "The Battles of the Rio Grande." *Southern Quarterly Review* N. S., 2, no. 4 (November, 1850): 427–463.

Hitchcock, Ethan A. *Fifty Years in Camp and Field: Diary of Major General Ethan Allen Hitchcock, U.S.A.* Edited by W. A. Croffut. New York and London: G. P. Putnam's Sons, 1909; reprint Freeport, New York: Books for Libraries Press, 1971.

Holland, James K. "Diary of a Texan Volunteer in the Mexican War." *Southwestern Historical Quarterly* 30, no. 1 (July 1926): 1–33.

Hollingsworth, John McHenry. "Journal of John McHenry Hollingsworth: A Lieutenant in Stevenson's Regiment in California." *California Historical Society Quarterly* 1, no. 3 (January 1923): 207–270.

Irey, Thomas R. "Soldiering, Suffering, and Dying in the Mexican War." *Journal of the West* 11, no. 2 (1972): 285–298.

Jamieson, Milton. *Journal and Notes of a Campaign in Mexico: Containing a History of Company C, of the Second Regiment of Ohio Volunteers.* Cincinnati: 1849.

Johannsen, Robert W. *To the Halls of the Montezumas: The Mexican War in the American Imagination.* New York and Oxford: Oxford University Press, 1985.

Johnson, William S. "Private Johnson Fights the Mexicans, 1847–1848." Edited by John Hammond Moore. *South Carolina Historical and Genealogical Magazine* 67, no. 4 (1966): 203–228.

Jones, Nathaniel V. "The Journal of Nathaniel V. Jones, with the Mormon Battalion." *Utah Historical Quarterly* 4 (January 1931): 6–23.

K., G. W. "Vera Cruz." *Littell's Living Age* 13, no. 157 (1847): 328–329.

Karnes, Thomas L. "Gilpin's Volunteers on the Santa Fe Trail." *Kansas Historical Quarterly* 30, no. 1 (Spring 1964): 1–14.

Kendall, George W. "Mr. Kendall's Letters from the Army." *Littell's Living Age* 15, no. 183 (1847): 323–335.

King, John Nevin. "The Happy Soldier: The Mexican War Letters of John Nevin King." Edited by Walter B. Hendrickson. *Journal of the Illinois State Historical Society* 46, no. 1 (1953): 13–27; 46, no. 2 (1953): 151–70.

Lane, Henry S. "The Mexican War Journal of Henry S. Lane." Edited by Graham A. Barringer. *Indiana Magazine of History* 53, no. 4 (1957): 383–434.

Lane, W. B. "The United States Cavalry in the Mexican War." *Journal of the United States Cavalry Association* 3, no. 11 (December 1890): 388–408.

Lippitt, Francis J. *Reminiscences of Francis J. Lippitt.* Providence, Rhode Island: Preston and Rounds, 1902.

Lundie, Thomas Y. "Letters from Mexico: 1847–1848." Edited by James W. McKee. *Tennessee Historical Quarterly* 29, no. 2 (1970): 152–159.

Manigault, Arthur M. "A Letter from Vera Cruz in 1847." Edited by Robert A. Law. *Southwestern Historical Quarterly* 18, no. 2 (1914): 215–218.

Maury, Dabney. *Recollections of a Virginian in the Mexican, Indian, and Civil Wars,* New York: Charles Scribner's Sons, 1894.

McCaffrey, James M. *Army of Manifest Destiny: The American Soldier in the Mexican War, 1846–1848.* New York: New York University Press, 1992.

McCaffrey, James M. *"Surrounded by Dangers of All Kinds": The Mexican War Letters of Lieutenant Theodore Laidley.* Denton, Texas: University of North Texas Press, 1997.

McClellan, George B. *The Mexican War Diary of George B. McClellan.* Edited by William Starr Myers. Princeton, New Jersey: Princeton University Press, 1917.

McClintock, William A. "Journal of a Trip through Texas and Northern Mexico in 1846–1847." *Southwestern Historical Quarterly* 34, no. 1 (1930): 20–37; 34, no. 2 (1930): 141–158; 34, no. 3 (1931): 231–256.

McSherry, Richard. *El Puchero; or, A Mixed Dish from Mexico.* Philadelphia: Lippincott, Grambo, 1850.

McSherry, Richard. "A Mexican Campaign Sketch." *The New Eclectic* 3 (1868): 327–336.

McWhiney, Grady. *Braxton Bragg and Confederate Defeat.* New York and London: Columbia University Press, 1969.

McWilliams, William Joseph. "A Westmoreland Guard in Mexico, 1847–1848: The Journal of William Joseph McWilliams." *Western Pennsylvania Historical Magazine* 52, no. 3 (July 1969): 213–240; 52, no. 4 (October 1969): 387–413.

Meade, George Gordon. *The Life and Letters of George Gordon Meade.* 2 vols. New York: Scribner's, 1913.

"Memories of Mexico." *Harper's New Monthly Magazine* 3 (June–November 1851): 461–466.

Miller, Robert Ryal. *Shamrock and Sword: The Saint Patrick's Battalion in the U.S.-Mexican War.* Norman, Oklahoma and London: University of Oklahoma Press, 1989.

Morrison, George S. "Letter from Mexico by George S. Morrison, a Member of Capt. Albert Pike's Squadron." *Arkansas Historical Quarterly* 16, no. 4 (1957): 398–401.

Nauman, George. "A Lancastrian in the Mexican War." *Historical Papers and Addresses of the Lancaster County Historical Society* 12, no. 3 (1908): 109–129.

Nauman, George. "In Command at Vera Cruz, 1847–1848." *Papers Read to Lancaster County Historical Society* 18, no. 6 (June 1914): 157–60.

Nunnelee, S. F. "Alabama in Mexico War." *Alabama Historical Quarterly* 19 (1957): 413–433.

Oliva, Leo E. "Missouri Volunteers on the Santa Fe Trail, 1847–1848." *Trail Guide.* 15, no. 3 (September 1970): 1–20.

Oswandel, J. Jacob. *Notes of the Mexican War, 1846–1848.* Philadelphia, 1885.

Payne, Darwin. "Camp Life in the Army of Occupation: Corpus Christi, July 1845 to March 1846." *Southwestern Historical Quarterly* 73, no. 3 (1970): 326–342.

Perry, Oran, comp. *Indiana in the Mexican War.* Indianapolis: William B. Burford, 1908.

Peskin, Allan. *Winfield Scott and the Profession of Arms.* Kent, Ohio and London: Kent State University Press, 2003.

Proctor, Alfred N. "A Massachusetts Mechanic in Florida and Mexico—1847." Edited by Arthur W. Thompson. *Florida Historical Quarterly* 33, no. 2 (1954): 130–341.

Quesenbury, William. "William Quesenbury of Fayetteville Reports the Battle of Buena Vista, Mexico." *Flashback: Preserving the Past for the Future* 4, no. 2 (1954): 34–36.

Reid, Samuel C., Jr. *The Scouting Expeditions of McCulloch's Texas Rangers.* 1847, Reprint. Freeport, N. Y.: Books for Libraries Press, 1970.

Reilly, James. "An Artilleryman's Story." *Journal of the Military Service Institution of the United States* 33, no. 126 (1903): 438–447.

Richardson, William H. "William H. Richardson's Journal of Doniphan's Expedition." Edited by William B. McGroarty. *Missouri Historical Review* 22, no. 2 (1928): 193–236; 22, no. 3 (1928): 331–360; 22, no. 4 (1928): 511–542.

Roberts, B. H. *The Mormon Battalion: Its History and Achievements.* Salt Lake City: Deseret News, 1919.

Roberts, Thomas D. "Resaca de la Palma: A Traditional Episode in the History of the Second Cavalry." *Journal of the American Military History Foundation* 1, no. 3 (Autumn 1937): 101–107.

Robinson, Jacob S. *A Journal of the Santa Fe Expedition Under Colonel Doniphan.* Portsmouth, N. H.: Portsmouth Journal Press, 1848, Reprint. Princeton, New Jersey: Princeton University Press, 1932, Reprint. New York: Da Capo Press, 1972.

Rogers, William P. "The Diary and Letters of William P. Rogers, 1846–1862." Edited by Eleanor Damon Pace. *Southwestern Historical Quarterly* 32, no. 4 (April 1929): 259–299.

Sandweiss, Martha A., Rick Stewart, and Ben W. Huseman. *Eyewitness to War: Prints and Daguerreotypes of the Mexican War, 1846–1848.* Fort Worth, Texas, and Washington, D.C.: Amon Carter Museum and Smithsonian Institution Press, 1989.

Skelly, James. "Diary of a Pennsylvania Volunteer in the Mexican War." Edited by James K. Greer. *Western Pennsylvania Historical Magazine* 12, no. 3 (1929): 147–154.

"Sketches of the Mexican War: The Texan Ranger." *Fraser's Magazine* 38, no. 7 (July 1848): 91–102.

Smith, George W. and Charles Judah. *Chronicles of the Gringoes: The U.S. Army in the Mexican War, 1846–1848.* Albuquerque: University of New Mexico Press, 1968.

Smith, Gustavus W. *Company "A," Corps. of Engineers, U.S.A., 1846–1848 in the Mexican War.* Willets Point, New York: Battalion Press, 1896.

Smith, Persifor F. "The Second Brigade, at Monterey." *Historical Magazine* 3, no. 1 (March 1874): 138–140.

Steele, John. "Extracts from the Journal of John Steele." *Utah Historical Quarterly* 6, no. 1 (January 1933): 2–28.

Sweeny, Thomas W. "Narrative of Army Service in the Mexican War and on the Plains, 1846–1853." *Journal of the Military Service Institution of the United States* 42, no. 151 (1908): 126–135.

Taliaferro, William Booth. "William Booth Taliaferro's Letters from Mexico, 1847–1848." Edited by Ludwell H. Johnson. *Virginia Magazine of History and Biography* 73, no. 4 (1965): 455–473.

Taylor, Zachary. *Letters of Zachary Taylor from the Battle-Fields of the Mexican War.* Rochester, New York: William K. Bixby, 1908, Reprint. New York: Kraus Reprint, 1970.

Tennery, Thomas D. *The Mexican War Diary of Thomas D. Tennery.* Edited by D. E. Livingston-Little. Norman, Oklahoma: University of Oklahoma Press, 1970.

Turner, Henry S. "Letters About Mexican War." *Glimpses of the Past* 2, no. 2 (1934–1935): 1–31.

Upton, Barna. "Our First Foreign War." Edited by William F. Goetzmann. *American Heritage* 17, no. 4 (1966): 18–27, 85–99.

Viall, Nelson. "Recollections of the Mexican War." *Rhode Island Historical Collections* 30, no. 3 (July 1937): 65–82.

Wallace, Edward S. "The United States Army in Mexico City." *Military Affairs* 13, no. 3 (Autumn 1949): 158–166.

Wallace, Lee A., Jr. "The First Regiment of Virginia Volunteers, 1846–1848." *Virginia Magazine of History and Biography* 77, no. 1 (1969): 46–77.

Watson, Henry Bulls. "The Journal of Second Lt. Henry Bulls Watson." *Fortitudine* (Summer 1985): 3–8.

Weber, R. B., ed. "The Mexican War: Some Personal Correspondence." *Indiana Magazine of History* 65, no. 2 (1969): 133–139.

Whitworth, Robert W. "From the Mississippi to the Pacific: An Englishman in the Mormon Battalion." Edited by David B. Gracy, II and Helen J. H. Rugeley. *Arizona and the West* 7, no. 2 (1965): 127–160.

Wool, John E. "General John E. Wool's Memoranda of the Battle of Buena Vista." Edited by K. Jack Bauer. *Southwestern Historical Quarterly* 77, no. 1 (1973): 111–125.

Wynne, James. "Memoir of the Rev. Anthony Rey, S. J." *United States Catholic Magazine* 6, no. 10 (1847): 543–552.

The End of the Mexican War until the Civil War

The following sources explore the lives of soldiers from the end of the Mexican War until the coming of the Civil War:

Averell, William Woods. *Ten Years in the Saddle: The Memoir of William Woods Averell.* Edited by Edward K. Eckert and Nicholas J. Amato. San Rafael, California: Presidio Press, 1978.

Babcock, Willoughby Maynard, ed. "Minnesota as Seen by Travelers: A Dragoon on the March to Pembina in 1849." *Minnesota History* 8 (1927): 61–74.

Bandel, Eugene. *Frontier Life in the Army: 1854–1861.* Translated by Olga Bandel and Richard Jente. Edited by Ralph P. Bieber. Glendale, California: Arthur H. Clarke, 1932.

Barry, Louise, ed. "With the First U.S. Cavalry in Indian Country, 1859–1861." *Kansas Historical Quarterly* 24 (Autumn 1958): 399–425.

Bender, Averam B. "The Soldier in the Far West, 1848–1860." *Pacific Historical Review* 8 (June 1939): 159–178.

Bennett, James A. *Forts and Forays: James A. Bennett, A Dragoon in New Mexico, 1850–1856.* Edited by Clinton E. Brooks and Frank D. Reeve. Albuquerque, New Mexico: University of New Mexico Press, 1948.

Bliss, Zenas R. "Extracts From the Unpublished Memoirs of Major-General Zenas R. Bliss, U.S.A." *Journal of the Military Service Institution of the United States* 38 (1906): 120–134.

Carr, E. T. "Reminiscences Concerning Fort Leavenworth in 1855–'56," *Collections of the Kansas State Historical Society* 12 (1911–1912): 375–383.

Clarke, Frank and Mary Clarke. *Above a Common Soldier: The West of Frank and Mary Clarke in the American West and Civil War, 1847–1872.* Edited by Darlis M. Miller. Albuquerque, New Mexico: University of New Mexico Press, 1997.

Coker, Caleb and Janet G. Humphrey. "The Texas Frontier in 1850: Dr. Ebenezer Swift and the View from Fort Martin Scott." *Southwestern Historical Quarterly* 96 (January 1993): 393–413.

Connelly, Thomas L. "The American Camel Experiment: A Reappraisal." *Southwestern Historical Quarterly* 69 (April 1966): 442–462.

Couts, Cave Johnson. Hepah, *California! The Journal of Cave Johnson Couts from Monterey, Nuevo Leon, Mexico, to Los Angeles, California, during the Years 1848–1849.* Edited by Henry F. Dobyns. Tucson: Arizona Pioneers' Historical Society, 1961.

Drum, Richard C. "Reminiscences of the Indian Fight at Ash Hollow." *Collections of the Nebraska State Historical Society* 16 (1911): 142–151.

Ewy, Marvin. "The United States Army in the Kansas Border Troubles, 1855–1856." *Kansas Historical Quarterly* 32 (Winter 1966): 385–400.

Freeman, W. G. "W. G. Freeman's Report on the Eighth Military Department." edited by Martin L. Crimmins, *Southwestern Historical Quarterly* 51 (July 1947): 54–58; 51 (October 1947): 167–174; 51 (January 1948): 252–258; 51 (April 1948): 350–357; 52 (July 1948): 100–108; 52 (October 1948): 227–233; 52 (January 1949): 349–353; 52 (April 1949): 444–447; 53 (July 1949): 71–77; 53 (October 1949): 202–208; 53 (January 1950): 308–319; 53 (April 1950): 443–473; 54 (October 1950): 204–218.

Furniss, Norman F. *The Mormon Conflict, 1850–1859.* New Haven, Connecticut: Yale University Press, 1960.

Gove, Jesse A. *The Utah Expedition, 1857–1858: Letters of Capt. Jesse A. Gove, 10th Inf., U.S.A.* Edited by Otis G. Hammond. Concord, New Hampshire: New Hampshire Historical Society, 1928.

Graf, Mercedes. "Standing Tall with Sarah Bowman: The Amazon of the Border." *Minerva: Quarterly Report On Women and the Military* 19, nos. 3–4 (Fall-Winter 2001): 27–38.

Griffin, John S. "A Doctor Comes to California: The Diary of John S. Griffin, Assistant Surgeon with Kearny's Dragoons, 1846–1847." Edited by George Walcott Ames, Jr. *California Historical Society Quarterly* 21, no. 3 (1942): 193–224; 21, no. 4 (1942): 333–357; 22, no. 1 (1943): 41–66.

Hamilton, Henry S. *Reminiscences of a Veteran.* Concord, New Hampshire: Republican Press Association, 1897.

Hedren, Paul L. "On Duty at Fort Ridgely, Minnesota: 1853–1867." *South Dakota History* 7 (Spring 1977): 168–192.

Johnston, Eliza. "The Diary of Eliza (Mrs. Albert Sydney) Johnston: The Second Cavalry Comes to Texas." Edited by Charles P. Roland and Richard C. Robbins. *Southwestern Historical Quarterly* 60, no. 4 (April 1957): 463–500.

Kip, Lawrence. *Indian War in the Pacific Northwest: The Journal of Lieutenant Lawrence Kip.* Lincoln, Nebraska and London: University of Nebraska Press, 1999.

Lane, Lydia S. *I Married a Soldier; or, Old Days in the Old Army.* 1893; reprint Albuquerque, New Mexico: University of New Mexico Press, 1964.

Langley, Harold D., ed. *To Utah with the Dragoons and Glimpses of Life in Arizona and California, 1858–1859.* Salt Lake City: University of Utah Press, 1974.

Lawrie, John. "Letters on the War in Kansas in 1856." edited by V. E. Gibbens. *Kansas Historical Quarterly* 10 (1941): 369–379.

Lee, William. "Desert Documentary: The William Lee Diary Account of the James H. Simpson Expedition, 1858–1859." Edited by James P. Langellier. *Annals of Wyoming* 59 (Fall 1987): 36–47.

Leonard, Thomas C. "The Reluctant Conquerors: How the Generals Viewed the Indians." *American Heritage* 27 (August 1976): 34–41.

Lowe, Percival G. *Five Years a Dragoon ('49 to '54) and Other Adventures on the Great Plains.* Norman, Oklahoma: University of Oklahoma Press, 1965.

The March of the Mounted Riflemen: First United State Military Expedition to Travel the Full Length of the Oregon Trail from Fort Leavenworth to Fort Vancouver, May to October 1849. Edited by Raymond W. Settle. Lincoln, Nebraska: University of Nebraska Press, 1989.

Matson, Sylvester W. "With the Third Infantry in New Mexico, 1851–1853: The Lost Diary of Private Sylvester W. Matson." Edited by Jerry D. Thompson. *Journal of Arizona History* 31 (Winter 1990): 349–404.

Meketa, Jacqueline Dorgan. "A Soldier in New Mexico, 1849–18—." *New Mexico Historical Review* 66, no. 1 (January 1991): 15–32.

Mowry, Sylvester. "Lt. Sylvester Mowry's Report on His March in 1855 from Salt Lake City to Fort Tejon." Edited by Lynn R. Bailey. *Arizona and the West* 7 (1965): 329–346.

Myer, Albert J. " 'I Am Already Quite a Texan': Albert J. Myer's Letters from Texas, 1854–1856." Edited by David A. Clary. *Southwestern Historical Quarterly* 82, no. 1 (July 1978): 25–77.

Peck, Robert M. "Recollections of Early Times in Kansas Territory from the Standpoint of a Regular Cavalryman." *Transactions of the Kansas State Historical Society* 8 (1904): 484–507.

Prucha, Francis P. "Fort Ripley: The Post and the Military Reservation." *Minnesota History* 28 (September 1947): 205–224.

Prucha, Francis P. "The Settler and the Army in Frontier Minnesota." *Minnesota History* 29 (September 1948): 231–246.

Prucha, Francis Paul. "Distribution of Regular Army Troops Before the Civil War." *Military Affairs* 16, no. 4 (Winter 1952): 169–173.

Reese, J. W. "OMV's Fort Henrietta: On Winter Duty, 1855–1856." *Oregon Historical Quarterly* 66 (Dec 1965): 133–160.

Scott, Charles A. "The Nevada Uprising of 1860 as Seen by Private Charles A. Scott." Edited by John M. Ellis and Robert E. Stowers. *Arizona and the West* 3, no. 4 (1961): 355–376.

Simpson, James H. *Navaho Expedition: Journal of a Military Reconnaissance from Santa Fe, New Mexico to the Navaho Country Made in 1849 by Lieutenant James H. Simpson.* Edited by Frank McNitt. Norman, Oklahoma: University of Oklahoma Press, 1964.

Sprague, John T. "Journal of a Wagon Train Expedition from Fort Inge to El Paso del Norte in 1850." Edited by Ben E. Pingenot. *Military History of the West* 25 (Spring 1995): 69–105.

Stacey, May Humphrey. *Uncle Sam's Camels: The Journal of May Humprheys Stacey Supplemented by the Report of Edward Fitzgerald Beale (1857–1858).* Edited by Lewis Burt Lesley, Cambridge, Massachusetts: Harvard University Press, 1929.

Stark, William C. "First Lieutenant Edmund Russell, 4th United States Infantry, 1847–1853." *Periodical* 19 (Fall 1992): 31–36.

Stewart, George R. *John Phoenix, Esq.: The Veritable Squibob: A Life of Captain George H. Derby, U.S.A.* New York: Henry Holt and Company, 1937; reprint, New York: Da Capo Press, 1969.

Sweeny, Thomas W. *Journal of Lt. Thomas W. Sweeny, 1849–1853.* Edited by Arthur Woodward, Los Angeles: Westernlore Press, 1956.

Talbot, Theodore. *Soldier in the West: Letters of Theodore Talbot during His Services in California, Mexico, and Oregon, 1845–1853.* Edited by Robert V. Hine and Savoie Lottinville. Norman, Oklahoma: University of Oklahoma Press, 1972.

Tanner, George C. "History of Fort Ripley, 1849–1859, Based on the Diary of Rev. Solon W. Manney, D. D., Chaplain of the Post 1851–1859." *Collections of the State Historical Society of Minnesota* 10 (February 1905): 179–202.

Tracy, Albert. "The Utah War, Journal of Albert Tracy 1858–1860." *Utah Historical Quarterly* 13 (1945): 1–119.

The Utah Expedition 1857–1858: A Documentary Account of the United States Military Movement Under Colonel Albert Sidney Johnston, and the Resistance by Brigham Young and the Mormon Nauvoo Legion. Edited by Leroy R. Hafen and Ann W. Hafen. Glendale, California: Arthur H. Clark, 1958.

Utley, Robert M. *Frontiersmen in Blue: The United States Army and the Indian, 1848–1865.* Lincoln, Nebraska and London: University of Nebraska Press, 1981.

Whaley, John R. "A Virginia Soldier in the Frontier Army[:] The Letters of Sergeant John R. Whaley, Second U.S. Artillery, 1854–1859." Edited by Robert P. Weittman, Jr. *Military History of the West* 29, no. 1 (Spring 1999): 63–88.

Whilden, Charles E. "Letters from a Santa Fe Army Clerk, 1855–1856." Edited by John Hammond Moore. *New Mexico Historical Review,* 40 (April 1965): 141–164.

Xántus, John. *John Xántus: The Fort Tejon Letters, 1857–1859.* Edited by Ann Zwinger. Tucson: University of Arizona Press, 1986.

SOLDIERS' LIVES: TOPICS

Health

The following sources deal with the health of the American soldiers:

Andrews, Joseph Gardner. "A Surgeon's Mate at Fort Defiance: The Journal of Joseph Gardner Andrews for the Year 1795." Edited by Richard C. Knopf. *Ohio Historical Quarterly* 66, no. 1 (January 1957): 57–86; no. 2 (April 1957): 159–186; no. 3 (July 1957): 238–268.

Ashburn, P. M. *A History of the Medical Department of the United States Army.* Boston and New York: Houghton Mifflin, 1929.

Ayars, Charles W. "Some Notes on the Medical Service of the Army, 1812–1839." *Military Surgeon: Journal of the Association of Military Surgeons of the United States* 50 (May 1922): 505–524.

Bigelow, Henry Jacob. "Insensibility during Surgical Operations Produced by Inhalation." *Boston Medical and Surgical Journal* 35, no. 16 (November 18, 1846): 311–317.

Bill, Joseph H. "Notes on Arrow Wounds." *American Journal of the Medical Sciences* 44 (1862): 365–387.

Black, Wilfred W. "The Army Doctor in the Trans–Mississippi West, 1775–1860." *Southwestern Social Science Quarterly* 24, no. 2 (1943): 118–128.

Breeden, James O. "Health of Early Texas: The Military Frontier." *Southwestern Historical Quarterly* 80, no. 4 (April 1977); 357–398.

Brieger, Gert H. *Medical America in the Nineteenth Century: Readings from the Literature* Baltimore: Johns Hopkins University Press, 1972.

Brooks, Stewart. *Civil War Medicine*. Springfield, Illinois: Charles C. Thomas, 1966.

Brown, Harvey E., comp. *The Medical Department of the United States Army from 1775 to 1873.* Washington, D.C.: Surgeon General's Office, 1873.

Bryan, Leon S. "Blood-letting in American Medicine, 1830–1892." *Bulletin of the History of Medicine* 38 (1964): 516–529.

Cassedy, James H. "An Early American Hangover: The Medical Professor and Intemperance 1800–1860." *Bulletin of the History of Medicine* 50 (1976): 405–413.

Coolidge, Richard H., comp. *Statistical Report on the Sickness and Mortality in the Army of the United States, Compiled from the Records of the Surgeon General's Office, Embracing a Period of Sixteen Years, from January, 1839 to January, 1855.* Washington, D.C.: A. O. P. Nicholson, 1856.

Courtwright, David. "Opiate Addiction in the American West, 1850–1920." *Journal of the West* 21, no. 3 (July 1982): 23–31.

Crimmins, M. L., ed. "Experiences of an Army Surgeon at Fort Chadbourne." *West Texas Historical Association Year Book* 15 (1939): 31–39.

Cutter, Irving S. "John Gale, A Pioneer Army Surgeon." *Illinois State Historical Society Journal* 23 (1931): 630–641.

Duffy, John. "Medicine in the West: An Historical Overview." *Journal of the West* 21, no. 3 (July 1982): 5–14.

Duncan, Louis C. "Sketches of the Medical Services in the War of 1812." *Military Surgeon: Journal of the Association of Military Surgeons of the United States* 81 (1932): 436–440, 539–542; 82 (1932): 48–56.

Duncan, Louis C. "A Medical History of General Zachary Taylor's Army of Occupation in Texas and Mexico, 1845–1847." *Military Surgeon: Journal of the Association of Military Surgeons of the United States* 48, no. 1 (1920): 76–104.

Duncan, Louis C. "Medical History of General Scott's Campaign to the City of Mexico in 1847." *Military Surgeon: Journal of the Association of Military Surgeons of the United States 47,* no. 4 (1920); 436–470; 47, no. 5 (1920): 596–609.

Eaton, Leonard K. "Military Surgery in the Battle of Tippecanoe." *Bulletin of the History of Medicine* 25 (1951): 460–463.

Edgar, James D. "The Army Medical Department in the War of 1812." *Military Surgeon: Journal of the Association of Military Surgeons of the United States* 60 (1927): 301–313.

Ennis, Lisa A, and Hugh T. Harrington. "Joseph Howland Bill, M.D., Arrow Wounds and Treatments on the Western Frontier: ... a fatality greater then [than] that produced by any other weapon." http://www.ehistory.freeservers.com/vol2/Arrow%20Wounds.htm, accessed November 6, 2003.

Erwin, Marie H., comp. "Statistical Reports on the Sickness and Mortality of the Army of the United States, 1819–1860." *Annals of Wyoming* 15 (1943): 315–375.

Fisher, B. J. "Medical Conditions at West Texas Military Posts in the 1850s." *West Texas Historical Association Year Book* 62 (1986): 108–118.

Gailland, P. C. "On Some Points of Hygiene, and Their Connection with the Propagation of Yellow Fever and Cholera." *Charleston Medical Journal and Review* 4 (1849): 280–295.

Garrison, Fielding H. "Notes on the History of Military Medicine." *Military Surgeon: Journal of the Association of Military Surgeons of the United States* 50, no. 6 (1922): 691–718.

Gillett, Mary C. *The Army Medical Department, 1775–1818.* Washington, D.C.: Center of Military History, U.S. Army, 1981.

Gillett, Mary C. *The Army Medical Department, 1818–1865.* Washington, D.C.: Center of Military History, U.S. Army, 1987.

Haller, John S., Jr. *American Medicine in Transition, 1840–1910.* Urbana, Chicago, London: University of Illinois Press, 1981.

Hammond, William A., ed. *Military Medical and Surgical Essays, Prepared for the United States Sanitary Commission.* Philadelphia: J. B. Lippincott Co., 1864.

Henderson, Thomas. *Hints on the Medical Examination of Recruits for the Army and on the Discharge of Soldiers from the Service on Surgeon's Certificate. 1840, Rev. ed. by Richard H. Coolidge.* Philadelphia: J. B. Lippincott, 1856.

Herrick, W. B. "Surgery at Buena Vista." *Illinois and Indiana Medical and Surgical Journal* 4 (1847–1848): 300–305.

Herrick, W. B. "Surgery in the Hospitals after the Battle of Buena Vista." *Illinois Medical and Surgical Journal* 4 (1847-48): 302, 414–418.

Herrick, W. B. "Remarks upon the Organization of the Medical Department of the Army, and the Effects of Marching and Camp Life in Producing and Modifying Disease." *Illinois and Indiana Medical and Surgical Journal* 2, no. 3 (1847): 225–232.

Horine, Emmet F. "Episodes in the History of Anesthesia." *Journal of the History of Medicine and Allied Sciences* 1 (October 1946): 521–526.

Horner, W. E. "Surgical Sketches: A Military Hospital at Buffalo, New York, in the Year 1814." *Medical Examiner and Record of Medical Science* 8 (1852): 753–774; 9 (1853): 1–25, 69–85.

Japp, Phyllis M. "Pioneer Medicines: Doctors, Nostrums, and Folk Cures." *Journal of the West* 21, no. 3 (July 1982): 15–22.

Jarvis, Nathan S. "An Army Surgeon's Notes on Frontier Service, 1833–1848." *Journal of the Military Service Institution* 39 (1906): 131–135, 275–286, 451–460; 40 (1906): 435–452; 41 (1907): 90–105.

Jarvis, Nathan S. "An Army Surgeon's Notes on Frontier Service—Mexican War." *Journal of the Military Service Institution of the United States* 40, no. 147 (May 1907): 431–452; 41, no. 148 (1907): 90–105.

Long, Edwin Ramsey. "An Essay on Delerium Tremens." *Illinois and Indiana Medical and Surgical Journal* 1, no. 2 (June 1846): 97–107.

Murphy, Lawrence R. " 'The Enemy Among Us': Venereal Disease Among Union Soldiers in the Far West, 1861–1865." *Civil War History* 31 (September 1985): 257–269.

Nichols, Roger L. "Scurvy at Cantonment Missouri, 1819–1820." *Nebraska History* 49, no. 4 (Winter 1968): 333–347.

Norwood, William Frederick. *Medical Education In the United States Before the Civil War.* Philadelphia: University of Pennsylvania Press, 1944.

Olch, Peter D. "Medicine in the Indian-Fighting Army, 1866–1890." *Journal of the West* 21, no. 3 (July 1982): 32–41.

Patton, Alfred. "Recollections of Medical Service During the War With Mexico." *Indiana Journal of Medicine* 5, no. 4 (August 1874): 145–150.

Porter, John B. "Medical and Surgical Notes of Campaigns in the War with Mexico, during the Years 1845, 1846, 1847, and 1848." *American Journal of the Medical Sciences* 23 (January 1852): 13–37; 24 (July 1852): 13–30; 25 (January 1853): 25–42; 26 (October 1853): 297–333; 35 (April 1858): 347–352.

Powers, Ramon S. and Gene Younger. "Cholera on the Overland Trails, 1832–1869." *Kansas Quarterly* 5 (Spring 1973): 32–49.

Randolph, B. M. "The Blood Letting Controversy in the Nineteenth Century." *Annals of Medical History* 7 (1935): 177–182.

"Requirements of the United States Army and Navy Boards of Medical Examiners. Also Those of the British Army and Navy." *Transactions of the American Medical Association* 2 (1849): 311–325.

Rothstein, William G. *American Physicians in the 19th Century: From Sects to Science.* Baltimore and London: Johns Hopkins University Press, 1972.

Scheips, Paul J. "Albert James Myers, an Army Doctor in Texas, 1854–1857." *Southwestern Historical Quarterly* 82, no. 1 (July 1978): 1–24.

Shafer, Henry Burnell. *The American Medical Profession 1783 to 1850.* New York: Columbia University Press, 1936.

Steele, Volney. "Arrow Wounds and the Military Surgeon in the West." *Military History of the West* 30, no. 2 (Fall 2000): 155–170.

Trent, Josiah Charles. "Surgical Anesthesia, 1846–1946." *Journal of the History of Medicine and Allied Sciences* 1 (October 1946): 505–514.

Tripler, Charles S. "Case of Gunshot Wound to the Spine." *New York Journal of Medicine and the Collateral Sciences* 7 (1851): 21–23.

Wilbur, C. Keith. *Revolutionary Medicine, 1700–1800.* Chester, Connecticut: Globe Pequot Press, 1980.

Clothing, Equipment, and Weapons

The following sources deal with the soldiers' clothing, equipment, and weapons:

Arthur, Robert. *The Coast Artillery School, 1824–1927.* Fort Monroe, Virginia: Coast Artillery School Press, 1928.

Branch, Paul. "Hot Shot Furnace to Become a Reality." *Ramparts.* Fall 1995, at http://www.clis.com/friends/HotShot.htm, accessed on March 8, 2005.

Bruce S. Bazelon. "How the Nineteenth Century Soldier Got His Stuff." *Bulletin of the American Society of Arms Collectors* 70 (1994): 35–47.

Chartrand, René. *Uniforms and Equipment of the United States Forces in the War of 1812.* Youngstown, New York: Old Fort Niagara Association, Inc., 1992.

Coates, Earl J., James L. Kochan, and Don Troiani. *Don Troiani's Soldiers in America 1754–1865.* Mechanicsburg, Pennsylvania: Stackpole Books, 1998.

Donnelly, Ralph W. "Rocket Batteries of the Civil War." *Military Affairs* 25, no. 2 (Summer 1961): 69–93.

Edwards, William B. *The Story of Colt's Revolver: The Biography of Col. Samuel Colt.* New York: Castle Books, 1957.

Falk, Stanley L. "Artillery for the Land Service: The Development of a System." *Military Affairs* 28, no. 3 (Autumn 1964): 97–110.

Field, Ron. *Brassey's History of Uniforms: Mexican-American War 1846–48.* London: Brassey's, 1997.

Gluckman, Arcadi. *Identifying Old U.S. Muskets, Rifles & Carbines.* New York: Bonanza Books, 1965.

Hickey, Donald R. "Andrew Jackson and the Haircut: Individual Rights vs. Military Discipline." *Tennessee Historical Quarterly* 35 (1976): 365–378.

Hicks, James E. "United States Military Shoulder Arms, 1795–1935." *Journal of the American Military History Foundation* 1, no. 1 (Spring 1937): 22–33; 1, no. 2 (Summer 1937): 75–79; 2, no. 1 (Spring 1938): 36–42.

Howell, Edgar M. and Donald E. Kloster. *United States Army Headgear to 1854: Catalog of United States Army Uniforms in the Collections of the Smithsonian Institution,* Volume 1. Washington, D.C.: Smithsonian Institution Press, 1969.

Howell, Edgar M. *United States Army Headgear 1855–1902: Catalog of United States Army Uniforms in the Collections of the Smithsonian Institution,* Volume 2. Washington, D.C.: Smithsonian Institution Press, 1975.

[Jacobs, James R.] "Colonel Thomas Butler and General Wilkinson's 'Roundhead Order.' " *Pennsylvania Magazine of History and Biography* 17 (1893): 501–512.

Kahler, Herbert E. and F. Hilton Crowe. "Hot Shot Furnaces." *The Regional Review* 2, no. 2 (February 1939), at http://www.cr.nps.gov/history/online_books/regional/vol2–2d.htm, accessed on March 7 2005.

Long, Oscar F. "Changes in the Uniform of the Army 1774–1895." http://www.qmfound.com/changes_in_the_army_uniform_1895.htm.

Manucy, Albert. *Artillery Through the Ages: A Short Illustrated History of Cannon, Emphasizing Types Used in America.* Washington, D.C.: U.S. Government Printing Office, 1949, reprint 1962.

McCaig, A. D. "'The Soul of Artillery': Congreve's Rockets and Their Effectiveness in Warfare." *Journal of the Society for Army Historical Research* 78 (2000): 252–263.

Moore, Robert J., Jr. and Michael Haynes. *Tailor Made, Trail Worn: Army Life, Clothing & Weapons of the Corps of Discovery.* Helena, Montana: Farcountry Press, 2003.

Olejar, Paul D. "Rockets in Early American Wars." *Military Affairs* 10, no. 4 (Winter 1946): 16–34.

Peterson, Harold L. *Round Shot and Rammers.* New York: Bonanza Books, 1979.

Ripley, Warren. *Artillery and Ammunition of the Civil War.* New York: Promontory Press, 1970.
Smith, Amasa. *A Short Compendium of the Duty of Artillerists: …* 2e, Boston: Isaiah Thomas, Jr., 1818.
Smith, Merrit Roe. *Harpers Ferry Armory and the New Technology.* Ithaca, New York and London: Cornell University Press, 1977.
Smith, Winston O. *The Sharps Rifle: Its History, Development and Operations.* New York: William Morrow, 1943.
Todd, Frederick P. *American Military Equipage 1851–1872.* Providence, Rhode Island: The Company of Military Historians, 1974.

Day-to-Day Routine

The following sources deal with the soldiers' day-to-day routine:

Anderson, Thomas M. "Army Posts, Barracks and Quarters." *Journal of the Military Service Institution of the United States* 2 (1882), 421–447.
Atherton, Lewis E. "The Merchant Sutler in the Pre–Civil War Period." *Southwestern Social Science Quarterly* 19 (September 1938): 140–151.
Barrett, Arrie. "Western Frontier Forts of Texas, 1845–1861." *West Texas Historical Association Yearbook* 7 (June 1931): 115–139.
Brown, William L., III. *The Army Called it Home: Military Interiors of the 19th Century.* Gettysburg, Pennsylvania: Thomas Publications, 1992.
Clary, David A. *These Relics of Barbarism: A History of Furniture in Barracks and Guardhouses of the United States Army, 1800–1880.* Harpers Ferry, Virginia: U.S. Department of the Interior, National Park Service, 1985.
Culpin, Alan. "A Brief History of Social and Domestic Life Among the Military in Wyoming, 1849–1890." *Annals of Wyoming* 45, no. 1 (Spring 1973): 93–108.
Cunningham, Mary Jo. "Army Bread: Pocket to Pouch." *Periodical* 22 (1995): 91–99.
Davis, W. N. "The Sutler at Fort Bridger." *Western Historical Quarterly* 2 (January 1971): 37–54.
Field, Ron. *Forts of the American Frontier 1820–1891: Central and Northern Plains.* London: Osprey, 2005.
Frazer, Robert W. "Army Agriculture in New Mexico, 1852–1853." *New Mexico Historical Review* 50, no. 4 (October 1975): 313–334.
Gamble, Richard Dalzell. "Garrison Life at Frontier Military Posts, 1830–1860." Ph.D. diss., University of Oklahoma, 1956.
Gamble, Richard D. "Army Chaplains at Frontier Posts, 1830–1860." *Historical Magazine of the Protestant Episcopal Church* 27, no. 4 (1958): 287–304.
Gardner, Hamilton. "Romance at Old Cantonment Leavenworth: The Marriage of 2d Lt. Philip St. George Cooke in 1830." *Kansas Historical Quarterly* 22 (Summer 1956): 97–113.
Giese, Dale Frederick. "Soldiers at Play: A History of Social Life at Fort Union, New Mexico, 1851–1891." Ph.D. diss., University of New Mexico, 1969.
Graham, Stanley S. "Life of the Enlisted Soldier on the Western Frontier, 1815–1845." Ph.D. diss., North Texas State University, 1972.
Graham, Stanley S. "Routine at Western Cavalry Posts, 1833–1861." *Journal of the West* 15 (July 1976): 49–59.
Haas, Irvin. *Citadels, Ramparts and Stockades: America's Historic Forts.* New York: Everest House, 1979.
Hintz, Kalina Ingraham. " 'My military life as a cadet here': The West Point Years of Major General John F. Reynolds." *Gettysburg* 25 (June 2001): 23–39.
Hoagland, Alison K. "Village Constructions: U.S. Army Forts on the Plains, 1848–1890." *Winterthur Portfolio* 34, no. 4 (Winter 1999): 215–237.
Hoagland, Alison K. *Army Architecture in the West: Forts Laramie, Bridger, and D. A. Russell, 1849–1912.* Norman, Oklahoma: University of Oklahoma Press, 2004.

Holt, Daniel D. and Marilyn Irvin Holt. " 'The Pleasures of Female Society' at Cantonment Leavenworth." *Kansas History* 8 (Spring 1985): 21–35.

Holtz, Milton E. "Old Fort Kearny 1846–1848: Symbol of a Changing Frontier." *Montana: The Magazine of Western History* (Autumn 1972): 44–55.

Huseas, Marion M. " 'Tuched Nothing to Drink ...': Frontier Army Leisure." *Periodical: Journal of the Council on America's Military Past* 12 (January 1981): 11–23.

Ingalles, Joan. "Family Life on the Southwestern Frontier." *Military History of Texas and the Southwest* 14, no. 4. 203–213.

Jacobsen, Jacques, ed. *Regulations and Notes for the Uniform of the Army of the United States: 1851.* Staten Island, New York: Manor Publishing, 1972.

Konstam, Angus. *American Civil War Fortifications: Coastal Brick and Stone Forts.* Oxford: Osprey, 2003.

Lewis, Emanuel. *Seacoast Fortifications of the United States.* Washington, D.C.: Smithsonian Institution Press, 1970.

McWhiney, Grady. "Sex, Women and the 'Old Army' Officers." *Southerners and Other Americans.* New York, 1973.

Miller, Darlis A. "Foragers, Army Women and Prostitutes." *New Mexico Women: Intercultural Perspectives,* 141–168. Edited by Joan M. Jensen and Darlis A. Miller. Albuquerque: University of New Mexico Press, 1986.

Miller, Darlis A. "Cross-Cultural Marriages in the Southwest." *New Mexico Women: Intercultural Perspectives,* 95–119. Edited by Joan M. Jensen and Darlis A. Miller. Albuquerque: University of New Mexico Press, 1986.

Miller, Darlis A. "The Perils of a Post Sutler: William H. Moore at Fort Union, New Mexico, 1859–1870." *Journal of the West* 32, no. 2 (April 1993): 7–18.

Myres, Sandra L. "Romance and Reality on the American Frontier: Views of Army Wives." *Western Historical Quarterly* 13 (October 1982): 409–427.

Ney, Virgil. "Daily Life at Fort Atkinson—on the Missouri—1820–1827." *Military Review* 57 (January 1977): 36–48; (February 1977): 50–66.

Obst. Janis. "Abigail Snelling, Military Wife, Military Widow." *Minnesota History* 54 (Fall 1994): 98–111.

Oliva, Leo E. *Fort Union and the Frontier Army in the Southwest.* Santa Fe, New Mexico: National Park Service, 1993.

"Promotion of the Rank and File of the Army." *Military and Naval Magazine* 3 (1834): 121–124.

Rorabaugh, W. J. *The Alcoholic Republic: An American Tradition.* New York and Oxford: Oxford University Press, 1979.

Samuelson, Nancy B. "Revolutionary War Women and the Second Oldest Profession." *Minerva* 7 (1989): 16–25.

Shirk, George H. "Mail Call at Fort Washita." *Chronicles of Oklahoma* 33 (Spring 1958): 14–35.

Steinhauer, Dale Richard. " 'Sogers': Enlisted Men in the U.S. Army, 1815–1860." Ph.D. diss., University of North Carolina at Chapel Hill, 1992.

Stewart, Miller J. "Army Laundresses: Ladies of 'Soap Suds Row.'" *Nebraska History* 61 (Winter 1980): 421–436.

Stewart, Miller J. "To Plow, to Sow, to Reap, to Mow: The U.S. Army Agriculture Program." *Nebraska History* 63 (Summer 1982): 194–215.

Tapson, Alfred J. "The Sutler and the Soldier." *Military Affairs* 21, no. 4 (Winter 1957): 175–181.

Weaver, John R., II. *A Legacy in Brick and Stone: American Coastal Defense Forts of the Third System,* 1816–1867. Missoula, Montana: Pictorial Histories Publishing Company, 2001.

Widder, Keith R. *Reveille Till Taps: Soldier Life at Fort Mackinac 1780–1895.* Mackinac Island, Michigan: Mackinac Island State Park Commission, 1972.

Wooster, Robert. *Soldiers, Sutlers and Settlers: Garrison Life on the Texas Frontier.* College Station, Texas: Texas A & M University Press, 1987.

Training

The following sources deal with the soldiers' training:

Abstract of Infantry Tactics; including Exercises and Manoeuvres of Light Infantry and Riflemen; for the Use of the Militia of the United States. Boston: Hilliard, Gray, Little, and Wilkins, 1830.

Cooper, S[amuel]. *A Concise System of Instructions and Regulations for the Militia and Volunteers of the United States, Comprehending the Exercises and Movements of the Infantry, Light Infantry, and Riflemen; Cavalry and Artillery; Together with the manner of doing duty in Garrison and in Camp, and the forms of Parades, Reviews, and Inspections, As established by authority for the government of the Regular Army.* Philadelphia: Robert P. Desilver, 1836.

Danckert, Stephen C. "Baron von Steuben and the Training of Armies." *Military Review* 74 (May 1994): 29–34.

Gilham, William. *Manual of Instruction for the Volunteers and Militia of the United States.* Philadelphia: Robert P. DeSilver, 1861.

Graves, Donald E. " 'Dry Books of Tactics': U.S. Infantry Manuals of the War of 1812 and After, Part I." *Military Collector and Historian* 38, no. 2 (Summer 1986): 50–61.

Graves, Donald E. " 'Dry Books of Tactics': U.S. Infantry Manuals of the War of 1812 and After, Part II." *Military Collector and Historian* 38, no. 4 (Winter 1986): 173–177.

Green, Joseph H. "The Evolution of Infantry Drill." *Infantry Journal.* 40 (March–April 1933): 109–116.

McNeill, William H. "Keeping Together in Time." *MHQ: The Quarterly Journal of Military History* 7 (1994): 100–109.

Ross, Steven. *From Flintlock to Rifle, Infantry Tactics, 1740–1866.* London: Frank Cass, 1996.

Steuben, Friedrich Wilhelm Ludolf Gerhard Augustin, Baron von. *Baron von Steuben and His Regulations.* Edited by Joseph R. Riling. Philadelphia: Ray Riling Arms Books, 1966.

"The Union Cavalryman in the Civil War." http://www.bufordsboys.com/UnionCavalrymanIII. htm, accessed December 13, 2004.

THE MILITARY JUSTICE SYSTEM

The following sources deal with the military justice system:

Callan, John F. *The Military Laws of the United States Relating to the Army, Marine Corps, Volunteers, Militia and to Bounty Lands and Pensions, from the Foundation of the Government to the Year 1858.* Baltimore: J. Murphy and Company, 1858.

De Hart, William C. *Observations on Military Law, and the Constitution and Practice of Courts Martial, with a Summary of the Law of Evidence, as Applicable to Military Trials: Adapted to the Laws, Regulations, and Customs of the Army and Navy of the United States.* New York: Wiley and Halsted, 1846, 1859; reprint: Buffalo, New York: William S. Hein and Co., n.d.

"Extracts from Court-Martial Records: Trouble in the Sixth Infantry, 1811." *Army and Navy Life* 9 (1906): 513–528.

Fisher, B. J. "Military Justice on the Texas Frontier." *West Texas Historical Association Year Book* 64 (1988): 123–139.

Hare, John S. "Military Punishments in the War of 1812." *American Military Institute Journal* 4 (1940): 225–239.

Hunt, Robert R. "Crime and Punishment on the Lewis and Clark Expedition." *Military Collector and Historian* 41, no. 2 (Summer 1989): 56–65.

Knopf, Richard C. "Crime and Punishment in the Legion, 1792–1793." *Bulletin: Historical and Philosophical Society of Ohio* 14, no. 3 (July 1956): 232–238.

McDermott, John D. "Crime and Punishment in the United States Army: A Phase of Fort Laramie

History." *Journal of the West* 7, no. 2 (April 1968): 246–255.

O'Brien, John. *A Treatise on American Military Laws, and the Practice of Courts Martial, with Suggestions for Their Improvement.* Philadelphia: Lea & Blanchard, 1846.

Vargas, Mark A. "The Military Justice System and the Use of Illegal Punishments as Causes of Desertion in the U.S. Army, 1821–1835." *Journal of Military History* 55, no. 1 (January 1991): 1–19.

MISCELLANEOUS SOURCES

Davies, Wallace E. "The Mexican War Veterans as an Organized Group." *Mississippi Valley Historical Review* 35, no. 2 (September 1948): 221–238.

Glasson, William H. *Federal Military Pensions in the United States.* New York: Oxford University Press, 1918.

Morrison, James L. "The Struggle Between Sectionalism and Nationalism at Ante-Bellum West Point, 1830–1861." *Civil War History* 19, no. 2 (June 1973): 138–148.

Oberly, James W. "Gray-Haired Lobbyists: War of 1812 Veterans and the Politics of Bounty Land Grants." *Journal of the Early Republic* 5 (Spring 1985): 35–58.

Tidball, John C. "Getting Through West Point: The Cadet Memoirs of John C. Tidball, Class of 1848." Edited by James L. Morrison, Jr. *Civil War History* 26, no. 4 (December 1980): 304–325.

INDEX

ABOUT THE AUTHOR

JAMES M. McCAFFREY is Professor of History at the University of Houston-Downtown. Among his publications are *"Only a Private": A Texan Remembers the Civil War: The Memoirs of William J. Oliphant* (2004), *"Surrounded by Dangers of All Kinds": The Mexican War Letters of Lieutenant Theodore Laidley* (1997), *Wake Island Pilot: A World War II Memoir* (with John F. Kinney, 1995), *Army of Manifest Destiny: The American Soldier in the Mexican War, 1846–1848* (1992), and *This Band of Heroes: Granbury's Texas Brigade, C.S.A.* (1985).